Peter Cook Remembered

'I could have been a judge but I never had the Latin, never had the Latin for the judging, I just never had sufficient of it to get through the rigorous judging exams. They're noted for their rigour. People come staggering out saying. "My God, what a rigorous exam" – and so I became a miner instead. A coal miner. I managed to get through the mining exams – they're not very rigorous, they only ask one question, they say, "Who are you?", and I got seventy-five per cent on that.'

The opening to 'Sitting on the Bench',
from *Beyond the Fringe*

LIN COOK
Spring 1982–January 1995
Peter's acquaintance, platonic friend,
dearest friend, girlfriend (one of), 'constant
companion', 'live-in' permanent
relationship, wife, widow.

Peter Cook Remembered

by Peter Alliss, Clive Anderson, Michael Bawtree, Peter Bellwood, Alan Bennett, John Bird, Eleanor Bron, John Cleese, Lin Cook, Stephen Fry, William Goldman, Jonathan Harlow, Joseph Heller, Christopher Hitchens, Barry Humphries, Eric Idle, John Lloyd, Victor Lownes, Elisabeth Luard, Nicholas Luard, Shane Maloney, Joe McGrath, Dudley Moore, Lewis Morley, Michael Palin, Adrian Slade, Geoffrey Strachan, Barry Took, Auberon Waugh, John Wells, Roger Wilmut.

Edited by Lin Cook

Mandarin

Published in the United Kingdom in 1997 by Mandarin Paperbacks

1 3 5 7 9 10 8 6 4 2

First published in the United Kingdom in 1996 by Methuen London
as *Something Like Fire: Peter Cook Remembered*

Mandarin Paperbacks
Random House UK Limited
20 Vauxhall Bridge Road, London SW1V 2SA

Random House Australia (Pty) Limited
20 Alfred Street, Milsons Point, Sydney, New South Wales 2061, Australia

Random House New Zealand Limited
18 Poland Road, Glenfield, Auckland 10, New Zealand

Random House South Africa (Pty) Limited
Endulini, 5a Jubilee Road, Parktown 2193, South Africa

Random House UK Limited Reg. No. 954009

A CIP catalogue record for this book is available from the British Library

Papers used by Random House UK Limited are natural, recyclable products made from wood grown in sustainable forests. The manufacturing processes conform to the environmental regulations of the country of origin

Typeset in Palatino by Deltatype Ltd, Birkenhead, Merseyside
Printed and bound in Great Britain by Cox & Wyman Ltd, Reading, Berkshire

ISBN 0 7493 2312 4

During the last few weeks
I've been trying to think of something
absolutely original and devastating.
I've been trying to lay my hands
on some idea that'll revolutionize
the world in some way.
Something like fire, or the wheel . . .

Contents

List of Illustrations

All photographs not credited come from Lin Cook's personal archives. Every effort has been made to trace the copyright holders for pictures used in this book. We apologise for any inadvertent omissions, which will be corrected in future editions if notification is sent to the publisher.

Editor's Note

An acquaintance or two; a few old friends who had lost touch and some who hadn't; some new friends; and, of course, those who loved Peter Cook most dearly and knew him better than most: these are the people who were invited to contribute memories of him, following his death in January 1995.

The purpose was to present a mosaic, a composite portrait of someone who was in a class of his own, someone who was always affectionately regarded and considered a friend, not only by people who knew him but also universally by those who only knew of him.

To my knowledge, all the contributors wrote independently without comparing their texts. Different people recalling the same events often remember them differently. As far as possible, where dates are given in the individual writers' texts, they have been checked for accuracy, as has the chronology at the end. But this is a book of overlapping and contrasting impressions, expressed with love or admiration, often both, not a definitive biography.

Peter was much loved and is now much missed. This book has gathered memories together as one might gather beautiful blooms to place in his arms as we say a gentle 'goodbye'.

L.C.

Acknowledgements

It is not possible for me to name every person who has been involved in putting this book together. However, I would like to thank those who have helped in any way and all the photographers whose pictures we have used.

I am indebted to each of the contributors: Adrian, Alan, Auberon, Barry (Humphries and Took), Christopher, Dudley, Eleanor, Elisabeth, Eric, Geoffrey, John (Bird, Cleese, Lloyd and Wells), Clive, Jonathan, Joseph (Heller and McGrath), Lewis, Michael (Bawtree and Palin), Nicholas, Peter, Roger, Shane, Stephen, Victor and William, who have written about Peter with such affection. I much appreciate their cooperation and the time they have taken as, for many, it was not an easy task.

I would also like to especially thank Geoffrey Strachan, my editor at Methuen, for his guidance, friendship and invaluable help. I am grateful to Mary Chamberlain at Methuen and Anna Davis at David Higham Associates for their patient assistance in the preparation of this book. Last but not least, my thanks go to Bruce Hunter who has held my hand throughout.

Prologue

Sitting on the Bench

Yes, I could have been a judge but I never had the Latin, never had the Latin for the judging, I just never had sufficient of it to get through the rigorous judging exams. They're noted for their rigour. People come staggering out saying, 'My God, what a rigorous exam' – and so I became a miner instead. A coal miner. I managed to get through the mining exams – they're not very rigorous, they only ask one question, they say, 'Who are you?', and I got 75 per cent on that.

Of course, it's quite interesting work, getting hold of lumps of coal all day, it's quite interesting. Because the coal was made in a very unusual way. You see God blew all the trees down. He didn't just say 'let's have some coal'. As he could have done, he had all the right contacts. No, he got this great wind going you see, and blew down all the trees, then over a period of three million years he changed it into coal – gradually, over a period of three million years so it wasn't noticeable to the average passer-by . . . It was all part of the scheme, but people at the time did not see it that way. People under the trees did not say 'Hurrah, coal in three million years', no, they said 'Oh dear, oh dear, trees falling on us – that's the last thing we want' and of course their wish was granted.

I am very interested in the Universe – I am specializing in the Universe and all that surrounds it. I am studying Nesbitt's book – **The Universe and All That Surrounds It, an Introduction.** *He* tackles the subject boldly, goes through from the beginning of time right through to the present day, which according to Nesbitt is October 31, 1940. And he says the earth is spinning into the sun and we will all be burnt to death. But he ends the book on a note of hope, he says 'I hope this will not happen'. But there's not a lot of interest in this down the mine.

The trouble with it is the people. I am not saying that you get a load of riff-raff down the mine, I am not saying that. I am just saying we had a load of riff-raff down my mine. Very boring conversationalists, extremely boring, all they talk about is what goes on in the mine. Extremely boring. If you were searching for a word to describe the conversation, 'boring' would spring to your lips – Oh God! They're very boring. If ever you want to hear things like: 'Hallo, I've found a bit of coal.' 'Have you really?' 'Yes, no doubt about it, this black substance is coal all right. Jolly good, the very thing we're looking for.' It's not enough to keep the mind alive, is it.

Whoops. Did you notice I suddenly went 'Whoops'? It's an impediment I got from being down the mine. 'Cause one day I was walking along in the dark when I came across the body of a dead pit pony. 'Whoops', and that's another reason I couldn't be a judge, because I might have been up there all regal, sentencing away, 'I sentence you to Whoops' – and you see, the trouble is under English law that would have to stand. So all in all I'd rather have been a judge than a miner.

And what is more, being a miner, as soon as you are too old and tired and sick and stupid to do the job properly, you have to go. Well, the very opposite applies with the judges. So all in all I'd rather have been a judge than a miner.

Because I've always been after the trappings of great luxury, you see, I really, really have. But all I've got hold of are the trappings of great poverty. I've got hold of the wrong load of trappings, and a rotten load of trappings they are too, ones I could've very well done without. (Looking round suddenly.) Oh, he's gone.

Peter Cook Remembered

Jonathan Harlow

Peter Cook's Schooldays, or What You Will

Peter Cook arrived at St Peter's College, Radley, in the same term as I did, the autumn of 1951. That is a long time ago[1] and I do not remember exactly how or when we first met. We were in different houses[2] and different forms, so it was not immediate. But some time in that first term I found myself queuing in a gloomy brown-panelled corridor near a boy with a Mephistophelean eyebrow and a sardonic cast of face and phrase. It was Peter; or rather, it was Cook – Christian names were not used by boys or by masters, until the acquaintance was well matured. We were both rather precociously, not to say affectedly, sophisticated and got on well together.

Radley was and is a boarding school for boys, of the kind perversely known as 'public'. In 1951 it was rather like much else in Britain at that time, not so much getting over the war as trying to maintain, despite rationing and

[1] To bring back the five years we shared, I have just read them up in the school magazine, *The Radleian*, which both of us edited at some time. Otherwise unattributed quotations in what follows are from its pages.
[2] Radley has a peculiar, mildly Oxonian, vocabulary: the Head is the Warden, a Master is a Don, a House is a Social, and its Housemaster a (Social) Tutor. Mindful of Peter's bogus reminiscences of a boyhood in Latin America, playing 'the local game of *futabala*', I have used the commoner forms.

austerity, that it had never happened. Those who had attended such a school in the 1920s or 30s, or perhaps just read *Chums* or the works of Talbot Baines Reed, would have recognized much that must seem strange (or so I should hope) today.

It was traditional: Chapel every day (in white surplices on Sunday); organized games every afternoon; Corps (military training) once a week; Latin grace to mark the beginning and end of meals. Not only were these rituals unchanging, but there was no sense that their continuation was even open to review.

Sporting and athletic prowess mattered. (Radley was named as top sports school of the year by *The Field* in 1952.) There was no animus against brains or artistic talent; but membership of school teams carried more kudos. Everybody turned out to watch school and house matches; and the entire school went by train daily to Henley for the Regatta.

The school, or at least the student body, was insular, poorly informed and largely Conservative (as an opinion poll in the early fifties showed). Peter was no more left-wing than any of us. The only time I recollect his being moved by public affairs was when he took a dislike to a Labour MP, Colonel Wigg, who was given to asking insistent questions in the Commons. Peter could deliver a shrill fantasia on the man's name in an ecstasy of scorn that lasted for minutes.

It was rigidly hierarchical, by seniority. We new boys, aged thirteen, were at the bottom of the heap. In our first few weeks we had to learn, from the 'Grey Book' (which of course was not grey), the names and offices of those to whom our respect was due: all those, I think, in our own house and all prefects and other persons in authority. We also learned the names of all the masters, but theirs was an indirect rule. (An American exchange student described the system as 'a casual association of men and boys living together through joint condescension'.) Our daily lives were ruled, and sometimes ruined, by older boys.

Rank was very visibly embodied in privileges. We in our first year must be sure to keep all the buttons on our jackets done up, gaining status at the rate of one loosened button a year. All had black gowns, from the full black-beetle of the new and generously fitted to the merest halter of black cloth between the elbows; but prefects might carry theirs rolled casually over the arm. They could walk in the open way past the Clock Tower, while others jogged in single file along a narrow causeway to the school shop at break. They could use the lavatories (white-tiled, outdoor, oh! so cold in winter) behind closed doors which others must leave open.

There was not much privacy elsewhere. At night, and for a compulsory twenty minutes Rest after lunch, we retired to flimsily partitioned cubicles in large dormitories, but these were not immune from inspection or invasion. The bathrooms were definitely communal: not just the rooms only, but even the hot water in the six baths which had to serve some fifty boys after games. In the morning, it was cold dips for all, and yes, someone was counting.

The first year was the worst. By day we were based in a junior house common room. Younger boys were a good deal bullied by their immediate seniors. Misfits might continue to be tormented by the socially dominant until the blessed fifth term when they attained to a tiny study shared with one or two others. Having friends was important; and though mixing between houses was not encouraged, Peter's and mine were in the same block and our common rooms next door to each other. We could meet and comment on the absurdities with which, it will be apparent, our lives abounded.

We were not rebels. Incidents or individuals we might deplore or scoff at. But I think that throughout our time there we accepted the system. It had, after all, a sort of serial democracy. Each year's intake in turn would succeed by

3

chronological progression to a growing degree of immunity, tolerance and privilege, enhanced opportunities for self expression and, finally, authority for itself. And the traditionalism, the values which were simply assumed rather than spelt out, with the cloistering from any countervalues, exerted an insidious but powerful pressure to conform.

It was a very good school. The apparently remote masters knew and cared for us. They taught well, sometimes brilliantly (brilliantly though not well in one or two blessed instances). They promoted and guided an enormous range of clubs and activities. There was space and time, especially on Sunday, without compulsory activity. One could read for hours in the Library, or tinker in the Craft shops, or the Art block, or walk with someone like Peter around the playing-fields to the edge of Bagley Wood where the school buildings seemed far away.

It may sound odd to speak of 'someone like Peter', but in those first years he was not especially distinguished. It goes without saying that he was neither a promising nor a keen games-player. He was not picked out for accelerated academic progress. He did not act in plays. Of course he mimicked masters, especially his and my housemasters and the chaplain. But so did we all. Either his gifts as performer or ours as audience were not yet developed – I don't remember that we thought him much better at this than the rest of us. On the other hand, he did not make himself obnoxious and get bullied much, nor did he break rules. In fact, I think the first time he got beaten – corporal punishment was the normal sanction – was in our third year when some officious prefect saw us buying beer to stow in our punt at Henley.

Peter seemed to be less affected than most of us either by the miseries or the exaltations of adolescence. Perhaps he merely talked less about himself – even when we knew each other very well, he never mentioned his home or his parents. But if he did not seem particularly unhappy, he was not yet master of that permanent good humour which was to mark him later. He could stare with cold cod's eyes from a long pale deadpan of a face, like someone gripped by terminal ennui or obsessive disorder.

His gift was slow to emerge. As late as December 1953, when he was sixteen, his performance as the Socialist Duchess in *Stuck in a Lift* achieved the peculiar distinction of being completely ignored in *The Radleian*'s review, and I remember nothing of it myself though, as it was compulsory, I must have seen it. With his rather faraway look, willowy form and carelessly waved hair, one might have sooner cast him as Sidney Carton than as a farcical peeress. But in the spring of 1954, he played Doll Common in the senior production of *The Alchemist* 'with breadth and gusto . . . richly authentic'. In the following autumn, in his house's production of *The Love of Four Colonels*, he 'did as much as could be done' with the Wicked Fairy – the part which Peter Ustinov himself took in the original London production. In the intervening summer he won the Medrington Trophy for short stories.

His prize-winning story was called *Bric-à-brac*. A girl baby-sits for a sinister couple who live over a second-hand shop. The baby dies in her arms, she panics, runs through crashing furniture and shattering glass from the shop. The couple knock at her door later that night – to tell her that she left the wireless on. Punch-line for an extended sketch? The couple just could have been played as Henry and Min Crun from the Goon Show. But the final paragraph reasserts the straight horror story. I think Peter retained a penchant for the borderline between Gothic and shaggy dog – but this may have been the last time he was tempted to play it for anything but laughs.

His last year brought triumphs. He won more prizes, for Speech and for German. He was one of the masterminds behind the impromptu *Gold Mine Revue*, and revelled in the absence of script and of rehearsal, to recreate (with Bill Butters) the pair of commentators who had shared the adjudication of the recent house plays in mutually deferring antiphon. Then came his wonderful Don Armado in *Love's Labour's Lost*, fantastic, florid, foreign, more than a little touched, more than a little touching – not a solo *tour de force* but exuberant within the discipline of text, production and ensemble. And finally, the musical *Black and White Blues* which he wrote with Michael Bawtree. That was for the Marionette Society, a wonderful institution which seemed able to use every talent for art or craft. *Black and White Blues* is not a fair sample of his wit. To call the plot perfunctory would be gross flattery. The master in charge insisted on rhyming couplets 'to cover possible weaknesses', but this was not Peter's natural idiom and it did more to cover possible strengths. It was also necessary to avoid offence to public decency and reference to recognizable members of staff. (I was glad to be reminded, on replaying my record of the show, that both restrictions had at times been evaded.) Peter himself played the part of an Old Etonian tribal chief in tones of strangled cultivation; and even sang or recited in a sort of Rex Harrison style.

The last year or so also saw Peter expand as a person. He was now, as were his friends, among the establishment of the school, enjoying with some complacency, as we all did, the fruits of freedom and privilege which grew at the top of the tree. He had the space and the liberty to make full and uninhibited use of his comic gifts. These, I think, were three, though they tended to run into each other. He had a tremendous ear, and caught at once distinctive speech patterns and vocabulary – the sort of noise a particular type might make. He had a quick mind and could cut the general tenor of his theme with slashes of verbal wit, play on words, substitution and malapropism. Above all, he could spin a whole fantastic web of absurdity from the merest thread of an idea or phrase. A scrap of speech, initially perhaps just the sort of idiosyncrasy which we would all use to characterize a master, would become the starting point for a whole persona so wild and wonderful that the original could never again be seen as ordinary mortal. Thus our benign and blameless chaplain was transformed before our very ears into a monster of depravity, ruthlessness and Jesuitical guile: Richelieu, Torquemada, Alexander VI and Pope Joan rolled into one. Thus too Mr Boylett.

Mr Boylett deserves a paragraph if not a biography to himself. (The spelling of his name varies, and not even the Bursar's office can supply an authorized version.) He was an elderly man, mostly cheerful, with a dry manner of speech. Among his tasks was to wait at High Table which stood on the dais at the end of the main dining Hall. Two prefects dined there each day, with the master on duty. There came an occasion when Mr Boylett accidentally swept the breadcrumbs from the table into the lap of one of the prefects. 'Well, they were your crumbs,' he said. From that moment he became a celebrity. High Table was no longer a chore: we would linger to savour his every word, and take away as much as we could to those who had missed it. 'I saw a stone the other day – I think I saw it meoove' – that was one of his legendary remarks. In due course, much of the man, the myth rather that he had become, went public as E.L. Wisty.

Of course, there were ready-made personae too, like the entire cast of the *Goon Show* (for which Peter wrote a script which got him to lunch with Spike Milligan) but the home-brewed tasted best.

The other great characteristic of Peter at that time was a comprehensive and generous conviviality. He seemed to have decided life was a continuous joke, which he was happy to share. He was the comic genius, but he was no monopolist. Everybody could join in and, as Peter juggled with the balls we threw, we became part of the performance and felt ourselves wondrous witty too. We could even regale ourselves with items from his repertoire when he wasn't there. And he never, that I can recall, directed his humour *against* people (the animus against Colonel Wigg had disappeared with adolescence). He did not put people down or show them up.

7

This made him not just a funny man, but a very good companion and friend. A man to go tiger-shooting with, if such a ridiculous pursuit could have survived his commentary. Certainly a man to go camping with ('gemping' is nearer the received pronunciation). Which we did, in the summer of 1956. Five of us, from medium to outsize, in a small car. A couple of little tents, primus stove cookery, not much money and the shadow of National Service hanging over us. And Peter, nobody's outdoor man, made delight of every misadventure.

Peter was exempted from National Service – a loss perhaps, as it might have extended even his appreciation of the wilder stretches of human unreason. By the time I got to Cambridge, Peter was ahead of me and had already done *Pieces of Eight*. He was, of course, still very funny, though I am not sure that he was funnier. He was also still great fun to be with and still with that gift for including the entire company in the non-stop improvisation. My last distinct memory of him is at a supper which he overlaid with an extravagant embroidery on the theme of *Nuwee San Jorj*. And my last memento is a copy of Samuel Beckett's *Watt* which he gave me in 1959. He did not read widely, but he was a naturalized citizen of the darkly comic world of the Irish writers, from Joyce through Flann O'Brien to Spike Milligan.

Peter went down from Cambridge, and up to Edinburgh, in 1959. I saw *Beyond the Fringe*, of course, but then I went to Africa, and lost touch not only with Peter but with his work. I have enjoyed this opportunity of remembering our friendship and feeling again something of the warmth and sparkle he generated. As I write I seem to see, as in an autocue, his face and arms writhe as he launches himself into the role of the man who was at school with someone who became famous. It makes me laugh just to think of him doing it.

Michael Bawtree

Black and White Blues

Even at school, Peter had a greater capacity for making
people laugh than anyone I have ever met then or since. The
monologues would fairly stream from him, making use of
everything around – people, situations, animals, birds,
silliness: whatever met his eye and ear.

We didn't know each other well until the last eighteen
months or so of our time at Radley, when he became a
somewhat unlikely head of his house, and I became a little
less unlikely head of mine. This meant that we were among
the eight school prefects who shared the prefects' study,
and here we spent a lot of time – a place of privilege and a
source of terror for junior boys. Little did they know the
nonsense that went on that year behind its grim oak door.

Peter never seemed to have much interest in classes,
using them primarily to gather satirical material about the
schoolmasters. They were all ruthlessly mimicked: the
gurgling, boy-loving Ivor; the rasping, malodorous Tonk
('Then it was that Louis put his spoke into the Hapsburg
pie'); the slow-moving Ray King, with his nasal delivery
and laborious wit; 'Lummy' Joe Eason, etc. etc. Radley in
those days was rich in characters.

Prospecting for material seemed, in fact, to be Peter's
main occupation at school. Every trivial incident was a
source of mirth, and as soon as some formal event like

9

chapel, or classes, or dinner at High Table, was over, we would dash into the prefects' study and burst with laughter. On Field Days out in the Berkshire Downs, we would find a hedge away from the harried officer masters, and sit behind it in continuous hysterics while Peter droned on, he himself giggling quite as much as we. Occasionally we would chip in with our own additions to the theme, and Peter would enjoy that too, building on them, improving them, turning them inside out, as he did his own. This was his developing style: some remark or observation, situation or object was noted and laughed at, and then became a pretext for endless variations, each spinning off into further absurdity while we rocked with laughter at the newest and yet more improbable flight of fancy.

Of all the people who became food for Peter's amiable ridicule, Mr Boylett was the most improbable. He was the waiter at High Table in Radley's dining-hall, which was much like High Table at a college except that the school prefects processed in behind the Warden and sat with him there, together with any special visitors to the school that day. We were being encouraged, no doubt, to engage in adult conversation and learn how to deal graciously with servants! Mr Boylett was in his fifties at that time: short, with grey hair around a balding pate, and a mouth that reminds me now of those Thurber mouths, open like birds' beaks. He would dress in shabby tails, grey waistcoat and tie, like a waiter in some Hungarian nightclub. Boylett worked with a fixed and affable smile always on his face – complemented somehow by a complete, utterly complete, absence of humour. However we teased him, he continued to smile, responding with remarks of sublime simpleness.

In our arrogant way, we never stopped to think twice about Mr Boylett. He was part of the landscape. But it was Peter who took painstaking note of the man, and mythologized him, turning him into a kind of clay divinity. The more pathetic and simple the poor man was, the more Peter saw in him an absurdist superhero. He used to quote

Warden Milligan, in Milligan's gushing tones: 'Dear old Boylett: he's simply amazing, wonderful – a real character . . .' and point out that the wonderful thing about Boylett was that he was so very ordinary, so very grey, so unremarkable. Peter had a way of seeing the world through the eyes of such people, weaving around them a world of cosmic triviality.

My own association with Peter came closest when the two of us became involved in our last term with the Radley College Marionette Society. This was a splendid institution, founded in the late forties by art master Chris Ellis (another almost mythological character: Old Etonian, and not only an artist but maths scholar, classicist, flautist, carpenter, art teacher, round-the-world yachtsman, and winner of the George Medal for removing an unexploded bomb from St Paul's during the war). The Society used to mount an operetta or opera each spring, and had dazzled the school with remarkable productions of *The Pirates of Penzance, Ruddigore, The Magic Flute* and *The Beggar's Opera*.

In 1956, Chris decided it was time to create an original musical, and approached Peter and myself: Peter to write the text and lyrics, myself to compose the songs. Mercifully I recall none of the music, and little of the story: it was entitled *Black and White Blues*, and its central character was an evangelical, Mr Slump, who took his jazz band to Africa to convert the natives – I think he came close to being cannibal stew. The dialogue was in crude rhyming couplets, and I remember being pained (in those far-off, more rigorous days) at the casual half-rhymes which Peter perpetrated:

> We must rise early tomorrow morn:
> The Slump Jazz Band will march at dawn.

Peter played the voice of Mr Slump; I played piano in a small combo. It all sounds primitive, but I have to say that the piece was a wild success. We recorded it in a studio at Oxford and sold four or five hundred albums to boys, masters and parents. There must still be some around somewhere.

When he left Radley, Peter soon acquired, first at Cambridge and then in London, a group of friends and colleagues for whom his perpetual monologue became a required performance, and he continued to develop his characters and themes in the same brilliant improvisatory way we had seen in its beginnings at Radley. When I went up to London to visit him in the early sixties at the *Establishment Club* and later in the offices of *Private Eye* we would laugh as always. He was very, very nice to me, and I think he valued our friendship as I did. He came over from Cambridge in '59 and the two of us put on a twenty-minute satirical revue for the Worcester College Commem. Ball. When he was preparing *Beyond the Fringe* for Edinburgh – or was it for London? – he stayed at my house outside Oxford (my parents ran a hotel) and commuted each day for meetings with Alan Bennett and the others.

I always felt I was a kind of straight man in Peter's life – for whom he did not have to hide behind the voices. And yet without the voices Peter always seemed vaguely uneasy, and blushing even: when he was not being funny in his brilliant, gothic, extravagant way, he was surprisingly awkward. I remember in fact staying with him – one of the last times – when he lived on Church Row in Hampstead around 1967, and was making *Bedazzled*. He told me he was seeing a psychiatrist. For middle-class English people in those days, to say one was seeing a psychiatrist was an extraordinary and even shaming admission. I asked why, and he said, 'I have been talking in other people's voices for so long that, when I don't, I have a terrible sense of emptiness. I don't know who I am.'

Adrian Slade

Peter Cook: Thirty-Seven Years a Very Rare Friend

The role of President of the Cambridge Footlights Club in the 1950s was obscure. There was no club room for which you were responsible and no obvious committee to whom you were answerable. All you knew was that it would be your fault if the twice-termly 'smokers' and the obligatory cabarets at Cambridge occasions were dull. Smokers were essentially cabaret evenings for members at which new talent pitted itself against the old stagers. And if later on as President you picked the wrong director for the revue, the chattering circles would soon let you know.

I was particularly lucky. One October day in 1958, as I sat in my room contemplating our first not wildly successful cabaret of the term, I was interrupted by the arrival of a long, thin, hesitant person with dashing, darting eyes. He said he had heard that I was the one to see if he wanted to join the Footlights. His name was Peter Cook and, apart no doubt, from a few close friends, he was unknown to the rest of Cambridge or the world at large.

'Have you ever written anything?' I said. Silly question in retrospect but it seemed necessary at the time. Yes, he happened to have a script on him (it was the one that he and Dudley Moore did together some years later in which they discussed exploration in, I think, 'Gumbara'). It was funny. He and I could do it at the first smoker, I suggested.

Had he got any more? Oh yes, quite a few, he said. Then what had he been doing in the past year? (He was in his second year by then.) He had been playing football. He was much too frightened to approach the Footlights, he said.

· Despite the non-stop wit and nervous energy for which he later become well known, here was a surprisingly shy extrovert. I believe he remained so. Take him off whatever stage others had put him on and he was often quiet and sometimes ill at ease. If there was any vanity in him in those early days it was confined to the need regularly to check his undoubted good looks in any passing mirror. Otherwise I never spotted an ounce of conceit or arrogance in him.

But to return to our conversation. If he had not been involved in theatre at Cambridge, what about school? Two hilarious hours of reminiscence followed that included his insistence that he avoided National Service by claiming an allergy to feathers and his endless impersonations of a Mr Boylett, apparently a manservant at Radley when he was at school there. It seemed that the curious Mr Boylett indulged in all sorts of unusual fantasies about life and the world. As far as I can remember, they involved almost anything from the Queen's German ancestry and the way that ants and bees organized their working schedules to Mr Boylett's own ambitions for world government. The world was, of course, coming to an end. All this was recounted in detail.

'Why not do that at the smoker?' I suggested.

'Do what?' he said.

'Mr Boylett,' I said.

'But it's not a sketch and anyway why would anyone think it funny?' he said.

'Well, I do,' I said.

'What would we call it?'

'Mr Boylett Speaks,' I suggested.

And so, as well as doing the sketch we had earlier agreed, Peter emerged for the first time from behind a curtain dressed in dirty mac and hat and simply rambled on Boylett-style. The success was instant. A phenomenon was born and the Peter Cook language was immediately universally adopted. From that moment Cambridge cabaret and revue never looked back. A new genre of Footlights writing was born. The surrealist Cook humour with its lateral thinking and devastating eye for contradiction, pretension and the absurd and owing only a touch to Ionesco and N. F. Simpson, spawned a generation of Footlights originals, many of whom freely acknowledge their debt to him.

By the summer of 1959 Mr Boylett had begat Mr Grole, he who was the first to pester complete strangers in public places. In the 1959 revue the luckless victim was Timothy Birdsall, caught alone in a railway carriage.

'I've got a viper in this box you know ... Oh no, it's not an asp ... Some people can't tell the difference between the viper and the asp ... More fool them, I say.'

'Yes.'

'Cleopatra had an asp but I haven't got one. Prefer the viper myself.'

'Much nicer, I expect ...'

'Not that they're cheaper to run. If anything the viper is more voracious than the asp. My viper eats like a horse ...'

'Like a horse, eh?'

'Oh yes, I'd like a horse ... mind you, you'd never cram it into this little box. It's not a horse-box, you know ... A viper yes, but a horse ... *no*,' etc, etc.

And, of course, later again Mr Grole begat E.L. Wisty.

Long before that revue Peter had quickly become the star of our cabaret team, with a little support and team discipline from myself and fellow cabaret performer Geoffrey Pattie, later one of Mrs Thatcher's longest serving ministers. One thing we learned very quickly. He could not sing ... but, as later TV viewers know, this never stopped him trying, and anyway there was enough of all that from the rest of Footlights.

If Peter needed an early baptism of fire it was probably the performance we all had to give at a Woburn Abbey dinner organized to launch the Duke of Bedford's memoirs in the spring of 1959. The audience included Peter Sellers and Bernard Braden and the contrast between their stony faces when listening to Cyril Fletcher reciting his odes and the choking laughter with which everyone received Peter was a good indication of the way British comedy was likely to go in the future.

I suspect that, if Peter had not been available, John Bird, then a serious Cambridge theatre director, would not have been persuaded to direct the 1959 May Week revue *Last Laugh*, the first Footlights revue to include a touch of political satire, mostly written by John himself. Politics or no, the stars of the revue were Mr Grole and Mr Boylett ('I'm the man who comes along at about this time and sings a song about the man who comes along at about this time . . . to fill in the gaps while people are busy trying to change the scenes behind the curtain, etc.'), because at that stage neither Peter nor I were particularly political animals so together we wrote what suited us best.

Nevertheless it was almost certainly *Last Laugh* which, thanks to John Bird's influence, sowed the seeds of Peter's later more political writing for *Beyond the Fringe* and led more immediately to his writing *Pieces of Eight* for Kenneth Williams, a revue that opened at the Apollo Theatre in Shaftesbury Avenue in September 1959.

I kept in touch with Peter for some years after Cambridge but then there was gap of about fifteen years during which I saw very little of him until politics reunited us. I had been elected to the Greater London Council as a Liberal. The Tories had chosen to use me as a test case to prove Liberal election overspending. They failed. Nevertheless, a technicality landed me with a large proportion of the costs and I rashly decided to try and see if some of my theatrical friends would participate in a fund-raising evening at Drury Lane.

Without a moment's hesitation, Peter was the very first of those friends to offer to appear. Eleanor Bron, David Frost and Angela Thorne (an old school friend of my wife's), also kindly offered. Then, thanks to the considerable help of my cousin Humphrey Barclay who directed the whole evening, another Footlights generation joined in i.e. John Cleese, Tim Brooke-Taylor, Graeme Garden, Graham Chapman, Bill Oddie and Rowan Atkinson, not to mention further invaluable contributions from Barry Took, Harvey and the Wallbangers, the very new French and Saunders, my brother Julian, and my daughter Nicola. *An Evening at Court* was held at Drury Lane on 23 January 1983 and was a huge success.

I retain an unreleased tape of the show including a sketch performed by Peter and John Cleese on a park bench that as far as I know has never been seen or heard elsewhere. Its subject, prompted by the evening, was 'inalienable rights'.

'Hullo ... I see you're reading *The Times*.'

'Yes.'

'As you are fully entitled to do. That is one of your *inalienable* rights. Aren't we lucky in this country to have *inalienable* rights?'

'I suppose so.'

'*You only suppose so* ... In Russia you wouldn't be allowed to sit on a bench reading *The Times*. You would not have inalienable rights in Russia. You'd have to sit on a bench reading *Pravda*.'

'Or *Izvestia*.'

'Or *Izvestia* ... and they are both pretty dull reads ... unless you speak Russian. Do you speak Russian?'

'*No I don't.*' ...

'*No, you don't, you poor sod.* And you have an inalienable right not to speak Russian in this country. In Russia they have to speak Russian ... I have a smattering ... well, just the one word actually.'

'Just the one, eh?' ...

'*Nyet.* Do you know what that means?' ...

'*No.*' ...

'Neither do I.'

And later in the sketch . . .

'Have you ever wanted wanted to eat a swan?'

'Now that you mention it . . . No.'

'My heart goes out to those people who crave the flesh of the swan. You see that it is not one of our *inalienable* rights. Only the Queen and her direct relatives are allowed to cram huge wodges of roast swan down their gobs. It's not one of *our* inalienable rights . . . it's one of *hers*, you see. All the swans in the United Kingdom belong to the Queen . . . and vice versa . . .'

Over the last twelve years of his life, Peter and I met regularly again, sometimes to record a spot of advertising that I had persuaded him to do, more often just to have lunch and natter about himself, his life with his wife Lin, and the politics in which he was now fanatically interested. He had first met Lin in 1982 and he married her in 1989. He still felt beset by problems from his previous marriages but otherwise he did not seem unhappy. He did not hanker for Hollywood or some other life, except that for a brief moment in the late eighties he nurtured modest political ambitions.

He had always felt more at home with the Liberals than any other party and he told me that he relished the idea of taking on Glenda Jackson, who had just become Labour candidate for Hampstead. The Hampstead Liberal Democrat candidacy was still vacant and for a short time he was on the verge of being persuaded by me to put himself forward for the next General Election (1992). Discussions had almost become official when a new project intervened and he backed away. It would have been an intriguing and explosive contest.

Very close Cambridge friendships never change. Ours didn't and nor, I believe, did he. Everyone knows that his three dimensional wit never left him but neither did his generosity to real friends nor his fundamental vulnerability. Too little has been written and said about his kindness and loyalty, his very real love of Lin and his increasing dependence on her. In latter years she was his life and chief support. It is a shame that insecurity made him his own worst, and probably only real, enemy. Beneath a dilapidating exterior remained a brilliant brain, an uncannily sharp eye and ear, a relentless tongue and a very warm heart. Friends like that only come once in a lifetime.

Peter Bellwood

The Seven Wild Strawberries are Flying

The smartest thing I ever did when I left York and went up to University was to take the ukelele my Uncle Noël had given me. He'd played it while serving in Coastal Command during World War II and it had the signatures of his squadron scribbled on the sound box and a beautiful mellow tone. By the time I got to St Catharine's College, Cambridge, I could play banjo lines to Chris Barber, Omer Simeon and Humphrey Lyttelton records plus a modest repertoire of George Formby songs ... *'On I-Tiddly-I-Ti Island'*, *'When I'm Cleaning Windows'* and *'Leaning on a Lamppost'*.

It was Geoffrey Pattie who propelled me quaking onstage to sing a Formby number one night at a Cat's 'Midnight Howlers' smoking concert at which Adrian Slade was also present. This resulted in my first appearance at a Footlights smoker, which in turn led to my being cast in that year's Footlights Revue, *Last Laugh*, directed by John Bird, which is how I met Peter Cook.

At some point thereafter, half-way through rehearsals, Peter came to tea bearing sticky buns, a long, lean, angular figure with a pale complexion, thick dark-brown hair parted way down on the starboard side, the bulk of it swept over to port in a huge wave, grey herring-bone jacket, drainpipe trousers and winkle-picker shoes. Looking around my digs, he drolly complimented me on my Vat 69 lamp with the booze-label-covered shade and how perfectly he felt my livid tartan bedspread blended with the cobalt-and-orange walls and how he wished he could have both of them for his very own. I thanked him and told him no. The light of lunacy was never far from his eyes . . .

He loved North Country humour – the thicker the accent, the better – Jimmy James, the Crazy Gang, Hylda Baker, music-hall, Spike Milligan . . . He loved my tapes of Al Read's old radio shows – 'Ay-up, here's two birds. Jam that door, Tommy . . . I don't like yours much.' Peter's laugh was explosive, infectious – his knees would buckle and his torso contort backwards whenever he had a fit of the giggles, which was frequent. His normal voice was deep and resonant, but could switch in the blink of an eye to the nasal, weird, surrealistic, back-of-the-throat drone he'd developed at Radley, based on Mr Boylett.

Strange people flowed from his imagination, denizens of his own personal Twilight Zone . . . The Phantom Bee-Fang Gluer, a lunatic on the loose in Amsterdam going round gluing sets of fangs onto dead bees . . . A man who was convinced the Soviets had planted a camera in his bath, incensed by the notion that at his expense, 'a bunch of Russian sailors were having a giggle in the Baltic' . . . Another who bought a walking stick because 'I thought I saw it move' . . . And a man who'd managed against all odds to purchase a heap of rotting grass only to learn that the bottom had just dropped out of the rotting grass market . . .

And then there was Peter's own 'Grit Song', in which he's on stage in his usual mac and trilby, string around his neck supporting a cardboard tray on which is scrawled 'GRIT FOR SALE', as he sings, tunelessly and relentlessly –

> Come along, come along
> And buy your grit from me.
> Come along, come along
> And buy your grit from me.

Here's the place to get your grit
Because I have lots of it
Come along, come along
And buy your grit from —

A prospective buyer interrupts: 'Excuse me. Half-a-pound of grit, please.'

Cook: 'Oops, Sorry. I'm right out.'

He thought it obsessive of me to keep a diary, amused by the notion of a man incapable of making any move or decision without consulting his diary, and bombarded me with streams of vital imaginary entries: '7.30 Look in diary. 7.45 Get up. 7.47 Check who you are in diary. 7.50 Go to lavatory. 8.15 Breakfast. 8.20 Look in diary. 8.25 Lavatory again . . .'

To Peter, lampooning the pomposities and inanities of the English upper classes was like shooting fish in a barrel. We'd all been exposed, through family, public school or both, to the Victorian concept of the gentleman amateur who disdains professional success and goes to whatever lengths are necessary to avoid it. One of his obituaries even described him as 'the last amateur'. To me, the notion that Peter deliberately planned his career to conform to this value system is rubbish. It's pretty strange stuff, the British admiration for the idea of failing gloriously (like Scott of the Antarctic) rather than succeeding.

It was the 'little people' who fascinated Peter, a group for whom he had the utmost affection. John Lahr, in a *New Yorker* article, quoted from one of Cook's earliest interviews in 1959, just after *Pieces of Eight* had opened in the West End: 'Sometimes I think of old men who live in single rooms. I see them listening to their portable radio sets and charting news bulletins, which then take on great importance in their pathetic little lives. They become amusing, not because one pokes fun at them, but because they make unimportant things seem important and base their lives on false premises.'

In *Pieces of Eight* Kenneth Williams and Fenella Fielding

brought Peter's take on those characters brilliantly and hilariously to life:

Kenneth	If I'd had wings I could've got around more.
Fenella	(*thrilled*) Wings would have helped you to see the world.
Kenneth	I didn't have 'em. And then there's my weight. If I'd had more flesh on me I could've got that job as the fattest man in the world –
Fenella	You nearly got it as it was. All you lacked was the build –
Kenneth	(*shouts*) I didn't have the flesh, woman! People want to see great mounds of the stuff all quiverin' on yer ...

Peter and I often went to the pictures. He even came up with the title of a film he wanted to make as an homage to Ingmar Bergman: *The Seven Wild Strawberries are Flying*. One afternoon early in 1960, we took the afternoon off to see Olivier's *Richard III* at the Regent Cinema. The film had already started, but we bought tickets, loaded up with unhealthy eats and drinks and headed for the dark. In those days cinemas had 'usherettes', who in Cambridge tended to be sweet old ladies in orange aprons who carried a torch to show you to your seat. We decided to stagger our entrance into the theatre. I went in first, handed the usherette my ticket, leaned in close to her ear and whispered 'Excuse me, but have I missed the nude bathing scene?' Startled, she switched the torch beam up to my face for a moment, looked hard at the screen then whispered, 'I'm not sure there is a nude bathing scene in *Richard the Third*.' Nodding thanks, I went and sat down.

Moments later, Peter entered, whispered to the same usherette, 'Excuse me, but have I missed the nude bathing scene?' She recoiled and in a voice shrill enough to be heard down the stalls said, 'I just had another gentleman in here asking me that!' Of course, there wasn't a bathing scene, nude or otherwise – but glancing back, we did notice all three usherettes standing at the rear, staring intently at the screen.

Peter's sketches seemed perfect. They were elliptical, concise, hilarious, three minutes long and seemed to spring from his vivid imagination fully formed. It was quite by chance, visiting him one day in his newspaper-strewn rooms, that I happened to be standing on one leg, scratching at a blister on my left heel – which put me, as he later said, 'present at the creation' of 'One Leg Too Few'.

Another of his Footlights sketches had him waiting in a queue to buy a ticket at a railway station. Finally he reaches the clerk, peers in through the mesh grill:

Peter	Good morning. Third class return ticket to Grantham, please.
Clerk	Yes, sir. That'll be four pounds, twelve and six.
Peter	(*claps hands*) Give you ninepence.
Clerk	I'm sorry, sir but –
Peter	Ninepence. Take it or leave it.
Clerk	Sir, the return fare to Grantham is four pounds, twelve and six –
Peter	All right. All right. You're doing your job, I can see that – one-and-six –
Clerk	No, sir –
Peter	Tell you what I'll do. I like you. I like your face – (*Claps hands.*) One-and-six and a ride on the engine! Final offer –
Clerk	(*angry*) I'm sorry, sir, but –
Peter	See this watch? (*Shows watch.*) I've been abroad, I've been to Egypt. I've been to the bazaars. Haggle-haggle. That's all they understand. Haggle-haggle-haggle. How much d'you think I paid for this watch? Go on! How much? Take a guess –
Clerk	I don't care –
Peter	Three quid! Haggle-haggle-haggle. 'Agu Be-naya-ki,' I said – I speak the

24

language – (*Claps hands.*) Beat him down to
fourpence-hapenny! . . .

One of Peter's sketches performed by the *Establishment* at
the Strollers Theater Club in New York in the early sixties
involved a man with staring eyes being led out into a single
spotlight and placed centre-stage. He's holding an open
book. His fingers fly over the page as he speaks:

Man	Good evening. I am blind. And yet I am reading this message. I am reading it on the wonderful system known as Broil –
	He pauses, backs up his fingers, checks text again, proceeds more cautiously . . .
	I am reading it on the wonderful system known as Broil . . . which was invonted . . . by a min . . . of the same nome . . . God-nit.
	Blackout. Then an amplified voice over the speakers:
Voice	Thank you, ladies and gentlemen. That was an appeal on behalf of the blond.

At the sketch's first performance there was a hissing from
the audience – but a blind man present asked to be taken
back to meet the actor who'd performed it. Tears of laughter
fell from his sightless eyes. To him, it was the funniest thing
he'd ever heard.

The truth is, Peter's humour wasn't sick, it was absurdist,
surreal. He didn't even consider himself much of a satirist –
except perhaps for his 'savage' piece on Macmillan. There
was a breathtaking elegance to his comic riffs, to the
seemingly effortless way he could toss them off – as in a
sketch, based on the Great Train Robbery of 1963, which he
did in the New York version of *Beyond the Fringe*:

Alan	Good evening, Sir Arthur.
Peter	Good evening.
Alan	I am going to ask you a few questions about the train robbery, if I may.
Peter	Good, the very thing we are investigating. I'd like to make one thing quite clear at the

outset – when you speak of a train robbery, this in fact involved no loss of train. It's merely what I like to call the contents of the train which were pilfered – we haven't lost a train since 1946, I think it was, the year of the great snows, we mislaid a small one. They're very hard to lose, you see, being so bulky – a train is an enormous thing compared for example to a small jewel, a tiny pearl for example might fall off a lady's neck and disappear into the grass, or the gravel, or wherever she was standing – in the sea, even, and disappear underwater – whereas an enormous train, with its huge size, is a totally different kettle of fish . . .

Alan   I think you've made that point rather *well*, Sir Arthur . . . who do you think may have perpetrated this awful crime?

Peter   We believe this to be the work of thieves, and I'll tell you why. The whole pattern is extremely reminiscent of past robberies where we have found thieves to be involved – the tell-tale loss of property, that's one of the signs we look for, the snatching away of the money substances – it all points to thieves.

Alan   So you feel thieves are responsible?

Peter   Good heavens, no! I feel that thieves are totally irresponsible. They're a ghastly group of people, snatching your money away from you . . .

Alan   I appreciate that, Sir Arthur, but . . .

Peter   *You* may appreciate it, but most people don't. I'm sorry I can't agree with you. If you appreciate having money snatched you must be rather an odd fish . . .

I never heard such laughter . . . and if there's a heaven and Peter's there, he'll be in a place which looks very like the old *Establishment* on Greek Street. Every flat surface will be strewn with newspapers, he'll have busty substances on demand, there'll be the Big Bopper, Buddy Holly, Chuck Berry, Ray Charles, Gene Chandler's 'Duke of Earl' and the Stones on the juke-box. God in his mercy will keep him supplied with endless cigarettes, champagne will be flowing and men with wings in cloth caps and raincoats will be flying about in a maelstrom of leaping nuns and one-legged Tarzans. He's one of the dearest and funniest men I ever knew ... Some amateur ...

John Bird

1: Good Behaviour

Speaking at the memorial service for Peter Cook, Eleanor Bron described the first time she had heard his name mentioned; I had called on her after going to see him, and told her: 'I have just met the funniest man in England.' It was 1958, and all three of us were at Cambridge, and while it has the ring of remarks undergraduates tend to make to each other, it is distinguished from most such remarks by being the flat truth. It is characteristic of my truly appalling memory that I don't recall anything about that occasion, but the judgement it gave rise to stood for the many years I worked closely with Peter Cook and the many subsequent years – to my regret and I'd say shame – in which my only contact with him was as just another member of an audience.

The crucial you forget, the trivial stays with you. One weekend, we paid a visit to his parents in Lyme Regis. The ambience appeared to me then probably rather more upper-middle-class than it actually was. The two of us went for a walk across the local golf club (I think Peter was a member himself); the cliff-top course was completely deserted since there was such a gale blowing and we were unable to hear ourselves speak even if we shouted. My foot caught in a rabbit hole and I fell over, to which I said 'Bugger!' in a loud voice. The future creator of the Derek and Clive tapes was genuinely shocked by this breach of golf-course etiquette: he put a finger to his lips and went 'Shh!' No one in sight for miles around: Peter managed to bring a touch of the surreal to what might be thought a display of extreme conventionality.

The first time I actually worked with Peter was a year later. I was then in my fourth year at Cambridge, having embarked upon a rather shaky postgraduate course, with a determination to 'give up' the theatre to concentrate on scholarly pursuits. This resolve lasted about a month, until I happened to see the text of N.F. Simpson's *A Resounding Tinkle*, published as one of the prizewinners in a playwriting competition organized by the Royal Court Theatre and the *Observer*. It seemed to me (and still does) one of the funniest plays I'd ever read, and I put it on at the Amateur Dramatic Club's theatre as an independent production. Undergraduate theatre in Cambridge was at that time taken very seriously by its practitioners, myself among them; insufferably so, in fact. Cook wasn't part of that crowd, restricting himself to mainly solo cabaret performances, but I wanted to cast the play with people who I thought would be in tune with Simpson's humour, so I asked him if he would play the lead opposite Eleanor Bron. She was one of the few 'proper actors' in a cast which also included the late Timothy Birdsall (the cartoonist), Geoff Pattie (now Sir Geoffrey, an ex-minister in the Thatcher government) and Penelope Balchin (now Leach, the distinguished child psychologist).

It has sometimes been claimed that Cook was strongly influenced by Simpson's work; in fact, Cook's style was already fully developed before I introduced him to *A Resounding Tinkle*. Indeed, that was precisely the reason I wanted him to be in it, because something close to Simpson's idiom was perfectly familiar to him, without being identical, and I knew he'd have no problem negotiating it. If anybody had any problems with the idiom it turned out to be me, as I later discovered I'd directed the play in a manner entirely at odds with the intentions of Simpson and his director at the Royal Court, William Gaskill. They wished it to proceed at a grave and stately pace, with long pauses, whereas Peter and Eleanor complained that the only direction I ever gave them was 'faster!' Still, the Court generously arranged for us to give a Sunday night performance, which was Peter's début on the London stage.

Alan Bennett

Thoughts and Afterthoughts

It is thirty-five years, almost to the day, that I first set eyes on Peter, at lunch in a restaurant, I think on Goodge Street, with Dudley Moore and Jonathan Miller, the meeting arranged by John Bassett, whose idea it was that we should all work together writing the review that turned into *Beyond the Fringe*.

Having already written while still an undergraduate a large slice of the two West End shows *Pieces of Eight* and *One Over the Eight*, Peter was quite prosperous and it showed. He dressed out of Sportique, an establishment – gents' outfitters wouldn't really describe it – at the west end of Old Compton Street, the premises I think now occupied by the Café España.

There hadn't really been any men's fashions before 1960; most of the people I knew dressed in sports coat and flannels, as some of us still do; but when I first saw Peter he was wearing a shortie overcoat, a not quite bum-freezer jacket, narrow trousers, winkle-picker shoes and a silk tie with horizontal bars across it. But what was most characteristic of him, and which remained constant throughout his life, regardless of the sometimes quite dramatic changes in his physical appearance, was that he was carrying, as he always seemed to be carrying, a large armful of newspapers. He had besides a book on racing form and I remember being impressed not merely that this was someone who bet on horses but here was someone who knew how to bet on horses, and indeed had an account at a bookmaker's.

But it was the newspapers that were the clue to him. He was nurtured by newspapers and there's a sense that whatever he wrote or extemporized, which he could at that time with a fluency so effortless as to make us all feel in differing degrees costive, was a kind of mould or fungus that grew out of the literally yards of newsprint that he daily digested. Newspapers mulched his talents and he remained loyal to them all his life, and when he died they repaid some of that loyalty.

In those days I never saw him reading a book. I think he thought that most books were a con or at any rate a waste of time. He caught the drift of books, though, sufficient for his own purposes, namely jokes; picking up enough about Proust, for instance, to know that he suffered from asthma and couldn't breathe very well; he decided in the finish, according to Peter, that if he couldn't do it well he wouldn't do it at all, and so died – this was one of the gems from the monologue in *Beyond the Fringe* about the miner who wanted to be a judge but didn't have the Latin. How Proust had managed to work his way into the sketch I can't now remember because it was less of a sketch than a continuing saga which each night developed new extravagances and surrealist turns, the mine at one point invaded by droves of Proust-lovers, headed by the scantily-clad Beryl Jarvis. Why the name Beryl Jarvis should be funny I can't think. But it was and plainly is.

In those days Peter could tap a flow of mad verbal inventiveness that nothing could stem: not nerves, not drink, not embarrassment, not even the very occasional lack of response from the audience. He would sit there in his old raincoat and brown trilby, rocking slightly as he wove his ever more exuberant fantasies, on which, I have to admit, I looked less admiringly then than I do in retrospect. I had the spot in the show immediately following Peter's monologue, which was scheduled to last five minutes or so but would often last for fifteen, when I would be handed an audience so weak from laughter I could do nothing with them.

Slim and elegant in those days, he was also quite vain, sensing instinctively as soon as he came into a room where the mirror was and casting pensive sidelong glances at it while stroking his chin, as if checking up on his own beauty. He also knew which was his best side for photographers.

There were limits to his talent; one or two things he thought he could do well he actually couldn't do for toffee; one was an imitation of Elvis and another was to ad lib Shakespeare. Both were deeply embarrassing, though of course Peter was immune to embarrassment; that was one of his great strengths.

What makes speaking about him a delicate task is that he was intolerant of humbug: detecting it (and quite often mistakenly), he would fly into a huge self-fuelling rage which propelled him into yet more fantasy and even funnier jokes. So it's hard to praise him to his face, even his dead face, that quizzical smile never very far away, making a mockery of the sincerest sentiments. So he would be surprised, I think, to be praised for his strength of character, but in his later years when some of his talent for exuberant invention deserted him I never heard him complain. It must have been some consolation that the younger generation of comic writers and performers drew inspiration from him but he never bragged about that either. Nor did he resent that Dudley had gone on to success in Hollywood and he hadn't. The only regret he regularly voiced was that at the house we rented in Fairfield, Connecticut in 1963 he had saved David Frost from drowning.

In later years I saw him quite seldom, though if he'd seen something you'd done on television he'd generally telephone, ostensibly to congratulate you but actually to congratulate you on having got away with it yet again.

There's a scene in *Brideshead Revisited* where Charles Ryder has an exhibition of his worthy but uninspired paintings which is a great success. Then Anthony Blanche turns up, who knows exactly what's what. 'My dear,' he says, 'let us not expose your little imposture before these good plain people; let us not spoil their moment of pleasure. But we know, you and I, that this is all t-terrible t-tripe.' And sometimes what Peter was telephoning about had been tripe and sometimes it hadn't, but you didn't mind because there's always a bit of you thinks it is anyway and it was to that part of you that Peter always spoke. And since he did it without rancour or envy it was a great relief. I suppose it was partly this that made him in his latter days such an unlikely father-figure for younger performers.

In the press coverage of his death one could detect a certain satisfaction, the feeling being that he had paid some sort of price for his gifts, had died in the way the press prefer funny men to die, like Hancock and Peter Sellers, sad and disappointed. I don't know that that was true and it certainly wouldn't have found much favour with Peter. Trying to sum him up in his later years, the television in the afternoon, the chat shows, the golf in Bermuda, one thinks of one of the stock characters in an old-fashioned western, Thomas Mitchell, say, in John Ford's *Stagecoach*, the doctor who's always to be found in the saloon and whose allegiance is never quite plain. Seldom sober, he is cleverer than most of the people he associates with, spending his time playing cards with the baddies but taking no sides. Still, when the chips are down, and slightly to his own surprise, he does the right thing. But there is never any suggestion that, having risen to the occasion, he is going to mend his ways in any permanent fashion. He goes on much as ever down the path to self-destruction, knowing that redemption is not for him – and it is this that redeems him.

As for us, his audience, we are comforted by the assurance that there is a truer morality than the demands of convention, that this is a figure from the parables, a publican, a sinner but never a Pharisee. In him morality is discovered far from its official haunts, the message of a character like Peter's being that a life of complete self-indulgence, if led with the whole heart, may also bring wisdom.

Required to amplify this memorial address for the purposes of this book, I still find it hard to separate out particular memories of Peter from the common recollections I have of the four of us in *Beyond the Fringe*. Peter's role in the group was as the metropolitan sophisticate but I've no doubt that that was as approximate and ill-fitting as I felt mine was as shy northern lad. Some memories, though, accord with that stereotype as Peter did have considerable charm and a slight old-fashioned Englishness (real or assumed) that stood him in good stead, particularly in America. When we were in New York, playing on Broadway, I think he may have seen something of Jackie Kennedy. Certainly when the President and his wife (at her urging) came to see *Beyond the Fringe* I have a vision of the presidential party in the Green Room having drinks in the interval, with Mrs Kennedy absently stroking Peter's hand as they chatted.

While his personal life was never so volatile nor so highly charged as Dudley's (whose performance on the stage was often merely a perfunctory interruption of the more pro-longed and energetic performance going on in his dressing-room), Peter did have his moments. On tour in Boston he was dating a young woman who I think may have been a Playboy bunny: there was certainly something odd about her knees and the overall resemblance was to Popeye's partner, Olive. I don't think we were ever told her real name as she was always referred to (though presumably not introduced) by Peter as Miss Kitty Nisty. On one occasion her father, taking exception to Peter's attentions, burst in upon the couple brandishing a (rather clichéd) shotgun, whereupon Peter, all sophistication gone, had to flee the apartment in his underwear.

Conventionally middle class as they seemed to me then, Peter's parents were in those days rather daunting; but when I met his mother and his sisters in later years we all got on very well, with Peter inordinately grateful that one had, as he saw it, spared the time, even though it was just to have tea. His family must have meant more to him than one realized, though, because after the death of his mother, which was not all that long before his own, he regularly referred to himself as an orphan. This seems to me so strange and uncharacteristic, both in Peter or in any man in his mid-fifties, that it made me feel that I perhaps hardly knew him at all.

In another respect, though, I believe I got him right. After the memorial programme about Peter on television the columnist Christopher Booker disputed my version of the Frost drowning story, claiming that so far from making a sardonic joke of it Peter was 'extremely proud of his feat, as anyone might be who had saved a fellow human being from drowning'. This is pious humbug. Peter wasn't extremely proud of *anything* and not to appreciate that or to see how drenching irony and a profound sense of the ridiculous informed everything he thought and did (and sometimes blunted his best endeavours) is to miss the point of the man. I'm not sure, though, which he would enjoy most, the thought of himself going through life with a sense of secret pride and sporting an invisible Royal Humane Society medal, or the spectacle of his surviving friends squabbling over the finer points of his character.

One of the most perceptive remarks about Peter on the same TV programme came from John Bird. When they were both at Cambridge and in Footlights, John was astonished by Peter's unresting flow of fantasy, as everybody who knew or worked with him must have been. But what also struck him was the difference between Peter and other writer/performers such as John Fortune and himself: for them (as for the other three of us in *Beyond the Fringe*), writing and performing and being funny was something we chose to do, did when required, then switched off. For Peter, on the other hand, there was no switching off; the torrent of verbal association which was his trademark flowed on, unstoppable in his head. We clocked in, as it were, whereas Peter never clocked out: he was utterly at the mercy of language. It was this unstoppable flow, as John Bird said, that made Peter almost to be pitied.

The flow did stop later, of course, and he might be pitied for that too, though never by himself.

1 May 1995 and March 1996

Nicholas Luard

The Man Who Lit a Bonfire

It's improbable but entirely appropriate that Peter and I should have been introduced to each other by a bishop.

He wasn't in fact a bishop then, although he is now – the distinguished Bishop of Coventry. Not much older than we were, then he was simply the Revd Simon Barrington-Ward, chaplain of Magdalene College at Cambridge, a lover of theatre and cabaret, a talented performer himself (he did, although I never heard it, a wicked impersonation of myself), and the statutory faculty head of the Footlights, the university's revue club.

Barrington-Ward decided the Footlights' management group needed strengthening. Peter and I were both under-graduates in different colleges but in the same year. Peter was already a star of Footlights and soon to become its president. Barrington-Ward felt we'd like each other and work well together.

In many ways it was a strange connection for the good chaplain to make. Both Peter and I were public schoolboys. Aside from that, we didn't appear to have much in common. Apart from his already-proven brilliance on stage, Peter had the reputation of being slightly feckless and indolent. Tall and languid, wonderfully good-looking and highly intelligent, even at twenty he'd been marked down as one of nature's anarchists, a passing traveller through university life. He'd somehow avoided military service. Improvising wildly, Peter had claimed, he said, bad breath, contagious purple pimples, fear of the moon that made him howl at the night sky, and uncontrollably dangerous homosexual tendencies, not to mention feet that sloped the wrong way. The authorities had believed him. The entire British war-machine, they were convinced, would be in deep jeopardy if Peter were admitted to its ranks. I, on the other hand, was a former special forces soldier, a dedicated scholar, and an athlete who boxed for the university. At first sight it wasn't one of those unions predestined by the constellations.

Yet Barrington-Ward got it right. Peter and I had more in common than what separated us. We both spoke languages fluently. We'd both seen political-satirical cabaret in France and Germany. We loved living theatre in all its expressions. Most important of all, we were both bold and irreverent: while my feet sloped the right way and I didn't bay at the moon, I'd only barely avoided a court-martial for an assault on a superior officer. We had little respect for the past. In different ways we felt an instinctive repugnance for the blandness and patronizing condescension of the Macmillan years. The post-war world we'd grown up in was breaking down. We wanted to drive bulldozers through the stifling dullness and greyness of the landscape of our inheritance.

Neither Peter nor I at the time would have framed it in those words; yet, with hindsight perhaps, I still think they're essentially true. We weren't making any sort of political statement. We certainly weren't spearheading a movement, although what we did touched a deep nerve with many. By chance, we arrived at the hour and caught the wind. Old men, discredited values, dubious so-called 'professions' varnished with respectable labels, those were our legacy. Lloyd's insurance business, we sensed long before its humiliating collapse, amounted to nothing more than what racecourse bookies do with much greater honesty every day. Sotheby's and Christies belonged to the world of street-corner pawnbrokers. The great merchant banks, like Barings, were incompetently run money-lenders, loan-sharks masquerading under fine names. We looked at our world, we found it comic and grubby, we thought we might change it a bit. No grand design, no grand plan. Just an intuition and, instead of bulldozers, laughter as the weapon of demolition.

The laughter came from Peter.

No one has ever been able to generate laughter like Peter. He wasn't a comedian, an actor, a performer in the usual sense. At intervals he made a fair fist of trying to be all three; none of the roles really suited him, none really worked. What he was – and the word might have made him chuckle – was a visionary, the wise fool. It wasn't a costume he could adopt, drawing on a harlequin's gown when required. It was what he was saddled with, what he was made of. Nature or nurture, genes or a good hard caning at school, a cold frost at his birth or long warm summers as he grew up, Peter emerged as uniquely Peter. He was touched, not in the head but by magic. He emerged to see and laugh.

Not by the way of jokes or crafted comic situations or sharp one-liners – although Peter could encompass all three – but in endlessly-spinning Catherine wheels, rockets and firecrackers of wit and perception and invention. Peter looked at the world or a naked light bulb hanging in the offices of *Private Eye*, and found both the world and the light bulb funny. He examined both. And he started to improvise on them. Descartes and Edison, God and the spider who'd wound his web round the bulb (and was given to strange sexual exploits), the Queen and Mother Theresa, E.L. Wisty and Greta Garbo (all of their bodily functions and libidinous activities came into it too – it was astonishing to be told what Her Majesty gets up to after muffins and Earl Grey tea on damp Tuesday afternoons), would find their lives threaded together by a sixty-watt glow from the ceiling.

What Peter did was cavalier, impulsive, irresistible – to

him and the audience who gathered round him, Pied-Piper-led, wherever he went. He couldn't stop himself from creating; his listeners couldn't stop themselves from laughing, not with the 'paid' laughter of those who've forked out good money to hear a comedian's jokes, but with the joyous, exuberant laughter of people who know they're hearing something gay and riotous, subversive and above all rare – rare beyond the telling. It was the true cornucopia which overflows, the well that never dries. And it reached everyone.

I once had dinner with Peter Ustinov, whose imagination, if more mannered and theatrical, worked in something of the same way. Ustinov had become known as the funniest man in the world, an absurd but welcome title for anyone. I asked him if it wasn't also something of a burden. 'It used to be,' he replied. 'No longer. I've been watching Peter Cook. The weight's off my shoulders now. The accolade, for what it's worth, belongs to him. It's a vast relief.' Ustinov chuckled. It was a generous but, I think, sincere and certainly deserved tribute.

At Cambridge, Peter and I plotted and planned. We had an idea, no more than a shadowy fragment of an idea, to open a little theatre in London where we could present the sort of satirical entertainment we'd seen abroad. I went off to the USA on a graduate fellowship, leaving Peter behind to ponder the possibility. I finished my studies, took my master's degree, and boxed in the Golden Gloves tournament. After being outpointed in a furious battle by the future world champion, Lenny Mathews, I headed south to lick my wounds in the Mexican sun. I got as far as New Orleans when I received a cable from Peter. 'Have premises,' he said, 'Come home.' Which I did.

Peter had found a seedy, derelict, ruined, abandoned strip-joint on Greek Street in the heart of Soho. It was the least appealing property I'd ever seen, but its chain of bankrupt owners meant its lease was available from the liquidators for a song – and to prove it Peter greeted me with an aria from *Tosca* when he first took me there. We bought the tail-end lease. Our friend, the brilliant Irish architect and designer Sean Kenny, gutted the building and reshaped it. We opened it as the *Establishment* theatre club in October 1961.

In his later life Peter, having quite rightly shed the nonsensical socialist notions so many of us then held, and having moved towards the relative sanity of conservatism (not political conservatism but conservatism with a very small 'c'), tended to deride the sixties. His contempt for socialism, the deceitful flatulence of its rhetoric, its spite and envy against the world, its demeaning of the individual, its degrading inefficiency and bungling bureaucracy, was one of the very few grievances he ever expressed. Unfortunately the sixties were years of Labour government, and the socialist sixties became twinned and debased in Peter's mind with what also happened at the time.

They should not have been. Fashionable as it is now to decry the sixties, they were in reality an epoch of splendour and freedom, a casting-off of the past and an attempt – inept, fumbling, tentative, exploratory – to chart a new road towards the future. Roads take people where they want to go, where they're already heading. From the Celtic drovers and the Romans onwards, the directions of the best roads have been chosen by seers. The Celts used to consult their bards about where they should drive their herds. Peter, the wise fool, however much he'd have denied and laughed at the notion, was unwittingly a bard of the new intellectual road-system. Nothing transcends the pure delight of laughter for itself alone, but one of the additional functions of all great humour – intentional or unintentional – is to change people's minds and perceptions. Peter did just that. No one who ever heard or saw Peter, and television meant that millions did, was able to look at the world in quite the same way again.

By the time the *Establishment* opened, the theatre revue *Beyond the Fringe* was a major success in the West End.

Peter's colleagues in the revue – Dudley Moore, Alan Bennett, and Jonathan Miller – have all gone on to express their bountiful talents in different fields. Dudley is a superb musician and now an accomplished Hollywood film actor. Alan writes engaging books and plays. Jonathan throws his energies and occasional frustration – he keeps threatening to leave Britain for Italy, generating waves of national panic unknown since the threat of nuclear war over the Cuban missile crisis – into directing 'modern-style' opera productions.

Rich, gifted, and successful as they all are, none of them approaches Peter. They simply don't have his scale or measure. The three have the talents of sturdy and honest professionals. They do their work, take their pay, and go safely home to their beds. Peter didn't always go home to his bed. He drank a bottle or two of vodka, read the newspapers, watched the football on television, chuckled, and slept wherever he found himself. What he had, what distinguished him from his *Fringe* colleagues, can only be called genius – wayward, wandering genius, but genius that is utterly unmistakable. And not only the genius he expressed in himself, but which he could spot in others.

When the *Fringe* team went to New York, I was left alone on the bridge of the *Establishment*. From America Peter sent me suggestions for strange and singular performers he felt it right for us to present. Some appeared and vanished without trace; the highly eccentric Professor Irwin Corey proved incomprehensible to British audiences. A young Australian drag artist called Barry Humphries, simpering and whimpering in sequinned dresses, was an equal disaster – although he later rescued himself financially with gladioli and vulgarities as Dame Edna Everage.

Among the disasters there was the occasional – although sometimes double-edged – triumph. For some reason, Peter loved the morose, shambling, and deeply camp pier-end comedian, Frankie Howerd. Howerd's career had virtually foundered when Peter suggested we put him on. Against my best judgement I agreed. Frankie Howerd, winsome, roguish, naughty, and in some strange way genteelly menacing with his lisp and his flapping hands, was a huge success. His career was revived and the *Establishment* was packed.

The place was packed too when the American, Lenny Bruce, appeared. Lenny Bruce is often bracketed in accounts of American satire with Mort Sahl and Tom Lehrer, the alternative comedians of the time. In fact he was quite different, like Peter in a class apart. He too was a bard. He too was in the business of changing minds. Sharp and robust as they were, Sahl and Lehrer belonged to the old mainstream tradition of stand-up comics. Lenny was dangerous. Fragile, sick, white-faced, dressed in black and often with a hypodermic needle pressed to a vein in his arm, Lenny was the most unlikely of all superstars. He had sores. He was a drug-addict, although I sometimes wonder what on earth the term means applied to someone like him. Lenny had been given a heroin compound as a pain-killer after being wounded during an extraordinarily gallant career as a sailor in the Pacific during the Second World War. He continued to use heroin afterwards. He was savage, anarchic, 'foul-mouthed' – again, what on earth does that mean in the case of someone whose use of language was so rich and vital? – and immensely gentle.

What Lenny did in performance, in a way that no one before or since has done, was explore in words human relationships, human sexuality, and human rage – love and hate and all the compass points between. To listen to him was uncomfortable, distressing, to many intolerable. People used to walk out of the *Establishment*, disgusted and frightened. Newspapers, notably the *News of the World*, mounted headline campaigns against him. 'Get this vile creature out of Britain,' they clamoured, 'and do the country a favour.' The reporters had to do some fancy fingering of their typewriter keys to produce their eyewitness copy that damned him. They couldn't get into the *Establishment* to see the man they were writing about. But the campaign worked. Lenny Bruce finished his engagement. When we tried to bring him back, he was deported by the Home Secretary on his arrival at Heathrow airport as 'an undesirable alien and a threat to public order'.

All of which proves, if it needs to be proved, that the pen is indeed mightier than the sword. Words are more powerful, more dangerous, to a hierarchy than the slashings of razors. Lenny used words, not blades. The resident company we'd created used words too. John Fortune, John Bird, Eleanor Bron, Jeremy Geidt, and the others may have become somewhat traditionally theatrical in the years since. At the time they were young, bold, inventive, and beautiful. More than that, they had a dynamism to them. They weren't given lines to deliver. They created, improvised their own moments and dialogue on stage. Solemn and intense American journalists used to ask who wrote the *Establishment*'s sketches. To their bafflement they were told no one did. Night by night, hour by hour, the words came out of nowhere – or rather, out of the soaring firecracker imaginations of the cast.

Fires and firecrackers need ignition. Peter's pockets were always full of matches. The best place to light a bonfire that can be seen for miles is on top of a watershed. It's likely to be the highest point in the area. The *Establishment*'s bonfire was stacked on a watershed in post-war British life. Peter put a torch to it. It was an extraordinary time. People flocked from all over London and across the country to enjoy and warm themselves at the subversive flames. The resident cast performed the constantly changing cabaret. Dudley Moore played jazz in the cellar. Annie Ross, the finest, loveliest, gutsiest musician I've ever heard, sang. There were art exhibitions and heckling, disturbances and celebrations, protest demonstrations and jeering and cheering. Painters, writers, poets, gangsters, and politicians gathered at the bar. They made it their own. Every night outside on the street there would be crowds clamouring to get in.

Above all, of course, there was Peter. Peter, with his infinite courtesy and charm, loping – most people walk or stride or hurry, Peter loped – moving among them. Always laughing, always the peacemaker in the flare-ups that inevitably break out in places where ideas are debated and drink is served late at night. 'It's only because I'm the greatest coward in the world and don't want to get hurt myself,' he used to claim. Utterly untrue. He was a pacifist but, like many such, he was extraordinarily, almost reck-lessly brave. He simply lacked fear. On one occasion a famous Irish actress took violent exception to a sketch ridiculing the excesses of Irish nationalism and anticipating, as it turned out, the brutalities of the IRA. She consoled herself with liberal potions of vodka. Then she started to rant and shout. Peter tried to quieten her. Her response was to rake his face with her razor-sharp fingernails. 'There's an Irish heart inside me,' she bellowed, 'and it's bleeding!' 'There's an English face outside me,' Peter replied mildly. 'It seems to be bleeding too.' He found a taxi and paid for it to take her home. She was still cursing as she left. Peter, wiping the blood from his cheeks, was smiling benevol-ently, as always.

If the evening was good, if he hadn't been drained by the taxing demands of his appearances on stage with the *Fringe*, that night's audience might be lucky enough to see him perform – improvising, speculating, juggling the golden oranges of his mind. Among his gifts was a remarkable talent as a mimic. Unlike modern television impersonators, Peter did not use props – wigs or make-up or signature clothes. He had, of course, no video-tapes to study. Yet after watching a short black-and-white clip of Macmillan on television news, he could play the old poseur to absurdity almost better than Macmillan himself. All Peter needed to do was hood his eyes, make a few jerky and wildly inappropriate gestures, and ramble on with ponderous madness in a voice that shimmied between a Scottish croft and the Duke of Devonshire's London club – and the winds of change were suddenly blowing over Soho as well as Africa.

Best of all, better even than his impersonations of the famous, were his portrayals of the 'types' of the time – accountants, business recruitment executives, fashion designers, police sergeants, the stars of the emerging pop world. I used to watch him studying them as he talked to them. There wasn't in fact a hint that he was studying them. He leant forward from his considerable height, smiling courteously, slightly stooped like a heron, his bright candid eyes never leaving their faces. Afterwards, in swift, incisive, and achingly funny sketches, drawn with the economy of line of a Hogarth or a Rowlandson, he'd recreate them. The sketches were truer to the essence of their subjects than the subjects themselves ever managed to be in their own lives.

Perhaps he wasn't really a performer at all. Perhaps at heart he was a cartoonist of the quality of Goya. The trouble with Peter as a verbal Goya was that he lacked rage. He was too tolerant, too forgiving, too indulgent of the woeful lunacies of the world that surrounded him. Goya looked at the heart of things with bitterness and cursed. Peter cast a watchful teasing eye on what were in the end the same matters and laughed.

The ethos of the time and the focus for its expression, the *Establishment* spilled out beyond Soho into the everyday life of all of us who were involved – the two were seamlessly joined. We met in pubs or coffee bars, we lunched together, we had dinner in each other's houses. For one of Peter's birthdays his first wife, Wendy, gave one of the finest dinner parties I've ever been to. The guests included John Lennon and Paul McCartney, the columnist Bernard Levin, the actors Peter O'Toole and Tom Courtenay, the poet Christopher Logue, the designer Mary Quant, the world middleweight boxing champion Terry Downes, and half a dozen more. We ate a magnificent meal by candlelight round the kitchen table in Peter's Hampstead house. Then we sat up into the early hours playing music and talking – about politics and prize-fighting, painting and poetry, theatre, de Gaulle, and President Kennedy, the Chelsea Flower Show and the summer sun in Spain. Peter, in an ancient wooden rocking-chair, presided. He never imposed himself on the gathering, it would have been against everything in his nature, but his presence was unmistakable, a shy contented point of reference for everyone else. Occasionally his attention would be caught by some chance remark. He'd unfold himself from his seat and pace the room for a few moments, the elegant heron with its head lowered once more, delivering some brilliant surreal monologue before settling himself chuckling into his chair again.

I and my wife, Elisabeth (at just twenty-one, the youngest person there), were living in Hyde Park Square near Marble Arch. It's quite a way from Hampstead to Marble Arch. Normally we'd have taken a taxi to get back. That warm summer night we strolled home together beneath the stars, arriving as dawn was breaking. It seemed the only fitting end to a bewitching evening which belonged partly to the mood of the times. When since has a brilliant acerbic Jewish intellectual broken bread and discussed the meaning of life with a couple of Beatles and a flattened-nosed Bow Bells-born pugilist, to the equal enchantment of all four? This was partly thanks to the youthful and lovely Wendy Cook. But most of all undoubtedly to Peter. The wise fool, the bard, had gathered his companions at his hearth, and quietly but lavishly made them welcome. All feasts should be lavish. Peter's feast that night was lavish in every way.

It was of course too good to last. Times fill, hold their riches for a brief precarious while, then under pressure they empty. When Peter went to New York for the Broadway production of *Beyond the Fringe*, we sent the *Establishment*'s cast after him across the Atlantic, not to New York but to the Second City Theatre in Chicago. For a short time the Second City company played at the *Establishment* in their place in Greek Street. Individually and collectively, they were immensely talented – the company had already produced Mike Nichols and Elaine May – but they were a little too earnest, a little too rigid and contrived. They won respectful reviews from the theatre critics, but the impetuous anarchic joyousness of the *Establishment* originals was missing. It had been packed in the baggage of the original cast and trundled with them to Illinois. This American tour heralded the end of the *Establishment Club*. Anchored round Peter, the place was built on a few rare people and their talents. People and talent can be irreplaceable. So, in combination with business incompetence, it proved in Soho. Neither Peter nor I had any experience in business. Ideas, laughter, songs, throngs of clamorous, interesting, quarrelsome people, writers and rogues, poets and painters, politicians and random fornicators of any gender, yes, they were all red meat to us. Tidy columns of accounts, neat balance sheets, and management control systems weren't. Fifty crates of wine would be delivered. Forty-nine of the crates would 'walk' straight out of the cellar door. We never noticed but we paid. The wine went, the cast went, and eventually the roof fell in.

Before the rafters collapsed we'd found ourselves involved in other ventures. With Peter's support, I'd launched an innovative and interesting magazine called *Scene*. It ran the first major article on the Beatles, and took on as its theatre critic a gangling young man from Bristol who claimed to be called William Boot, strangely the name of the nature notes journalist in Evelyn Waugh's *Scoop*, although I missed the coincidence when I interviewed him. Boot later turned out, after probing, to be a Czech-born would-be playwright named Tom Stoppard. The magazine was splendid, but wildly overambitious, undercapitalized, and incompetently run. It sank in the sands. By the time it ended, Boot/Stoppard was the only journalist left, writing everything from the sports pages to the financial supplement.

A second venture was another magazine named *Private Eye*. *Private Eye* was started in autumn 1961 by a cabal of Oxford-educated public schoolboys. It swiftly ran out of steam and money, and for a whole variety of reasons, its founders approached Peter and me for a rescue operation. There should have been, in today's fashionable term, an obvious 'synergy' between the two arms of the so-called satire movement; the one in performance, the other in print. It didn't work out like that. Naïvely I brought the *Establishment* cast and the *Eye* team together for idea-exchanging working lunches. The *Establishment* group, state and scholarship-Cambridge-educated, thought the *Eye* lads were greedy, ambitious and supercilious members of the middle-classes. The *Eye* contingent found the *Establishment* boys and girls flint-hard, down-market, even threatening. The one group, the *Eye* people, as Richard Ingrams among others has chronicled, gloried in boozing, braying, and throwing-up in pubs. The other, the *Establishment* team, worked, drank coffee, discussed F.R. Leavis, and played poker for relaxation. Cultures clashed. Hostility flared and flickered like static electricity. I persevered with the meetings, but they weren't a success.

Peter never liked the business from the start. When I wrote to him to say that Andrew Osmond, the majority shareholder in *Private Eye*, had offered us his shares, he replied on a postcard. 'Nick, this isn't for me,' he said. 'If you want to go ahead, do it on your own. They'll do nothing but fight, and it'll all end in tears.' I ignored his advice, and agreed to buy Osmond's seventy-six per cent holding over lunch in a Soho restaurant.

Private Eye was the first venture since our alliance at Cambridge that Peter and I hadn't taken on in partnership. My effectively sole ownership of the magazine didn't last for very long, although it did span the time when the *Eye* started to become a national institution. Then when *Scene* and soon afterwards the *Establishment* closed, I handed over my *Private Eye* shares to Peter. Peter, swallowing his initial reluctance to have anything to do with the magazine, became the *Eye*'s owner. There was little else to be picked up from the debris, and I went off to Spain in search of new and warmer pastures – to travel, explore, and write.

Peter's hostility to *Private Eye* was, I think, due to little more than what's known now as 'bad chemistry'. He was fond of and fiercely protective towards the *Establishment* company. They were his creation, his clan, intellectually far brighter than the *Eye* people, more disciplined, and much funnier. They were also happy, a small band of companionable friends. The *Eye* people were strangers. He just didn't like what he called the cunning and quarrelsome dead fish – Peter was right, they were always at each other's throats and some of their feuds have lasted to this day – he had to deal with. Over the years that followed, his attitude changed and softened. He became immensely proud of the magazine. As he used to confide, Peter came to tolerate, if never particularly to trust or like, Richard Ingrams. It wasn't surprising. Peter was on the side of life, a scintillating vodka-drinking anarchist. Ingrams was a censorious teetotaller. Peter had a roving eye and was three-times married. Ingrams believed in fidelity and marriage for life, and pursued those who strayed like a hungry vengeful shark. Peter rocked with laughter at the hubristic pretensions of government ministers. Ingrams was immensely proud to be invited to receptions at 10 Downing Street – a summons from Harold Wilson to attend a reception notable for the presence of a comedian called Jimmy Tarbuck was, according to Ingrams's wife, Mary, one of the high points of his life.

They were complete opposites and yet, as Peter said the last time I saw him, 'We rub along together.' Ingrams remained editor for years under Peter's ownership of the *Eye*, before parting painfully from his wife, skipping off with a fragrant lady, and becoming a dry bar-fly at the Groucho Club, a flash drinking club of a kind that represents everything Ingrams once claimed to despise.

Rushton, the victim of a purge, became a fruity voice-over in television commercials. Osmond, perhaps the only man of substance among the original *Eye* team, emerged with his friend Douglas Hurd as a skilful novelist. Booker, another casualty of one of the magazine's endless palace revolutions, moved to the west country and into mainstream journalism.

Peter made his own adjustments to all of them as they came, stayed, or went. His contribution to the magazine's success was vast. Not just in the brilliance and vigour of his ideas, but in his constant search for and encouragement of talents to move it forward. One of his proudest claims, a story he loved telling, was of finding a young Italian waiter called Fantoni, who was attending art school. Peter taught him, not very successfully, how to play cricket and encouraged him to go on drawing. Fantoni became an entertaining cartoonist whose drawings often appeared in the *Eye*. Who else but Peter would have shown a balding Italian waiter how to bowl and helped him to become a successful artist?

And in terms of the relationship between him and myself that was largely that. Peter devoted himself to *Private Eye*, created his inspired second-wave performance relationship with Dudley Moore – one of the most inventive, perceptive, and brilliantly funny series of dialogues in modern comedy – and took on, with increasing weariness, a few other roles. I travelled, explored, wrote. We stayed in touch and frequently had dinner together, but time and geography increasingly parted us. Then, barely a month before his death, my own beloved eldest daughter died too. Peter had known Francesca since she was a child. The twin tragedies of their deaths had, in the rum way things have of shaking out, at least one positive consequence; it brought me back into touch with the gentle companion, and subsequently wife, of Peter's later years, Lin, gentle but also resolute and strong. I haven't the slightest doubt that with Lin Peter found peace and safety. Lucky old Peter – but men like him merit the fortune and the fair following wind that carries a Lin to them.

His genius for vision and laughter aside, Peter had other rare qualities. He was a man utterly without malice, envy, or rancour. He teased himself and others about Dudley's success as a Hollywood sex-symbol. I don't think Peter cared a damn. Peter lived his life with exceptional and unconscious grace. In the whole, wide scheme of things he had what he wanted. Vodka by the bucket, and why not? The strange panorama of human life that he scanned and chuckled over as the tabloids recorded our mischiefs, murders, and adulteries. His devotion to Spurs footballers. His mischievious calls to radio talk-show phone-ins, in the character and voice of a visiting Norwegian fisherman or a lunatic killer who'd been released back into the community from Broadmoor. His love for a late-night crack with his many luminous friends. Instinctively, Peter got the whole damn thing sorted out. Darkness comes soon enough. You didn't need to fulfil your promise, whatever that flatulent phrase means, or become rich or famous, Queen or Prime Minister, Lord Olivier or Mother Theresa or whatever. You needed a brimming glass, good company, a story, and a smile.

Peter, thank God, had them all in abundance. Peter *was* the promise – and the promise realized in gentleness and laughter. He looked deep, deep and far and often sideways, and he saw and chuckled. His vision of the world was matchless in its clearsightedness, as true and steady as the scanning gaze of a hunting falcon, and he was able to live with it. Most of us would have buckled and broken under the pressures of what Peter saw. He didn't. Peter poured himself another vodka and laughed. The man died happy. Bless him.

Elisabeth Luard

To Pin a Butterfly

The smile made the difference.

It had a sardonic edge as you might expect, but also a gentleness, a sweetness, a lack of disapproval, a refusal to judge or be judged. It had a detachment too, as if its owner did not quite believe that he was supposed to be in that place at that time. It was always there, just on the edge of the mouth, in the curve of the eyebrows, in the eyes themselves. A sadness too. That he saw the world more clearly than others saw it could not have been an easy load to bear.

Peter was never a clown, not even in the early days of *Beyond the Fringe*, or on the stage of the *Establishment Club*, where he starred nightly in cabaret. I saw Peter first behind the footlights, playing *The Fringe*, admired him, fell a little in love in with him, like all the young women of my generation and my kind – those whose brothers went to the great universities, whose intellects were no less than theirs whose educational good fortune we were not quite allowed to share. Believe me, it was so – in my family and many others. It was believed that clever girls didn't catch husbands, and we were kept as ignorant as lack of education could make us.

The other three of the quartet – Alan Bennett, Jonathan Miller, Dudley Moore – were daring, funny, admirable to us, their own generation, their own kind. They too were anarchic, iconoclastic. They too were saying the unsayable. But they had a kind of puppy eagerness, a willingness to play the game, which would ultimately lead them to reach for the rewards, to make their careers within the system.

Peter was different. More dangerous. Subversive. You could see it in the stillness, the tranquillity of the actor on the stage. He was never one to follow the rules. He was even then, and would remain always, an observer, an outsider, a man who had no appetite for compromise. You could see it already, in all his youth and beauty – and he had physical beauty, no doubt of that, as attractive to men as he was to women. But far more seductive, to me and those who like myself lacked formal education, was his accessibility, his lack of intellectual arrogance – a rare quality in the clever men of that time, perhaps of all time.

Nevertheless, he was a true satirist, a Swift, a Bacon, a pickpocket of the mind who could unravel the threads of the Emperor's cloak until his subjects saw the demigod in all his vainglorious nudity, the stripping fingers so swift and deft that the victim was unaware until the deed was done. He did it, and then he walked away. That was his role, as with all those who sweep away the cobwebs of the mind.

Later, when I was courting my future husband, Nicholas – and yes, we girls dared to do the courting, although our mothers would have despaired of our boldness – I knew him better. Peter and Nicholas were partners, co-owners of the *Establishment*, billed as London's first and only satirical theatre club. At that time I was working for the embryonic *Private Eye* (let's not get excited – females were confined to bookkeeping and stamp-licking – we women did not star on that early masthead).

Peter even then was impossibly glamorous. He had already married his first wife, Wendy Snowdon, in a flurry of tabloid headlines and posed photographs in glossy magazines. The golden couple, they were the first of our generation to play house, have babies – two daughters – and Wendy kept open house in a tall house in Hampstead. I remember stripped pine, polished brass and those dense dark colours – forest green, midnight blue, claret – newly fashionable. Objects on tables, too. Sean Kenny was responsible for the minimalist décor at the Club, but David Hicks did lifestyle for the readers of *Tatler* and *Queen*.

The kitchen was in the basement, social activity centred on a vast table permanently loaded with wine and food – although maybe, like the summers of our childhood, memory paints a rosy picture. We were as fashionable in the kitchen as we were in our Vidal Sassoon haircuts and our sharp little Mary Quant shifts. Elizabeth David had gripped our youthful culinary imaginations. Just as we, liberated by the Pill, did not share our mothers' sexual inhibitions (although, heaven knows, they had all kicked over the traces during the war), so we did not wish to cook as they did. Our independence manifested itself in garlic and olive oil. We were the moussaka generation. We cooked quiche. Ratatouille ruled where cauliflower cheese had once held sway.

The guests who crowded into Wendy's kitchen were, naturally, as fashionable as anyone might wish (although we did not yet know how fashionable – hindsight adds fame). Long-legged Charlie Rampling (starlet, not yet star); sly John Lennon and nice young Paul McCartney, a shy Cat Stevens towed in his wake. Waspish Ken Tynan, Judy Huxtable (before long, the second Mrs Cook), Ustinov, Sellers – Dudley, of course, not yet the tiny superstar, but a man who could make a fine fistful of the ivories.

And always Peter himself at the centre of it all, spinning word-pictures like candy floss around some notion, some absurdity, some story which had caught his magpie attention. Half were pure fantasy – the activities of the fictional Order of the Leaping Nuns, Leda explaining to a disbelieving husband how she fell for a passing swan; others were the stuff of politics – Christine Keeler's pillow-talk, Prime

Minister Macmillan scenting the wind of change through Dr Banda's arsehole.

Black or white, yellow or pink, Peter was no respecter of persons. If his politics were anarchic, he was not without allegiances. He was the moving force behind the first Oxfam concert at the Albert Hall. Wendy and I (certainly several months pregnant) did the catering for the party afterwards – rabbit stew with rosemary as I recall, but what would you expect? The venue was the Pheasantry – the party negotiated by Anthony Haden-Guest in the studio of the fashionable photographer, Clive Virgin. I remember that I danced with Peter – we did the twist, an odd couple, me some seven months gone, and Peter with his lanky limbs contorting like corkscrews. For company, the Rolling Stones, Tom Wolfe, Hockney, Boshier, Allen Jones – everyone who was anyone in what had just been dubbed Swinging London. It was not that Peter had a nose for the centre of things, he *was* the centre of things.

At that time in the early sixties, the *Establishment Club* was riding the crest of the satire wave, while *Private Eye* was struggling for life. My job (wages, £5 a week) was on the line. After the few newsagents who carried us had been threatened with libel-suits, the Club (and a few university bookshops in the provinces) was the only place we could sell the magazine. Peter did not approve of the *Eye* at first – it was Nicholas who gave us the chance of survival when the print-bill had to be paid. I think perhaps Peter thought the magazine too lightweight, too frivolous, too close to the slapstick comedy which pinches the fat lady's bottom and slides round the serious business of satire.

Under the *Establishment*'s umbrella, the magazine briefly moved offices to the waiters' changing-room, then relocated to a vacant first-floor two doors down Greek Street. The finances stayed behind, and I was shifted to full-time bookkeeping, so I had – geographically at least – changed allegiance. There were three of us girls in those backstage offices – the other two, Venetia Morshead and Helen

Nicholl, both beautiful and glamorous young women, whom Peter had decided should don pebble-glasses and answer to the name of Miss Rigby when outsiders came to visit. It was a game, all of it – there was no room for outraged feminism.

Soho was a dangerous place in those days. Perhaps no more dangerous than now – except that the villains were mostly home-grown. The Kray twins and Peter Rachman ran the manor, and you could never be certain whose side the policemen were on. The *Establishment*'s bar was a late-night venue, and like all such, filled up with the usual 'colourful' characters: poets and playwrights (Logue and Hastings, McGrath, Wesker); painters (Minton, Freud and Bacon among them); con-men; gamblers; bent coppers (Detective Sergeant Challenor, a man a little too eager to slip a brick into a CND protester's pocket); gangsters. Particularly gangsters.

Heady stuff, bad characters. But we were young and innocent, and couldn't tell the good from the bad. Naturally enough, protection money was looked for from those entrepreneurs who set up in business among the strip-shows and knocking-shops. Naturally enough too, London's first satirical nightclub could not recognize a collecting box even when it was being rattled energetically in its ear. 'Hate to see nice boys like you get into trouble' met with innocent agreement. This led to what can only be described as misunderstandings. The misunderstandings led to the appearance, one sunny morning, of a couple of heavies hell-bent on inflicting a spot of GBH on the owners of the premises.

Peter happened to come in early that morning. Finding the bar staff cowering behind the counter, and the two thugs (for all I know, they were the Kray twins themselves) terrorizing the office and smashing up the typewriters, Peter did one of the bravest things I have ever seen. Later he said it was blind panic – but whatever it was which possessed him, he managed quite literally to talk our assailants into a state of disarmed bewilderment, coaxing them back down the stairs and out onto the pavement outside, leaving them in a pool of helpless, hypnotized docility to be scooped up by a passing Black Maria.

I did not see him often in later years. He came to dinner occasionally, in the various family houses we had. Perhaps the invitation would have been triggered by finding him at one of the rare gatherings of those who were associated with *Private Eye* – tenth anniversary celebration, twenty-five years since first publication, whatever. At such nostalgic jamborees there were drink and noise, speeches, laughter, gossip; new faces (to me at least), famous or infamous, and the old familiar faces grown older – worried and lined with the struggle to bring up families, or heavy and soft with the trappings of success.

There were jokes, naturally. Professional comedians to entertain the faithful. *Private Eye* takes pride in its jokes. But it makes a distinction between campaigning journalism and the finger-pointing icon-tipping verbal cartoon which pricks pomposity, sometimes draws blood, but rarely changes the way we think. Peter did jokes too, but he did not manufacture them. He came to them without luggage, without plot or forethought, without the careful structure of the stage comedian. He did more than jokes, he changed lives.

How to explain that curious quality? Film clips and TV soundbites do not do him justice. He was not much of a man for the written word. Sensitive to his audience as any medieval jester, he was a penny-in-the-hat man, at his best as a raconteur, a spinner of that strange web which binds a storyteller to those who listen to his stories. A man for company: one would do but three was better, whose reactions he could judge, whose emotions he could play, whose laughter he could orchestrate. In a medieval court he would have had it easier, been merrily employed to shake his cap and bells at the pompous and the puffed-up, enlivening the long evenings, sneaking out to the stable to rescue a fair maiden by spinning dull straw into glittering gold.

At public gatherings, I would search Peter out. He would always be there somewhere, tall and tranquil at the heart of the maelstrom, an observer always, smiling that same smile. In later years with Lin, his third wife destined to be his widow, close by his side. He looked happier with her there, more content, as if the demons which had haunted him in earlier years had wandered away – never totally out of earshot, but no longer perched on his shoulder, poking sharp noses into his business.

And yet his peculiar genius remains elusive. You cannot pin a butterfly unless you first kill it. Its beauty can only be properly admired in life, from a little distance – dancing in sunlight or settled on a leaf. And yet reality is not always as it seems. Appearances can deceive. The butterfly, seductive though it may be to the eye, is not dainty in its habits. It is as likely to sip sustenance from a steaming cowpat as dip its tubular tongue into the throat of a lavender blossom.

What might appear (in dappled shade of woodland) to be the courtship ritual of a pair of Painted Ladies, is not a mating couple at all, but two males engaged in a fierce territorial battle. Things are not always what they seem – but we love them all the same. We see in them what we wish to see – and their beauty illuminates our lives.

So too with Peter, and I shall miss that light. But above all, most of all, in any gathering where I might expect to find him, I miss that smile.

Barry Humphries

A Recollection

I first glimpsed Peter Cook in the saloon bar of the Lamb and Flag, off Floral Street. The cast of *Oliver!* drank there between matinées and evening shows – or those of us who drank did. Occasionally, some of the cast of that other concurrent hit, *Beyond the Fringe* at the Fortune Theatre, dropped into the pub as well, but then there were only four people in that show, and it was Dudley Moore we usually saw. His pretty, blonde girlfriend, Anna Leroy, was a flower-seller in Lionel Bart's operetta.

Peter Cook, who sometimes accompanied Dudley for an abstemious half pint, was aquiline to the point of undulation. Although he never diffused an aura of vanity, he held his fine features at a haughty tilt as though regarding himself dispassionately in an invisible looking-glass. By then his celebrity was well established and he wore a dark suit of shiny mohair in a modish cut. He retained the schoolboy's mannerism of flicking back an unruly forelock with an abrupt turn of the head.

When *Beyond the Fringe* moved to Broadway, auditions were held for a replacement cast, and I went along, even though my *Oliver!* contract was for the 'run of the show'. I had been assured by Mr Donald Albery that after a year in the musical my release would be sympathetically considered if I were offered something really spectacular.

I don't know who it was who sat in the darkened stalls on the day I auditioned, but Peter Cook was certainly there. I improvised a surreal monologue as Neville Chamberlain returning from Munich and, soon after, was offered a job in the new cast. Alas, a starring role in *Beyond the Fringe* was not regarded by the producer of *Oliver!* as sufficient justification for my release, and I revolved for another six months on Sean Kenny's famous Dickensian set.

I didn't see Peter again until the following year. I had done my first Australian one-man show, returned to London, and immediately been offered a few months in the States to help launch *Oliver!* on Broadway. By the time I got to New York, bribed by undreamed-of dollars, *Beyond the Fringe* was already an established success and Peter and his wife Wendy, with their faithful secretary Judy Scott Fox, were living in what seemed to me a sumptuous *ménage à trois* in Greenwich Village. Here and there in the rambling apartment were real Tiffany lamps – only then returning to fashion – and there was an abundance of rich textiles of crimson and mulberry silk and crushed velvet, which created an atmosphere of opulence. Or so I apprehended, living as I was, only a few blocks away in an austere cold-water flat above a poodle parlour.

Peter and I, somewhat warily at first, began a friendship which was to last, off and on, until his death. The possibility that he might predecease us all seemed unthinkable. Peter had, I noticed, Americanized himself. He had exchanged his London winkle-pickers for sneakers and his suits for jeans and T-shirts, often emblazoned with the slogans of popular baseball teams. On closer acquaintance, I was surprised – perhaps even slightly shocked – to find such a brilliant fellow preoccupied with sport and pop music. He did not, as far as I could tell, read anything other than newspapers, and may indeed have spent his entire sojourn in New York without having ever visited the Metropolitan Museum or the Frick collection.

To a rather self-conscious young highbrow from the

provinces like me, Peter Cook's studied philistinism was disconcerting. It seemed anomalous that such an apparently 'aesthetic', indeed, languid personage could enjoy life without books, or art, or music. It is true that he appreciated *some* music; we went to Harlem together and heard The Supremes at the famous Apollo Theatre and occasionally went to Village Vanguard when a famous band was playing. But Peter's perpetual, almost compulsive jocosity made intimacy difficult. Unable to discuss sport – his principal interest – or to enjoy rock 'n' roll for more than a few consecutive minutes, I felt excluded from the inner court of his friendship.

I had brought with me from Australia a 'microgroove' recording of my one-man show *A Nice Night's Entertainment* and Peter particularly enjoyed the Sandy Stone monologue, wherein a desiccated old suburbanite rambled on in minute detail about his exceedingly boring life. In later years, I rather felt that Cook's creation, E.L. Wisty might have been partially influenced by his Australian counterpart.

Just before my American contract in *Oliver!* expired, Peter invited me to perform my 'act' at his new club in Greek Street, the *Establishment*. He had already presented there, with great success, the notorious American comedian and drug addict, Lenny Bruce, and I secretly feared that my rather anodyne regional monologues, with their multiple Australian references, would be lost on the beau monde of Soho. However, Cook was convinced they would work, and offered me the amazing fee of £100 per week.

He never saw the show, fortunately, since he was still working in New York when I opened – and closed. The reaction of audiences and critics confirmed my worst fears and the large cheques on Coutts bank, signed by Peter in far-away Manhattan, were small consolation to a disgraced comedian. I wondered if I could ever look Peter Cook in the eye again after that, but when he returned to London he never referred to the *Establishment* débâcle, and instead offered me a role in his first film, *Bedazzled*, a modern chronicle of the Seven Deadly Sins. I was cast, somewhat appropriately under the circumstances, as Envy.

Not long after, Peter suggested that I collaborate with Nicholas Garland on a comic strip for *Private Eye*. At the *Eye*'s cluttered office in Greek Street pullulated the Cook coterie. A fan club of real talent like Ingrams, John Wells or Willie Rushton, diluted with a raggle-taggle of toadies, shameless sycophants and Cook impersonators. Peter seemed to thrive, as most of us do, in this climate of adulation. He viewed with a sublime indifference the wild crushes which he unconsciously and without effort inspired. One of my other monologues on the record I had given him in New York concerned a naïve Australian anglophobe in Earl's Court called Buster Thompson, whose life was a quest for cold Australian lager. This was the prototype of the Barry McKenzie strip, which ran, off and on, for the rest of the sixties. Cook had furnished the name of the character which derived from my own, and Garland contributed the 'look'.

Barry McKenzie took a while to catch on. I think Richard Ingrams was, in the early days, less enthusiastic than his proprietor, but as Nick and I slowly developed a coherent and offensive style, Ingrams supported us also. As the decade drew to a close, the adventures of Bazza had been banned in Australia and achieved cult status in Britain.

When I came back to London in 1971 after a long interlude in Australia, it was to make a film version of McKenzie with my friend Bruce Beresford. Peter's midwifery at Bazza's birth was appropriately acknowledged on the screen credits, and he even played a minor role in the film in his habitual languid manner. He wasn't really an actor and did everything with a half-smile and a curiously writhing movement of the head and shoulders, so that one watched his performance more than anyone else's.

Peter's first marriage ended some time in the seventies and he formed a long liaison with a blonde actress who had the face of a sprite. Her previous partner had been the famous designer, Sean Kenny, whose premature death, tragic though it was, was certainly not attributable to thirst. We saw each other only occasionally in these years, though I heard in the early eighties that Peter had sought professional help in conquering an addiction to alcohol. There were stories of his splendid resurrections and equally spectacular relapses. Meanwhile, his art suffered; or rather, his public suffered for the lack of it. There was a sudden renaissance when he and his old partner, Dudley Moore, impersonating two cronies called Derek and Clive, collaborated on a scabrous series of gramophone records. These obsessive dialogues, of a transcendental lewdness, mostly improvised, one surmised, under the influence of various popular stimulants, are amongst the funniest of Cook's and Moore's virtuoso turns.

In spite of sporadic appearances on talk shows through which he nonchalantly sauntered, Peter Cook, in his last years, devoted most of his time to golf and occasional inspirational visits to the offices of *Private Eye*. His shape had changed rather startlingly, and his appetite for vodka and cigarettes seemed undiminished. He was always available for his friends, however, and performed many private acts of kindness without getting found out. At a dark time in my own life when I had received an ominous letter from Australia which I dreaded opening, he sweetly performed that office, perused the letter and delivered an hilarious précis of its contents.

Two years ago he came to my birthday party at the Garrick Club. You knew he was present by the gales of laughter emanating from the large group in his corner of the room. We talked for a while before he and Lin went home, and I shook the hand of this most original, most generous of men. It was the last time.

John Bird

2: Impresario

Everybody thinks of Peter Cook now as an individual comic genius. I do too, but the Cook I knew was also an impresario, an imaginative and seemingly effortless one. Most people who go in for that sort of thing are interested in power but I think Peter just wanted certain things to happen because he fancied the idea of them, and the quickest and best way of achieving that was to do it himself. At Cambridge we had talked about the idea of having a satirical cabaret club in London; the model was the Berlin night-clubs of the twenties and thirties which did so much, as Cook put it, to prevent the rise of Adolf Hitler.

A factor not to be underestimated was the arrogance of Cambridge undergraduates: we thought it was only a matter of time before we took over the world; a world or at least a Britain creaking under a long-established Conservative Government and stifled by rigid social conventions. It was one thing, however, to sit in Cambridge coffee-bars imagining ourselves at the centre of London showbusiness and another to fix it up. Cook did it. He left Pembroke College in 1960; exactly a year later *Beyond the Fringe* had opened in the West End, and in October 1961 the *Establishment* started in the premises of a Soho strip-club, with a pre-opening membership of 7000 people, many of whom had paid for life membership. It was a ridiculous success. There were queues in Greek Street every night. Socialites, cabinet ministers, fashion models, intellectuals fought to get in. Doormen were bribed. We performed twice a night, six nights a week. In May the following year, I remember walking through the audience for the second show on a Monday night and seeing two empty seats: I was appalled. It turned out that somebody had just had a heart attack and had been compelled, presumably reluctantly, to give up his place. It was filled by the time the show began.

There was a practical point to having a club: at that time the Lord Chamberlain exercised a form of censorship over the public theatre and scripts had to be submitted in advance to his office. This was no mere formality: they would cut material they considered offensive, and sometimes suggest their own rewrites. (I had by now joined the Royal Court Theatre as a director and had first-hand experience of this. Some of the Lord Chamberlain's suggestions were based on mysterious precepts; he rejected the line 'God – he doesn't exist, the bastard' in Beckett's *Endgame*, offering as an alternative 'God – he doesn't exist, the sod.') Performances at members-only clubs were outside the Lord Chamberlain's control, allowing for stronger material. Today, when menstruation and the techniques of fellatio form the staple fare of our best-loved family entertainers, most of the *Establishment*'s material would seem tame indeed. We had a piece in which a (ludicrously stereotyped) north-country Labour politician was being instructed by a smoothie marketing executive in methods of advertising through subliminal sexual innuendo ('Vote Labour for bigger genitals') and negative suggestion ('If you don't vote Labour your genitals will drop off'); perhaps the most radical of our sketches was written for our American shows. Since so much of our material centred on class we wanted to demonstrate to the American audience the way the British at that time saw everything through a filter of class and accent recognition; we therefore began the show with a presentation of the crucifixion scene in which the thieves had East End voices and John Fortune as Christ deployed a decent upper-class accent. We brought this sketch back to London but if we'd performed it in a theatre we'd have been arrested.

The *Establishment* was Peter Cook's creation, floated initially on his name, or perhaps I should say his aura. The nuts-and-bolts things were somehow taken care of, too: money raised, premises found and rebuilt, staff engaged, publicity organized. Cook was heavily involved in all of this, but he must have done it in his lunch-time, or his sleep; as far as I was concerned, what he was really interested in was the show, which he co-wrote with John Fortune and myself. He also, incidentally, encouraged me to perform, something I'd never done or intended to do; I'm still doing it thirty-five years later.

The cast of the *Establishment* took two short breaks during the first year, and Peter's choice to fill those gaps was characteristically inspired: Frankie Howerd and Lenny Bruce. Howerd's stint there – seemingly a fish-out-of-water engagement, and with an act built at Cook's suggestion round that disjunction – in fact was a triumph, rejuvenating him and his career. He brought Lenny Bruce from America, and had to fight the Home Office to do it: Bruce, a very public drug-user, was declared a prohibited person by the Home Secretary. Cook not only had to persuade the authorities that Lenny was a clean-living paragon who wouldn't frighten the horses, he had on occasion to traipse round London at three in the morning trying to find heroin for him.

We spent a lot of time in early 1962 trying to get the BBC to buy a packaged television satire show based on the *Establishment*. Peter and I devised formats, wrote sample scripts and had long meetings with various Corporation executives. This turned out to be a doomed project; the BBC men nodded, made notes, and eventually came up with their own show, *That Was The Week That Was*, initially bearing some resemblance to ours. In those days they had no intention of taking packages from outside, though they didn't tell us that at the time; it was the one area where Peter was unable to extend his influence, or his control.

Since I found I needed the odd moment to eat and sleep I was only marginally involved in Cook's take-over of *Private Eye* – that story is told elsewhere in this book. Willie Rushton has described meetings that Peter arranged between the *'Establishment* people' (John Fortune, Eleanor Bron and me) and the *'Eye* people' as uncomfortable, even hostile encounters. I must say I don't remember that, in fact I scarcely remember the meetings. Probably what Willie refers to as my austere, left-wing reserve was straightforward semi-consciousness. Peter carried the whole process, as he did everything, on a floating carpet of laughter and unstoppable invention. He never seemed tired, or anxious; he always looked terrific. There was an atmosphere of open-top cars, chic restaurants, fashion shows. And, just to fill up the time, he was performing *Beyond the Fringe* every night.

Chicago had a cabaret theatre, much longer-established than the *Establishment*, called Second City. Mike Nichols and Elaine May had come out of there, Alan Arkin and lots more. Some time in summer 1962, Peter turned up and said, how would we like to do an exchange with their company? Eight weeks. I never knew how he got on to this, but *Beyond the Fringe* was going to Broadway that autumn so it seemed like a good idea. Restless, restless. We'd been in Chicago about a month when Peter, now in New York, rang me to say he'd had an idea: what did we think about opening an *Establishment Club* in New York? He'd found a really nice place on East 54th Street, some American partners, money. We could open around Christmas, which would be a good time. To fill in the gap between then and the end of our Chicago engagement he'd got us a month's booking at the Hungry I in San Francisco, then the most famous comedy club in America. I suppose he'd been in New York about a fortnight, must have got bored with just being a sell-out on Broadway.

A few weeks afterwards, this neat scheme received a setback: the New York print unions began a prolonged newspaper strike. It was the accepted view, certainly in the sixties, that to open a new show, let alone a new venue, in a period when you would be deprived of reviews, publicity and print advertising would be suicidal. We decided to postpone the opening till the strike was over, and Cook arranged a new engagement for us in Washington. But Christmas came and went, the strike dragged on, the premises on 54th St – it had been the old El Morocco night-club – stood empty, with the lease still having to be paid and no income coming in. Finally we felt we couldn't hang on any longer: newspapers or no newspapers, we had to open. Of course we weren't the only people with this problem; every new venture in New York was trying to think of ways to publicize itself without the benefit of press exposure, at a time when radio and television weren't quite as important as they are now. Every square inch of public space in Manhattan was plastered with flybills and posters and it was difficult to do something which stood out. Cook's solution was worthy of Diaghilev: it was effective, original, funny, with the additional advantage (for him) of paying off an old score.

The background to it was the negotiations which had gone on for the rights to produce *Beyond the Fringe* on Broadway, which had come down to a contest between David Merrick, then the most powerful American theatrical producer, and Alexander Cohen. Cohen won, which had irritated Merrick considerably, prompting him, as Cook told it, to slag off *Beyond the Fringe* and British talent in general whenever he had the opportunity. Merrick himself had trouble during the newspaper strike, and for a show he put on called *Subways are for Sleeping* he'd come up with the idea of getting people with the same names as the theatre critics on the New York papers to give laudatory quotes for the piece, which he than printed on handbills. Cook found – don't ask me how – a man in Philadelphia called David

Merrick (as it happened, a black postman), brought him to Washington to see the *Establishment* and pressed him for his verdict. He readily agreed that it was the best show he had ever seen. Since it was the only show he had ever seen, this was undeniably true; posters were printed with a photograph of this solemn-looking middle-aged black gentleman in a gabardine raincoat with the legend: 'The *Establishment* ... "this is the best show I have ever seen, I wish I had a piece of it" – David Merrick.' Just to make sure, Cook had a blow-up of the poster attached to balloons and floated it up past Merrick's skyscraper office window.

The New York *Establishment* was, if anything, even more successful than the London one; once again, Peter had created a place which attracted what used to be called the cream of society. I suppose there's an argument that a genuinely satirical venture ought to put off, rather than attract, the cream of society. This was a problem we had faced in London, where it might fairly be said that we in the show were actually hostile to much of our audience, particularly the young Guards-officer-and-their-bimbos element. Fashionable people were among our targets, we thought, so if it was fashionable to go to the *Establishment* it must also be suspect. This wasn't just tortuous, there was a suggestion of having one's cake and eating it. It was an issue which never bothered Cook, though. If people wanted to pay him good money to get a going-over, that was fine by him. It wasn't just a question of keeping up the cash-flow, either: Cook enjoyed setting up situations which tested people's sense of their own context, including his own. What didn't appeal to him was the sight of performers lining up on stage (as would be memorably done at the Royal Shakespeare Theatre) and glaring icily at the audience with the unspoken message: 'Yes! You are the guilty ones.'

Cook and his American partner David Balding immediately began work on turning the upper floors of the New York *Establishment* into a straight theatre, and that opened in May 1964 with a production of Ann Jellicoe's *The Knack*. If an impresario is judged by the quality of people he gives chances to, Cook scored well here: the then unknown George Segal starred with Brian Bedford, and the production marked the beginning of Mike Nichols's career as a director.

Peter Cook now had successful clubs in London and New York, a controlling interest in *Private Eye*; he himself was a hit in *Beyond the Fringe* (which was also still running in London with a replacement cast). But he was still irritated by his failure to get us on the BBC, and he regarded *That Was The Week That Was*, now running back home and news of which filtered across the Atlantic, as something of a rip-off, so he turned his attention to American television. In 1963 this was dominated by the three major networks, their output – particularly entertainment – dedicated to the massiest of mass appeal, sponsor-controlled and deeply conservative. Of all light entertainment programmes, the one with the biggest audience (over sixty million weekly) was the *Ed Sullivan Show*, put out by CBS. It was this that Cook improbably chose as our vehicle. Once again the producing machinery was conjured up apparently overnight: a company was set up with two American partners, Jean Vandenheuvel and Clay Felker, and a contract was signed with CBS for us to independently produce a weekly thirteen-minute segment for Ed Sullivan. Peter and I were to write and appear, Jonathan Miller to direct; we engaged some American writers, mostly from the *New Yorker*, and American performers. It was a happy and enthusiastic little team, and if Khrushchev had decided to run for the US Presidency he would have had more chance of success. Sullivan himself was a large man, a former sportswriter who, despite having hosted this show for years seemed paralysed by nerves on transmission (it went out live); he announced the acts standing stiffly at the side of the stage bellowing at the camera, working from cue cards with his entire script written on them, including the words, 'Hi, I'm

Ed Sullivan.' I'm not sure he knew what political satire was. He'd certainly never seen the *Establishment* and I guess somebody had told him that we and *Beyond the Fringe* were the most fashionable shows in New York. When he saw the run-through of our first offering his eyes glazed over, his mouth opened and shut but nothing came out. There were terrific rows, mainly involving Jonathan, as I recall, who kept walking out on principle. Sullivan's view was that our material – which we had deliberately kept mild, or so we thought – required cuts, starting with the first words of the script and ending with the last. My memory of Peter was that he was well aware of the impossibility of the enterprise which he had launched and rather enjoyed watching the fall-out. We did maybe two shows – God knows what went in them – and they paid us off. What had been remarkable was not that it didn't succeed, but that it had got as far as it did.

Cook had done it all in an astonishingly short space of time: it had been barely eighteen months since the *Establishment* had opened in London. It took an equally brief period for the whole thing – *Private Eye* excepted – to collapse. By the time I finally returned to London in November 1964 there was no *Establishment* in Greek Street, and the American version dribbled away not long afterwards. The next time I visited New York, not just the club and the theatre but the whole building had disappeared. Ironically for what had been created on the sixties fashion for British culture, it was now a branch of Habitat.

There were some straightforward reasons for the demise. Money: the considerable profits of the London *Establishment* had been sunk into a trendy 'lifestyle' magazine with the suicidal name *Scene*. This meant that some questionable figures were allowed to buy into the club; when the original cast members returned from New York to play a few weeks we were surprised by the number of large Levantines in slightly iridescent suits who seemed to be in charge. Still, it might have been possible for Cook to put the pieces of his 'empire' back together if he'd been so inclined: he had after all proved himself a resilient and imaginative entrepreneur. The problem was that his attitude to business was ambivalent. Essentially it was something that enabled him to do what he liked doing with people he liked doing it with, and although suites of offices, deep-piled carpets and attractive secretaries had their charms for him, business as such he regarded as an activity largely practised by self-important people with suspect inner lives. Which is why he relished taking them on in the numerous libel actions brought against *Private Eye*.

For someone to consider the exercise of power over others was for Cook an indication of a central flaw in their make-up, yet an impresario must exercise power, however gracefully. And there are many of us who were grateful to him for the power he did use in those early years, because he was an extraordinarily inspiring – and extraordinarily generous – employer, and we wished, I suppose, that he could have continued to reconcile these contradictions. That this was not possible had been already been made clear by E.L. Wisty in his programme for the World Domination League.

> How we aim to go about it is as follows: we shall move about into peoples' rooms and say 'Excuse me, we are the World Domination League, may we dominate you?' Then if they say 'Get out', then of course we'd give up.

Victor Lownes

Waiting in Line

Fact is, when I met Peter I had no idea that I'd ever come to live in England and it was before he became well known in America for his part in *Beyond the Fringe*. Peter was in Chicago to talk somebody at *Playboy* into getting that magazine to invest in his new publication, *Private Eye*. I think Peter must have tackled Hugh Hefner on this idea first. Then Hef turned Peter over to Augie Spectorsky, who was *Playboy*'s Associate Publisher and a man who shared the opinion that 'Satire is what closes on Thursday'.

Nevertheless, 'Spec' was a committed anglophile and especially philish about Oxford and Cambridge veterans. I think this had something to do with the fact that Spec had recruited top literary lights in England such as Ken Tynan, author-critic who was a regular contributor and editor for *Playboy*. Spec, who deplored the place, gave me the job of showing Peter our new sideline, the Playboy Club, a five-floor restaurant-cabaret-nightclub palace whose 'untouchable' servitors were the famed Playboy Bunnies, dozens of beautiful young ladies decked out in brightly coloured bunny costumes, complete with matching coloured satin ears and fluffy cotton tails. From the moment one stepped into this male chauvinist bastion on Walton Street just off Michigan Avenue in Chi-town one could see that it was a huge success.

The place was jammed. Just to get in one had to present a silver plated numbered key, with the famed *Playboy* rabbit-head trademark on the top part. The number was related to a huge cabinet chock full of plastic nameplates, the sort of thing that graces the desks of vice presidents at banks. But in this case they were slotted into brass bound slots on a whole wall, headed: 'AT THE PLAYBOY CLUB TONIGHT'.

This key-number-into-nameplate business was partly designed to massage the egos of our members but it also served the purpose of discouraging patronage by people who might not want anyone to know that they were right there at 107 East Walton Street . . . Well, like the mafia, for example. You see, when we opened this first Playboy Club, we met tremendous opposition from Chicago politicos, who felt a personal responsibility for trying, ineffectually as it turned out, to doom an organization that was not popular with Chicago's Roman Catholic Bishopric. (Good pun in there, somewhere.)

To keep our liquor licence, we were forbidden to call our members members; we had to call them *keyholders*. This was to avoid giving people the idea that we were a conventional club that belonged, not to a proprietor, but to its members. And then, we had to agree that we would take anyone in as a member provided they paid the not too forbidding membership fee of twenty-five dollars. Not surprisingly, we attracted some pretty notorious characters, as well as virtually everyone else. But the key–nameplate connection discouraged some of them from even putting in an occasional appearance.

I explained all this to Peter as we stood there in the lobby, looking at the 'AT THE PLAYBOY CLUB TONIGHT' wall, and waiting in a roped-off area for a table somewhere in the club to free up. I remember that Peter's comment, as he surveyed the passing Bunnies and considered our problem with the member–keyholder designation, was 'Beauty is in the eye of the keyholder.' An offhand jest that we virtually adopted as a club slogan.

The next thing that happened practically had everyone in the roped-off waiting area collapsing with laughter. I had just introduced Peter to the girl who was the key-checking 'Door Bunny' receptionist, Bunny Kitty, who also made announcements over a public address system, alerting room and floor directors of the need for tables for parties of x number. A well dressed Chicago businessman with a party of five others stormed through the front door, presented his key and demanded immediate seating for his group. Bunny Kitty took down his key number and told him that he and his group could wait with us for the next available 'six'.

'Wait? *Wait?* Do you know who I am?' he demanded.

Peter stepped in, even before a slightly flustered Kitty could get out his nameplate which would have answered that question. Peter wasn't one for letting this situation go to an easy resolution. Peter gently took the microphone for the PA system out of Kitty's hand and with a straight face and in his clipped British tones announced, 'We have a problem here in the front lobby which perhaps someone can help us with. We have a gentleman here who doesn't seem to know who he is. If anyone recognizes this man, will they please come down to reception and help us respond to his query?'

Peter handed the mike back to Kitty. The keyholder addressed his final remark to her: 'Fuck you!' Then, as he turned to leave, red-faced and angry, Peter, still with a straight face, addressed the pompous Chicagoan, 'You'll have to wait in line for that, too, I'm afraid.'

Right then I knew that Peter, unlike most of that manic-depressive school called comedians, was as likely to be as funny in ordinary life as he could be on stage or in print. I wanted this guy for a friend . . . even if I had to wait in line.

Christopher Hitchens
and Joseph Heller

Heller's Version

If – like me – you were groping your way to maturity in the early 1960s, there were two handy ways of keeping your sanity. And both of them involved a good deal of mania. Faced with ridiculous headmasters and a BBC that soon considered 'satire' to be too toxic to persist with (even when presented by David Frost) and confronted by an expiring Tory regime and with nights spent under the bedclothes brooding on things like the Cuban missile crisis, some of us were fortunate enough to find allies in the wider world. We found them by listening to *Beyond the Fringe* and by reading *Catch-22*. You could recognize a fellow-sufferer if, confronted by some ludicrous regulation or other, he knew enough to mouth the words: 'I never 'ad the Latin for the judgin'.' The boy at my school who could do this best was also the boy who helped me produce a desperate 'alternative' magazine. Pseudonyms and *noms de plume* were of the essence in such an enterprise. (Apart from adolescent posturing, there was the matter of concealing one's identity.) My friend chose the name Yossarian.

> Major Danby replied indulgently with a superior smile, 'But, Yossarian, suppose everyone felt that way?'
> 'Then I'd certainly be a damned fool to feel any other way, wouldn't I?'

1. Programme for *Pieces of Eight*, September 1959

2. 'So That's The Way You Like It'
(left to right: Peter, Dudley Moore,
Alan Bennett, Jonathan Miller)

4. (*Right*) Peter's solo, 'Sitting on
the Bench'

3. 'Bollard' (left to right: Alan Bennett,
Dudley Moore, Jonathan Miller,
Peter)

5. (*Right*) Programme from the
Fortune Theatre, May 1961
6. (*Far right*) Programme from the
John Golden Theatre, New York,
October 1962

BEYOND
THE
FRINGE

PROGRAMME : ONE SHILLING.

John Golden
Theatre

PLAYBILL

the weekly magazine for theatregoers

3/63

BEYOND THE FRINGE

DUKE OF YORK'S
THEATRE

MICHAEL CODRON

presents

one

over the

8

A NEW REVUE

PROGRAMME . . . PRICE SIXPENCE

7. (*Left*) Programme for *One Over the Eight*, April 1961

8. Peter outside the premises chosen for the *Establishment Club*, autumn 1961

9. The *Establishment Club*

Not Only...But Also

10. 'Bo Duddley'

11. Dud and Pete

12. The football fan

I can remember *exactly* where I was sitting, and what I was doing, when I first read those imperishable lines. They ranked with a cartoon in Lord Gnome's *Private Eye*, which showed a man about to hurl himself off a precipice. Another figure was admonishing him: 'Stop! If we let you do it, they'll *all* want to do it.' (What a thrill it was to send a donation to the first Gnome libel appeal, and to see one's name in the *Eye*.) Here was an anthology of response to all the stupid questions and bullying attitudes of authority.

The Fringe and the Catch were passwords by which one could survive living in Absurdistan. They prepared us for all that was to come, including the famous village in Vietnam that was destroyed in order to save it – an idea that seemed crazily stolen from Cook's 'Civil Defence' routine and Heller's 'Great Big Siege of Bologna'. I don't suppose that either man would have done anything but shriek and scoff at the notion of 'harmonic convergence'. But it was with an almost superstitious thrill that I learned that Peter Cook and Joseph Heller had become friends in New York in the early 1960s, and that Heller wanted someone to record the relationship for this volume.[1] If ever two people can have been 'meant' to meet ... well, you get the idea.

In the course of a lengthy and uproarious lunch in Manhattan, Joe Heller made me more envious than he can possibly have imagined by summoning up the days when he met Cook. '*Catch-22* had just caught on, having been published the previous year, and I was just starting to get asked everywhere. Peter was doing *Beyond the Fringe* and was also, with the others, the talk of the town. You want to know what being "lionized" means? It means being invited to parties by people you don't know. And there were a lot of parties. Peter was being lionized at the same time and in the same way, so we met. We both found it funny when we

[1] I should say that, as readers of his latest novel, *Closing Time*, will already be aware, Mr Heller is quite undimmed. But he has been recovering from back surgery and could not easily meet the deadline for this volume.

discovered that neither of us knew the host or hostess. In fact, we always found the same things funny. We laughed at the same jokes, and had the same attitudes. I don't know that we would have voted the same way but we had the same responses to things and to people.' Had he been influenced by *Catch-22*? 'You know, I have no idea. It wasn't the sort of relationship in which he was trying to impress me or I was trying to impress him. At any rate, I don't think there was any direct influence.' I asked Heller this question because, for all the appositeness of the friendship, it's quite difficult for my mind's eye to picture the extroverted New York Jew and the rather thin and reserved Englishman together. 'Well, I remember being surprised when he told me that his father had been a diplomat. He had been in Africa when the country had become independent, and Peter did a hilarious account of the dinner at which power was being handed over. One of the African leaders went on and on about what good riddance it was and how he hoped never to see the British again and all that, and then finished up by saying "*Au revoir*, Mr Cook." ' (Hearing this, I have a sudden intuition of how Peter's instinct for the ridiculous, and for the contrast between formality and absurdity, may have been nourished.)

'Peter was very shy and sensitive and nervous and highly-strung. I remember how we had dinner with him and his second wife Judy. This was when he and Dudley were in New York with *Good Evening*. He was terrified all the time that he was going to run out of pills. He had brought a supply of uppers *and* downers from London, but he only knew what they were called on his London prescription. He didn't know the generic name, or how to replenish his supply. My wife and I were living at the Apthorp in which he had sublet an apartment for a time. In those days, a building for actors on the way up. I tried to find him a doctor who could work out what he needed and get it for him locally.' Heller, indeed, seems to have more than once helped the younger man with the base practicalities of life. 'Earlier, when he was in New York with *Beyond the Fringe*, I think he realized that with four of them working seven nights a week and splitting the take four ways, they were being overworked and underpaid. So I found him an entertainment lawyer – Jerry Lurie of Cohen and Glickstein. Peter was starting a New York club, the *Establishment*, at the same time. Later, I was told that Peter was a good businessman and had made himself worth a lot of money. I was glad to hear it.'

The two began to see each other at a series of dinners, which sometimes also included Jonathan and Rachel Miller. 'I remember one dinner in our apartment where he had to spend the entire evening on the telephone. Lenny Bruce had been asked to do his act at the *Establishment Club* in London, but the British government had plans to keep him out and Peter had to arrange for him to be smuggled in through Dublin. Lenny was later the cause of him being a bit unkind to his second wife. She used to boast, it seemed, that she was the only girl Bruce had ever loved. He had told her so. Peter knew Lenny Bruce, and he knew that he said that to all his nineteen-year-old girls, and he told her so in a mocking impersonation of Bruce.'

In Heller's memory, 'Peter was not a comic in private, but his normal conversation was full of funny asides and images. He had no idea how funny he was, and was surprised – even jaw-droppingly surprised – when people would burst out laughing. I remember my friend George Mandel, the novelist, saying: "He really doesn't know how amusing he is." The occasion I remember most clearly is a social discussion in my home about English literature, with me and Frederick Karl (recently the biographer of George Eliot). The general tenor of the remarks led Peter quite naturally, and quite unpredictably, into a recitation of "Ode on a Grecian Urn" in which he used the London accent of the time – would it have been Cockney? – that Keats would have used. Frederick Karl was encountering Peter for the first time and and afterwards he exclaimed: "That man is *ferociously* brilliant." To which I replied: "Don't I know! And educated too." '

There was a surprise birthday party for Heller at which Cook arrived early. 'He had just seen his first copy of *Screw* magazine and couldn't get over it. He couldn't, I mean, get over the idea that anyone could get away with it.' (Like the Lenny Bruce banning incident, this recalls the time when the Lord Chamberlain and other censors still held sway over English life but, as Heller recalls, he himself was also a bit surprised that *Screw* could be published openly in New York.) At the party and on other occasions, he also noticed that Peter was that rarest of things – a good listener. And even more rare – a good laugher at other people's jokes. 'Mel Brooks was there one time and he likes to perform. Peter was happy to let him, just making the occasional remark. There were two twin doctors present – their name was Bader – and while one of them spoke, the other would mouth the words in synch even if he had no idea what the topic was going to be. "It's a stereo," said Peter. "They're so alike you don't need two of them." And I can remember another evening, this time at his place in the East Village, with his first wife Wendy during *Beyond the Fringe*, where Peter Ustinov was the guest of honour and Peter let him do the talking. But when he wanted to perform he could really do it. He would sometimes rehearse ideas and routines that he was working on for him and Dudley to do on stage. One evening he did the one where the lecturer on diarrhoea comes on the stage, looks at the audience, opens his mouth to announce his subject and then says "Excuse me" and dashes off through the wings. Then he comes back, still drying his hands, and tries to begin again only to rush off once more.' (I tell Heller that Cook only tried this once in public, at the *Establishment Club*.)

A recurrent theme in Heller's recollection of Cook is a certain insecurity or vulnerability. 'At about the same time that he was having this crisis about his pills – actually, I would say that he was in terror about them – I fixed up for him to meet Dustin Hoffman. Hoffman was making his film about Lenny Bruce and he's one of those actors who likes to "excavate" the part. God knows why – acting is so easy. Anyway, he wanted to meet Peter and we took him to see *Good Evening* before all having dinner together at Sardi's. Hoffman isn't much of a talker at the best of times and on this occasion he barely talked at all. So Peter did most of the talking – almost all of it what I would call scatological reminiscences about Lenny Bruce, at his worst as a house guest. As soon as I got home I got a call from Peter, who was living in the same building. It was late and this was about one hour after we had parted at the entrance. He was very distraught. Not only had Hoffman not talked at all. He had never said that he liked the show.'

The two men lost touch when Cook returned to England. It was when he was on a world tour, in 1985, that Heller visited Australia and met the wife of Barry Humphries. She urged him very strongly to contact Cook when he got to England, which he did. 'I found him dangerously depressed. Lin (at that time his girlfriend) said that Jonathan Miller had been very good about coming round to visit with him a couple of times, and the encouraging thing was how devoted to Lin he seemed to be. I knew him with all three of his wives and his marriage to Lin was by far the best and the closest. We went to Rules restaurant in Covent Garden [Heller is suitably impressed when I tell him that this gamey old-English establishment was the favourite resort of Graham Greene] and I remember that he ordered some very fine wine but didn't touch a drop of it. To me, this is almost a sure sign of someone on a programme of abstention. I guess this may have been a clue to his problem or depression or whatever.

'Another time we met in England was when I had an engagement party for myself and Valerie, my second wife. Peter's always been very nice to both my wives. Valerie said that she would really love to get married in Canterbury

Cathedral. Peter at once said that he could and would arrange it, adding that he could fix to have Archbishop Desmond Tutu come as well, and swing on a trapeze if necessary. I don't know who else would have thought of that. He was always coming up with amazing images. I remember we were talking about Kenneth Tynan once. Tynan had been among the first to popularize *Catch-22* in England, and Peter was going on about Tynan's hectic need for the discovery of new talent. "If he could have been there," said Peter, "Ken would have grabbed the Mona Lisa right off the easel and run through the streets with it. While the paint was still wet."'

It's still easy to see how the two would have been on the same wavelength. I told Heller during lunch about Peter Cook's 'greatest regret' remark – the one about saving David Frost from drowning. 'Yeah,' said Heller. 'When *Catch-22* came out, Norman Podhoretz reviewed it for *Show* magazine. He later told me that it had broken his writer's block. So I owe the world one as well.' And one notices – I'm sure I'm not being fanciful here – Cook-like echoes in the novel. Perhaps I was too opportunistically attuned. Having bought a presentation copy for Heller to sign, and having also brought my tattered paperback original for the same purpose, I obviously found myself re-reading it for the umpteenth time:

> 'When I was a kid,' Orr replied, 'I used to walk around all day with crab apples in my cheeks. One in each cheek.'
>
> Yossarian put aside the musette bag from which he had begun removing his toilet articles and braced himself suspiciously. A minute passed. 'Why?' he found himself forced to ask finally.
>
> Orr tittered triumphantly. 'Because they're better than horse chestnuts,' he answered 'When I couldn't get crab apples, I used horse chestnuts. Horse chestnuts are about the same size as crab apples and actually have a better shape, although the shape doesn't matter a bit.'

'Why did you walk around with crab apples in your cheeks?' Yossarian asked again. 'That's what I asked.'

'Because they've got a better shape than horse chestnuts,' Orr answered. 'I just told you that.'

Dud and Pete could have worked with that.

And Peter, surely, could have worked with the hopeless Colonel Cargill, an individual who 'could be relied on to run the most prosperous enterprise into the ground. He was a self-made man who owed his lack of success to nobody.' Or Yossarian himself, who 'had decided to live forever or die in the attempt'. In Heller's version of the *Aftermyth of War*, people use the telephone and claim to be T.S. Eliot before hanging up. And a cheerful, not to say defiant, obscenity and scatology prevails. While, if you remember the dialogue between Yossarian and Lieutenant Scheiss-kopf's wife on the nature of God, you are in the world that is also mapped in *Bedazzled*:

'Why in the world did He ever create pain?'

'Pain?' Lieutenant Scheisskopf's wife pounced upon the word victoriously. 'Pain is a useful symptom. Pain is a warning to us of bodily dangers.'

'And who created the dangers?' Yossarian demanded. He laughed caustically. 'Oh, He was really being charitable to us when He gave us pain! Why couldn't He have used a doorbell instead to notify us, or one of his celestial choirs? Or a system of blue-and-red neon tubes right in the middle of each person's forehead. Any juke-box manufacturer worth his salt could have done that. Why couldn't He?'

'People would certainly look silly walking around with red neon tubes in the middle of their foreheads.'

'They certainly look beautiful now writhing in agony or stupefied with morphine, don't they?'

Or – to annex a line from *Bedazzled* – 'Sing My Praises'. (Heller, incidentally, confirms the story that his novel was originally entitled *Catch-Eighteen*. But Robert Gottlieb, its editor, pointed out that the same house was bringing out

Leon Uris's *Mila 18* in the same season. 'I thought of *Catch-Eleven*, because it's the only other number to start with an open vowel sound. I guess we doubled that.' *Could* it have been the same book under any other name? We both agree that we wish we could have had Peter's opinion.)

'You know,' says Heller in closing, 'he always had the most subtle ways of showing his esteem. He didn't shower you with compliments. It wasn't until after he died and I got a letter from Lin that I knew what he thought of me. And I've been surrounded with good wisecrackers all my life, and I can wisecrack myself. So I don't just mean that he was witty. I actually felt, even though there were twenty or so years between us, that he was my age – or even older. A mentor. There was always a sensibility that underlay all the jokes – an education and an intelligence.'

Lunch is over and I like to think that Joe Heller is sorry – as I am – that he has to go back to Long Island. Not sorry to see the last of me, but to end a conversation that briefly brought back somebody we both wish we'd known better.

John Wells

The Mystic Spube

The most intense expression I ever saw in Peter's eyes was once when he was very drunk. He was clearly being assailed by wave after wave of wildly comic ideas he was at that moment unable to express. He'd been reading a piece in the paper about the Frederick West murder story: the police were removing bodies from West's back garden, and his lawyer was complaining that 'this kind of publicity might well damage his client's case'.

Peter had read out the quote, and we'd laughed, then he sat there thinking about it. He crooked his cigarette up to his mouth, rocking forward, shaking with laughter, half turning away, but when he looked back the expression was still there. It was intense, affectionate, full to overflowing with a kind of glittering amusement. You could regret he'd got himself into that state, but when he looked at you like that you could only love him.

Even when he was drunk, Peter still seemed seriously obsessed by jokes. Once, at the satirically-inspired Nether Wallop Festival, we were all in a back room at a local hotel after the show. Peter sat smoking into a jumbled collection of glasses, some empty, most of them half-full, occasionally tipping one into the other and drinking it.

Very slowly he had the idea for a practical joke. As we all watched he got up, none too steadily, and closed the door.

87

Then, chuckling to himself, he found a rather fragile chair, propped it with the back lodged under the handle of the door, and rang for the waiter. A few moments later the waiter tapped on the door, Peter shouted 'Come in!', convulsed with giggles, and the door opened easily, pushing the chair smoothly back with it. Peter said 'Damn!' and ordered some more drinks. He fixed the trap, as far as I remember, at least twice more, and every time it failed, the waiter as far as I could see unaware that the chair was even there. In the end Peter smashed it.

The drink was a terrible thing, and it is ridiculous to pretend that it didn't diminish him. The first time it became obvious was the opening night of *Behind the Fridge* in London in 1972. The house manager appeared just before the curtain went up, apologized that they were having trouble with the projection equipment and said that the show would probably be starting in about twenty minutes.

It was only at the end of the evening the audience realized there hadn't been any projection equipment: Peter had been dead drunk in his dressing-room, and they needed the twenty minutes to pour hot coffee down him. Dudley was said to have found him in the wings just before they began, and threatened him with death if he forgot his lines. 'You dry, you bastard, and I'll fuckin' kill you!' As often happens under such circumstances it was Dudley who twice missed his lines while Peter sailed through without a fluff, serenely confident and in control. It may have been that confidence that kept him drinking, the belief he could always give it up when he really needed to and be as good as new.

The first time I met Lin was in a television studio in Maidstone. Peter had been through a very bad patch, and suddenly there he was, sitting on a park bench doing his Wisty as well as ever, apparently back to his old self. I watched him from behind the cameras, and then noticed Lin. She was sitting, as he asked her to, where he could see her all the time. I had never known him so happily dependent, and it seemed that at last he had found someone who could help him to get off the booze.

Lin did as much as any loving human being could have done, but I suppose the truth is that he didn't really want to. Not that he would have admitted it, or found it possible to discuss it seriously. The nearest Peter came to confessing that he was sometimes unconsciously moved by urges beyond his control was in the front hall of Broadcasting House, some time in the late eighties. He'd just had yet another unsatisfactory meeting with someone in BBC Radio who was, Peter said, slipping into his throaty executive drawl 'tremendously excited, really *tremendously* excited' about him doing a show, 'ideally to go out at about four in the morning so we should be looking at a really *substantial* audience'. Then he went back into his own familiar nasal voice and mentioned that he'd been watching some old Dud and Pete tapes. 'I had no idea,' he said, almost remorseful, 'that I was so cruel to the little bugger.'

He may never have had any idea either that he gave himself such a bad time, or why he did it. He must have loved the excitement of drinking, just as he loved the excitement of sex or the excitement of language, weaving his way through invented words and relishing names like Sir Basil Nardly Stoads, Arthur Streeb-Greebling and the Clintistorit of Wintistering, straming as they frequently did the blages and in no uncertain manner, often murmuring coded phrases that included 'Farg' or 'Drebbidge'.

Sex did him no harm, the games he played with language will still be making people laugh in a hundred, or as he would have preferred to say, a million years' time, but the drink cut him off.

I think almost the worst moment was when he was taking some sort of pills designed to put him off alcohol, but which made him slur his words as if he were dragging them up from the cellar. He came into *Private Eye*. I was for some reason alone, there was a page to fill, so he got down to it. He sat down, put his feet on Richard Ingrams's desk, lit a cigarette, cocked his head on one side, unfocussed his eyes, and began to dictate. It was a story about a newly appointed politician, and Peter said very slowly, in his Major Streeb-Greebling voice, slower than usual and more slurred, that he was sure, as a member of the Tory Party, that the minister's arrival would come as – long pause – 'a breath of hot air'.

I first met Peter Cook among the sawing and hammering at his new *Establishment Club* in Greek Street in the autumn of 1961. The name in itself was a joke, taken from either a Henry Fairlie piece in the *Spectator* or Anthony Sampson's *Anatomy of Britain*, both of which popularized the term 'the Establishment' to mean the ruling élite. The 'Establishment clubs' were where that élite was seen to gather. Peter had succeeded in creating his own ruling élite in the satire business with the club as its headquarters. But even among the élite, which included John Bird, John Fortune and Eleanor Bron, Barry Humphries, Willie Rushton and Richard Ingrams from *Private Eye*, as well as visitors like Lenny Bruce, Peter was on his own, the Godfather. If you made a family tree of all the collaborations and acts and long-running *Private Eye* features and shows and books that followed in the next thirty years, everything would lead uncannily back to Peter. He gave us everything.

The morning I met him first he was wearing a suit – no one else was – and looked very elegant. I remember the formal way he shook hands, very English and polite. What seemed so remarkable then was that anyone of our age, just out of university, should be able to open his own nightclub in the West End, employ staff, install kitchens. But Peter was building an empire.

Soon after that he asked me to dinner with him and his first wife Wendy to meet Nick Garland, who was directing the shows at the club. I had co-written and acted in an Oxford satirical revue at the Edinburgh Festival in the summer of 1961, and by far the most exciting response, far outstripping the good notices, was a telegram from Peter, whom I had never met, offering to buy the show.

My co-writer and I had some harebrained scheme to bring the revue to London, and we initially hung on to the material, but Peter remained entirely gracious about it. The first time I went to supper he and Wendy had a flat overlooking Battersea Park. It seemed very opulent, newly decorated, with polished wooden floors and a polished wooden rocking-horse with a horsehair mane. I was teaching at the time, but he asked me to appear at the first night of the *Establishment*, very late, after him and the rest of the *Beyond the Fringe* team, doing a John Betjeman impersonation from our Edinburgh revue that could only by a severe stretch of the critical imagination be described as satirical. That first night was, I suppose, the real climax of the Satire Boom. Television lights blazed white, everyone who made up what would soon become known as Swinging London fought to get in to eat supper and drink and watch the cabaret.

The idea of that kind of entertainment at a night-club was again something entirely new to England which would never have happened without him. Peter had seen so-called satirical cabarets in Germany like the *Stachelschwein*, where you ate and drank and watched shows full of sharp-edged songs and jokes out of that day's newspapers. The same thing existed in Paris, at clubs like the Caveau de la République. No one had ever tried it in London, and Peter's *Establishment* initiated a whole new tradition of shows in pubs and clubs that was to resurface twenty years later in places like the Comedy Store. It also created the style of the Amnesty shows, in which he later played a leading part, and, through the people he worked with on stage in those, Peter also inspired another thirty more years of television comedy.

But even in those early days he was a legend. He was, to the day, a year younger than I was – we twice shared birthday parties – but I could never really get over the fact that he was a star. If he entertained fantasies when he was young about becoming the new Cary Grant – and he confessed himself baffled by Dudley's success in Hollywood with what Peter humorously referred to as his 'fine Jewish profile' – he was entirely justified in entertaining them. His occasional tentativeness in later years may have made him register less confidently on film, but look at *Bedazzled* and you will see the great leading man he was when he began.

It has been argued that he could only perform his own material. That could be true, and the argument goes close to the centre of the problem or problems: the drink problem and the problem of understanding him. His originality lay in a kind of despairing boredom with the ordinariness of life, and that often included the ordinariness of other people. No one should ever underestimate Peter's intelligence.

Alan Bennett is rightly credited with producing in *Beyond the Fringe* the definitive criticism of the Church of England Sermon, a sketch still used to train preachers in the nation's dwindling number of theological colleges. Peter's musings on the ultimate truths are a great deal more destructive. When, in one of their Biblical moments in *Behind the Fridge*, Dud as the local reporter in Bethlehem asks him as one of the shepherds who came to the manger, 'Was the Holy Ghost actually present at the birth?' and he replies after a short pause for recollection, 'It was hard to tell,' he is in the Voltaire class.

He is, equally, in the same league as Samuel Beckett in *The Dagenham Dialogues* discussing the brevity of life and the Humble Mayfly.

This constant awareness that life was 'unbelievably boring' did not make him an easy companion, even to himself. He found small-talk very difficult, except possibly about football and libel lawyers. His eyes would gleam in the friendliest way when he was listening, he'd lean forward and laugh at jokes, sometimes at his own which were by far and away the best, but he was always somehow on his own, guarded and remote, unable to see the point of 'work' or many other tedious things that less enlightened human beings cling on to for their security. When we were having supper alone together in a restaurant once, the thing I remember most clearly was him asking me if my food was all right. It may have been a habit he had picked up in America, but I can't imagine anyone else among our contemporaries at that time having that kind of old-fashioned good manners.

It may just have been that I was boring him, and even when I got to know him better that fear was certainly always there. But being alone with Peter was more alarming than that. What was terrifying, in the absence of small-talk, was his absolute lack of ordinariness. Looking back, it was like the mystics' descriptions of being in the presence of God. His blazing originality seemed to reveal all your own inadequacies. It was like being X-rayed.

For his part, the good manners were certainly defensive. In the early issues of *Private Eye* in 1962 there was a strip cartoon on the back page in the form of a series of cautionary fables and called *Aesop Revisited*. One was the story of the Satirist, called Jonathan Crake. Willie Rushton's drawing was a cartoon of Peter, at first fêted and wildly successful, eventually driven to drink and despair by the stupidity of his audience. Whatever he said, even if he was asking the way to the gents, everyone fell on the floor, weeping with laughter.

It was true. All of us fell on the floor for years and years, and I suppose it is possible that we reinforced his natural remoteness by doing so. But certainly at the outset he was very frightening. He had dominated the Cambridge Foot-lights, contributed sketches to West End revues while he was still at university, then with Jonathan Miller, Dudley Moore and Alan Bennett, taken the Edinburgh Festival and the West End by storm. Most of us who wrote and performed comedy sketches at university thought of ourselves, with reason, as amateurs. Everything Peter did had the authority of a professional, but was more than professional because it was so much better than what professional writers and actors were doing.

What was so surprising about *Beyond the Fringe* when it opened at the Lyceum in Edinburgh in August 1960 – which was the first time I ever saw him – was that it absolutely cut through all the showbiz rubbish. Other student revues, like our own, still had elaborate costume-changes and make-up and pathetic opening numbers, for which we were urged to clean our teeth and grin dazzlingly into the lights. In our jokes we made an effort, as my co-writer James Crossman put it, to take the audience further than the headlines and into the small print, but most of the sketches and monologues, with one or two exceptions, could have come out of any university show for the past twenty-five years.

When the curtain went up on *Beyond the Fringe* it wasn't like that at all: what we saw was four people of our own age slipping in and out of funny voices in the way we all liked to think we did in everyday life, being effortlessly funny. The difference between us and them, which we dimly but definitely sensed at the time, was that they were producing the Real Stuff. The wit of all four performers in *Beyond the Fringe*, and Peter in particular, drew on very great intelligence, wild imagination and association of ideas, and a great deal of professional hard work. The jokes are as good today, if you listen to the record, as they were then.

But even in that company Peter was unique. Alan Bennett famously complained that after being with Peter he couldn't write for days. Peter's effortless, glorious and spontaneous outpourings were a challenge to anyone. He was like some thirty-times-a-night Casanova, reducing rivals to impotence.

The rivalry at *Private Eye* was intense. Joint writing sessions with the Shrewsbury Mob – Christopher Booker, Richard Ingrams, Willie Rushton and Paul Foot, who had all been at school together – involved a great deal of eye-gouging, knee-in-the-groin work to get a joke in edgeways, and usually it was Richard Ingrams, as the hand that held the biro, who had the final word. When Peter appeared, absorbed into the public-school changing-room atmosphere first as 'Cook' and later, more affectionately, as 'Cookie', even Richard Ingrams took dictation.

I think I was still teaching when Peter took over *Private Eye*, but it roughly coincided with the demise of the *Establishment*. Rumours circulated that Peter had been swindled by his catering manager there, and the club was eventually sold. Losing the capital of his empire must have caused him grief, but he never spoke about it. Instead he transferred his allegiance for the rest of his life to *Private Eye*. The magazine's circulation had gone through the roof during the Profumo Scandal, then it began to dip, and it was at that point that Peter stepped in and bought it.

It must, even in terms of comic style, have been a shock. Peter, as a Cambridge man, had already had a whiff of Oxford when he joined *Beyond the Fringe*, but Alan Bennett and Dudley Moore were no real preparation for what he was to find at *Private Eye*. Christopher Booker, it is true, was a Cambridge man too, he shared their intellectual superiority, but his attitude always seemed to reflect more the dormitories of Shrewsbury than the dining clubs of Cambridge.

Recklessly, when the *Establishment* was still flourishing, Peter tried to bring together the two teams at a weekly lunch in the club to 'exchange ideas'. I only attended a couple of them, but the atmosphere was charged with mutual loathing. It was in the days before Richard Ingrams himself eschewed the booze, and *Private Eye* was virtually edited from a pub. The mood was rough, bluff, philistine and beery, puritanical but largely apolitical, flourishing on the exchange of coarse personal insults. The Cambridge lot, on the other hand, already gave off a hum of high-tech earnestness, producing precision-made satirical jokes. They were serious about politics, intelligence was openly revered, and their sketches searched deep into emotional and psychological problems nobody at *Private Eye* would have dreamed even existed.

In the upstairs room at the *Establishment* where Peter hosted the joint lunch there seemed to be a lot of pale blue close carpeting and lacquered black furniture, waiters from the club in white coats served sensible salads on black plates with the knives and forks wrapped in green paper napkins, and there was deadlock. John Bird looked across at us with his big cold blue eyes, and clearly decided we were a lot of public school wankers. Paul Foot may have escaped by being politically more committed to the left, but he probably failed on Eng. Lit. The rest of us were obviously not serious.

I don't think when Peter took over *Private Eye* that the lack of earnest political commitment worried him. Suffering from such cosmic boredom, he was always more interested in the jokes. For one issue, when Richard Ingrams was away and I was left in charge, he was full of approval at my choice of a photograph for the cover from *Health and Efficiency*. It showed a naked girl arching up crab-fashion, tummy in the air, supporting herself on her hands and feet, surrounded by a group of nude admirers. Peter looked at it for a long time as he always did when choosing the bubble caption, head on one side, then decided that the bubble was to come from a girl bystander: 'And where was *he* standing?'

Peter's Cambridge education did show, though, in the fact that his jokes, like John Bird's, were fuelled with an immense amount of reading. He read all the newspapers and political weeklies and, unlike John Bird, allowed his researches to carry him into *Rubberwear News*, *The Budgerigar Fancier* and *Frilly Knickers*. He took a particular delight in misprints, sub-editors' clichés and Fleet Street journalese, creasing up with laughter at Swoops, Grabs and Probes.

What Cambridge may have given him was a modicum of

restraint. They had treated him at the Footlights as a serious Surrealist: his work had, after all, been performed with that of Harold Pinter and N.F. Simpson. Given more academic discipline he might have become an Edward Lear or a Lewis Carroll, but I'm not sure he'd have been able to manage the limitations of their kind of life any better than he did the one he was dealt in the twentieth century.

At *Private Eye* his every whim was encouraged, every joke he made carried on far too long and usually taken far too far. When he read in the paper that Harold Wilson's wife, Mary, was intending to continue with writing her occasional poetry at Number Ten Downing Street and to keep a diary, it was Peter who decided on the idea of *Mrs Wilson's Diary* and led the writing of the first episode, leaving Richard Ingrams and me to continue it for eleven years. He masterminded the first letter in the *Dear Bill* series, and again left us in charge.

Some of his other comical ideas, wildly applauded and encouraged by us, got him into trouble. He was hugely amused by two photographs in a Scottish paper with misprinted captions. The figure on the left, a plump man with a bald head and glasses was subtitled 'Provost Knowles', the face on the right was that of Sir Alec Douglas-Home, and it was captioned 'Baillie Vass'. This led to years of fun with Sir Alec as the Baillie, and when it seemed likely that the Baillie was about to be booted out of Number Ten, Peter announced in the magazine that there would be a public rally in his support. It was called 'Mass for Vass' and would present an ironic petition to Number Ten, begging the Prime Minister to stay in office.

Someone must have cleared it with the police. It took place on a Sunday morning, and Richard Ingrams was appalled when he looked out of the first-floor window to see Greek Street thronged with beards and sandals and prams, the readers he preferred not to think about. Peter, by contrast, shy as he often was in public, greeted them all with enthusiasm. He hoisted his own placard *'The Baillie will no fail ye!'* and was wheeled at the head of the procession in a chair – he had broken his ankle and had his leg in plaster – accompanied by a senior police officer who told us that such demonstrations were 'easy enough to start but a bugger to stop'.

Other jokes, not always his own, landed the magazine in court and him personally in grave financial danger, but as the editors have testified, no proprietor could have been braver in defence of his paper. It was not easy. In the Lord Russell of Liverpool case, where the magazine had suggested that Russell's book *The Scourge of the Swastika* was pornographic – a suggestion that cost *Private Eye* £12,000 in damages alone – Peter stood in the witness box trying gamely to make jokes. In the atmosphere of the courtroom even he was like a man trying to strike matches underwater.

Having lost the case, Peter immediately organized a charity night, *Russell of Spring*, to pay the costs. Peter Sellers, Spike Milligan, the famous Alberts and a great many other stars turned up free of charge, and the show was so popular that similar entertainments were put on regularly at the St Pancras Town Hall, whether the magazine needed the money or not.

Peter's attitude to money was always mysterious. He told me once that he had filled a bureau with unopened demands from the Inland Revenue, and when that was full that he had bought another bureau. It would therefore be wrong to suggest that he was always socially responsible, or even entirely reliable. He had great fellow-feeling for Claud Cockburn. When he was staying with him once in Ireland, Claud, who was always short of money, waited till Patricia his wife had left the table, and said with his famous slow drawl, 'Er – Peter. I wonder whether I could possibly trouble you for a ... small loan?' Peter suggested two hundred pounds, and was delighted when Claud, without leaving a second's gap, said 'Four!'

There were long periods during his time as proprietor of *Private Eye* when he never appeared in the office, being only glimpsed occasionally at progressive parties given by pop-singers with his hair dyed orange. But even then there was a feeling at the back of all our minds that he was there if you really needed him, the absolute standard you could never hope to measure yourself against, and that is what makes his death still so terrible.

If more puritan elements at *Private Eye* disapproved of some aspects of his life, others of us saw it as charmed. There were tales of multiple Bunnies, and when he and I went together to his favourite strip-club in St. Anne's Court, I was deeply impressed when the stripper winked at him and threw him her bra.

John Fortune, too, remembers, as one of his happiest experiences, getting drunk with Peter in Knightsbridge and hammering on David Frost's front door at three in the morning. After a while the window was eased up, David's tousled head appeared, and John swears he said 'Peter! Super to see you!' Peter at that stage had taken to calling David 'Gypsy Dave', and called up 'Gypsy! We thought we might come in and have a drink or two!' According to John Fortune, David replied, 'Actually, Peter, I'm *with* someone,' and very courteously closed the window.

But the happiest times of all with Peter were when he was working. One of his most sustained fantasies, carried on in *Private Eye* from Christmas 1964 to May 1965, was a memoir on 'The Seductive Brethren'. Like 'The Memoirs of Rhandi Purr', which drew deeply on the *Kama Sutra*, it was composed officially by the committee, but when Peter lit his cigarette, licked his lips and stared into the middle distance all we usually did was to listen, howl with laughter, and write it down.

At one point Sir Basil Nardly Stoads, Chief Rammer and Dragger of the Seductive Brethren – a sect devoted to the Bodily Seizing of Young Women – has been denounced for the sin of St Arnolph by the Revd 'Knocker' Prume and has been betrayed by his close friend the Clintistorit of Wintistering. He has defended himself in court.

Liberty is not merely a word, or a group of ants. It is a substance that permeates every fibre of a righteous man. If it is a crime to give succour to a bee, then I am a criminal. If it is a crime to give honey to a newt, then it is your solemn duty to cast me forth into another place. If, however, you believe, as I do, in the flame of justice and the balls-aching tediousness of the Revd Prume and his ilk, then I am your man!

Now Sir Basil has escaped from prison, and is in hiding on the estate of the McDoon of McDoon. The McDoon's character is beyond reproach, but 'local glen-folk have been alarmed by recent events in the area of the Whistling Hole, a local ugly spot, traditionally the haunt of the Phantom O'Doon, a small bespectacled man clad only in butterfly wings . . .'

Only Peter could have written that. Reading it again, I remembered Peter's face, the centre of the room at 22 Greek Street, the rest of us laughing and occasionally making suggestions which he very generously incorporated. Little phrases like 'hobbling about' or a reference to a German work *Der Ring der Seduktiven* I recognize as my own and I wish I'd kept my mouth shut. Trying to collaborate, let alone compete with Peter was always incredibly difficult, and it is a great tribute to the imagination and comic genius of Dudley Moore, however cruel Peter thought he was to him, that he managed the Pete and Dud dialogues as subtly as he did.

Some of us tried improvising with Sir Herbert Gusset or Sir Navel Throbes when we recorded the plastic discs that were sold stuck to the cover of *Private Eye*. In one case the disc concealed a photo montage of Sir Alec Douglas-Home sitting on the lavatory with one of Peter's bubble captions saying 'Put that record back immediately!'

At these recording sessions, sometimes made in the office and sometimes in a local studio in Soho, Peter was by far the best organized, actually bringing along scripts that he appeared to have dictated to a secretary while the rest of us were in the pub or in bed with someone. Even so, a great deal was improvised, and I found myself more than once having to float off into what John Fortune calls 'the realms' with Peter entirely unrehearsed.

With anyone else the improvisation would have been two-handed, one beginning and the other developing it, following each other in whichever direction the imagination or the language took you. With Peter, that was impossible. Any intrusion into his world sounded flat and trivial. He also, for all his apparently free stream of warped, boredom-racked consciousness, had some intricate design at the back of his mind which he was slowly and often quite labori-ously working towards – his face would pucker up and he would narrow his eyes – when he could drop in the keyword, like 'breath of hot air' or 'ugly spot'. I wondered, as we got older, whether the hero-worship when we were young might have been exaggerated. Then I saw Peter in the *Saturday Night Live* studio in 1986, surrounded by all the best comics of the next generation who worshipped him if anything more passionately than we did. On that occasion he was recreating President Ferdinand Marcos of the Phillipines, who he decided, speaking in a very sniffy Point-to-Point voice, was known to his intimates as 'Ferdy'.

He got the same adoration at his birthday parties: younger comics obviously thought of an invitation as worth more than an Oscar. Our children, who had never seen him on television when they were young, rolled about the room laughing when he talked. On his last birthday I was out of London, but my daughter asked him whether he was enjoying it. 'Well, when you've had fifty-seven of them, birthdays get a bit boring somehow.'

I shall always remember Peter as he was when he was imagining his own world: like a medium, head cocked, looking sideways across the room, cigarette burning, licking his lips and then droning out some inversion of boring normality that made all our eyes flash and filled the room with laughter. Peter was unique. He was part of a tradition of surreal English humour that he himself loved and respected – Laurence Sterne, Edward Lear, Lewis Carroll – but he revitalized popular comedy. Without him, it is highly unlikely there would have been *Beyond the Fringe*, and without his success with *Beyond the Fringe* there would have been no *That Was The Week That Was*, no *Establishment*, and possibly no life beyond the late sixties for *Private Eye*. But the fact that his influence has continued to spread into so many different channels ever since is no consolation. He should never have died so young.

At a Christmas party at *Private Eye* a year before his death he had made an effort, given up the drink, and he looked thirty-five. He was thin, alert, moving through the room as he had when I first met him at the *Establishment*. If he had persevered he might be alive today, but if he had persevered I suppose he would not have been Peter Cook. That would have been accepting a kind of imprisonment, and freedom for Peter, as his *alter ego* Sir Basil Nardly Stoads put it, was not merely a word or a group of ants. It was a substance that permeated every fibre of a righteous man.

There is a happy epilogue to the story of Sir Basil. After he has been found dead by seventy-six policemen in a fur-lined coffin in the Green Room of the Southern Turret of Castle O'Doon, receiving the kiss of life from eighty-four-year-old 'Queenie' Simpson – the policemen all shed their clothes as a mark of respect and slow-march down the stairs with their truncheons reversed – Sir Basil vanishes from the coffin. Observers on the funeral train describe 'not unfrenzied activity' and the singing of 'spirited dirges', and as the train passes through one sequestered halt 'phials' believed to have contained 'unguents' are seen to be thrown from behind closely drawn blinds. Even more mysteriously, an 'unusual tribute' arrives, a postcard 'of an artistic nature' bearing a South American postmark. On the reverse is the message: 'Sorry to hear you are dead. See you Thursday. *Je t'embrasse*. Clinty.'

This is taken by the Seductive Brethren to imply a final

reconciliation between Sir Basil and the Clintistorit, and to affirm their belief in the 'Mystic Reincarnation of the Spube'. Remembering Peter, that seems to me to be a wholly reasonable belief.

Auberon Waugh

Peace Through Nudism

In my sixteen years on *Private Eye*, Peter's visits stand out as moments when everybody suddenly became possessed with a new energy. It was not like being visited by a celebrity, because Peter held the whole celebrity system in the deepest contempt. Perhaps that was why he had no enthusiasm for working in the United States. One of the bitterest things he was ever reported as saying, when the Pete 'n' Dud partnership was breaking up, was to explain his friend's choice. 'Perhaps if I had been born with a club foot and a height problem, I might have been as desperate as Dudley to become a star.'

Yet, if he was reported accurately, it was not really cruel, just a simple statement of fact. Peter did not have any desire for the trappings of stardom. On one occasion, when he was staying with us in Somerset during the breakup of one of his marriages, he asked to attend a ghastly school performance of Arnold Bennett's play *The Card* in which one of my daughters, then fifteen, was playing a major female part. The cast was somewhat thrown to find this superstar in the audience, but Peter was so gentle, so friendly, so ungrand and unpatronizing that they all fell in love with him. He had no sense of his own importance, no desire to be the centre of attention. He just liked making his jokes in the corner, from the periphery of the dynamic world of movers and shakers whose absurdity was his constant inspiration.

Most of the things we did together proved disastrous. At one time he was given a TV programme, whimsically called *Where Do I Sit?* which, he insisted, should go out live and unedited. He asked me to join him for the pilot and the first performance. It was an unmitigated catastrophe, withdrawn after three performances. When I left *Private Eye* and moved to a small magazine called *Literary Review* he adopted it, too, as if it was another of his children and showered kindnesses on it, from mystifying reviews of books he had plainly not had time to read, to appearances at its public functions. On one particularly unfortunate occasion he agreed to be part of a *Literary Review* panel at the Cheltenham Literary Festival. I had organized a star list, with Peter, William Rushton, Keith Waterhouse, Willie Donaldson and the lovely Anna Ford. The hall was packed. Unfortunately, we had not been able to get together in advance to arrange what we would do, so after short speeches by myself, as Editor, and Kate Kellaway, then Deputy Editor, we asked the audience of some three hundred if they had any questions to ask the Panel.

Nobody had a single question. Kate and I talked nervously to each other. Then, inspired, I asked the audience how many of them had ever seen the *Literary Review*. Nobody put up a hand. In desperation, I asked how many had ever heard of it. Rows of blank faces stared back. Eventually from the back of the hall, a voice asked why they were not given free copies of the magazine. They had paid £2.00 for their entrance tickets, he said. I had arranged for pretty young women in *Literary Review* sashes to sell copies of the magazine at the entrance. They did not sell many, and this man was insisting that they should have been given free copies. Perhaps he had a point, but suddenly Peter blew his top.

'How dare you expect to be given a free copy,' he shouted

at the only person prepared to ask a question. 'What have you done to deserve it? Are you so mean you wish to ruin the magazine?'

There were no further questions, and the meeting broke up after about twenty minutes. The wretched questioner had affronted Peter's sense of loyalty, which assumed that everyone present was drawn, as he was, by the highest of motives.

Perhaps the most ludicrous of our joint enterprises was the great *Private Eye* putsch of 1986. When I resigned from the *Eye* after sixteen years to join the *Literary Review*, a small luncheon party was given in my honour in a Soho restaurant at which I was presented with a silver-plated wine funnel. Richard Ingrams chose to use this occasion to announce his own retirement as Editor, and his appointment of Ian Hislop as his successor. Little was known about Hislop at this stage except that he was extremely young – some put it at twenty-two. In his acceptance speech, Hislop made some hurtful remarks about the importance of youth, the need to find younger readers or whatever.

An opposition group immediately formed under Peter McKay, an old *Eye* hand, later to become the Worst Columnist in the World, then, of all things, Editor of *Punch*. It included Nigel Dempster, the social commentator and *belle-lettriste*, then known as the Greatest Living Englishman. I was roped in and Peter Cook, to everybody's surprise, was inveigled into attending our emergency meeting. Perhaps he felt that as proprietor of the *Eye* he should have been consulted, I do not know. My memory of the event is as hazy as that of everyone else who attended, but the consensus appears to be that at lunch we decided that Peter should go and confront Ingrams, with the support of David Cash (the *Eye*'s boxwallah who was present in a slightly ambiguous role) and demand the sacking of Hislop and the appointment in his place of Peter McKay.

By the time the deputation reached the *Eye*'s headquarters in Carlisle Street, Cash and McKay had mysteriously disappeared and Peter was left to confront Ingrams on his own. Unfortunately, he had completely forgotten what it was he was supposed to tell him – with the result that Hislop remains Editor to this day, and the *Eye* flourishes.

The *Eye* crowd was a talented lot: Ingrams, Foot, Wells, Marnham, Rushton, Dempster, McKay – yes, Booker, too, and even Fantoni – but none was so conspicuously touched by genius as Peter Cook. It became fashionable to say that in his later years, Peter retired into indolence, an overweight, shambolic figure who smoked and drank too much, although he was capable of emerging for brilliant performances.

I think that is a short-sighted view. He may well have decided at quite an early stage that there are more important things in life than good health – against all the flow of modern thinking. But did he ever decide what they were? The love of a good woman, as he eventually found in Lin, perhaps. Scarcely the admiration of his friends. Least of all, the applause of the multitude. The simple truth, I suspect, is that he spent all his time on earth in search of the meaning of life, examining the explanations on offer, and finding them all equally ridiculous. That is the great clue to his *œuvre*, whether expressed through the lips of Pete in the Pete 'n' Dud manifestation, or in the voice of E.L. Wisty, whose memorable 'World Domination League' plainly summarizes all Peter's political conclusions.

Perhaps because Peter could express himself only through irony and satire, nobody ever pauses to consider whether Wisty's poem on 'Peace Through Nudism' might not represent a serious and settled conclusion about life:

> If all the world were nudists
> If all the world were bare
> Everyone would live in peace
> No war would they declare.
> If everyone went dancing
> Around with nothing on
> Everybody would be happy
> As a person I know called John.

Of course it is absolutely essential for E.L. Wisty to aver at this point that he does not know anyone called John. A likely story. Elsewhere, Wisty remarks:

> I think it's about time I started doing a few interesting things. It's time I found out something like the secret of eternal life, the meaning of the universe, or how to get hold of women, or something ... I must do something with my life. Something I'll be remembered for when I'm gone.

Perhaps it was because Peter had decided that there is no secret of eternal life, the universe has no meaning, that he decided to die at the age of fifty-seven. It was hard luck on his widow that he chose to make such a decision. But there is no danger that he will be forgotten for as long as the tapes, CDs and books survive. He expresses an aspect of the human condition which no Englishman had ever really explored before: the philosopher-king who has decided that wisdom reduces all philosophy to its elements of the absurd.

Joe McGrath

Not Only Dudley Moore But Also Peter Cook

I was introduced to Peter by Dudley Moore towards the end of 1964. Before *Beyond the Fringe*, when I was a fledgling director for ABC Television, Dudley had taken part in my 'graduation' programme some years earlier and we had remained friends. I had since moved to the BBC on a contract basis and produced such shows as Michael Bentine's *It's a Square World* and *A Degree of Frost*.

My contract was coming to an end. I was asked by Frank Muir and Bill Cotton (then Head of Light Entertainment) to come up with an idea for a comedy 'special'. I approached Dudley and asked him if he'd be interested in our working together again. (This time he'd get paid.)

Dudley said he was interested and suggested involving Peter. *Not only* was Peter fun to work with *but* he'd *also* be a wonderful contributor (which is how the show got its name). Peter was willing and so the billing was changed. Up until then it was to have been called *The Dudley Moore Show* starring Not Only Dudley Moore But Also Blossom Dearie (for example). It was now *Not Only ... But Also* starring Not Only Dudley Moore and Peter Cook ... But Also John Lennon (as it happened in this 'one-off' special). Concerning John Lennon, Norman Rossington, who had appeared in *A Hard Day's Night* took me to meet John and I outlined the idea of the show to him. As soon as he heard that Peter and Dudley were the stars he immediately agreed to take part. 'I dig what they're doing,' were his words.

Peter, Dudley and I got down to working out the basic format of the show. Since, in those days, the show was more or less 'live', in that almost no recording time was allowed to remedy any mistakes, we agreed to include some pre-filmed pieces, first of all to take some of the weight off ourselves during the actual recording of the show (which had a live audience of around five hundred) and secondly, because the three of us wanted to do some filming! We had *carte blanche*. (Difficult to believe nowadays when the accountants are in charge.)

I had always enjoyed Peter's work but it wasn't until I saw him performing in the television show in front of an audience, with all the attendant stress, that I knew what 'grace under pressure' meant. Up until then I had only heard it applied to George Best, and Peter was much much funnier.

Although it didn't seem as if the powers that be at the BBC were paying much attention to what we were doing, this actually wasn't true: a system of benign despotism was in operation. They were. We had a full house for this special – Dudley and Peter have always appealed to a wide audience. If there is a class divide in Britain, and I think there is, they straddle it. Especially Peter with his gallery of British eccentrics, my two favourites being E.L. Wisty and Sir Arthur Streeb-Greebling (the first man to attempt to teach ravens to fly under water), whom he introduced to a bewildered, entranced nation, rendered powerless with laughter, in that first show.

Michael Peacock, then Controller of BBC2, had seen it and he had us in to his office and commissioned a series. Peter, Dudley and I left and, in the circular corridor outside, exchanged smiles and nods. Peter admonished us, 'No running in the corridors boys!' and set off at top speed around the bend. After the first show was transmitted, Peter Sellers also telephoned me to ask if he might appear as a guest, which he later did. Peter told me during this first series that he enjoyed going in to the BBC TV Centre and doing the show. 'Just like university,' he said, 'but the grants are bigger.'

Watching Dudley play the piano at rehearsals, Peter would say in a loud voice, 'I wish I'd been forced to learn to play an instrument when I was a child.' It was well known to everybody concerned with *Not Only ... But Also* that Peter's secret wish was to be another, better, Elvis Presley. The closing song 'Goodbye' gave him his chance. He couldn't wait to get hold of the microphone on its cable and swing it around. Dudley and his Trio feared for their lives.

On some of the shows Peter's performance of the number reaches an emotional level of intensity that borders on hysteria. As Dudley plays the opening chord you can hear the audience's gasp of expectation. Peter's face contorts into an indescribable grimace of joy, before bursting into an uncontrolled, out-of-tune, series of interjections aimed to destroy Dudley's perfectly pitched falsetto. Peter said he enjoyed this moment most of all. Watching him, you believe it. They complement each other perfectly, and his joy is there for all to see.

I usually brought Peter and Dudley into the editing room for a look at each film piece before it was shown to an audience. Dudley almost always provided a musical backing and Peter a commentary, if necessary. The 'Leaping Nuns' sequence worked so well that Peter wrote a whole studio interview piece that had never previously been envisaged, and used the idea once again in the film *Bedazzled*. Peter's remarks, comments and one-liners during our editing sessions were invaluable and were generally incorporated in the final version of the film piece. Looking at the BBC video of the show is rewarding; it provides great clues to Peter's character. The shows were very well received by the studio audience; in those days no canned or added laughter was used. The laughter that you hear is what we got on the night.

On many occasions Peter and Dudley had to wait for the laughter to subside. In the 'Art Gallery' sketch it becomes almost riotous. Peter slips in a reference to Dudley's Aunt Dolly, 'who'll do anything for money', and watches Dudley 'corpse' almost as a matador watches a stricken bull. Dudley chokes on a sandwich and Peter does about a minute extra simply on this happening, then shoots a glance at the camera (me !), remarking that he's not surprised that Dud is choking because the sandwiches are terrible. In many of the sketches they were close to tears of laughter. Dudley was the main culprit in giving in to the emotion. He tried to handle it by choking. Peter usually looked away and swallowed, but even he succumbs in the 'Art Gallery' sequence and also in the very first 'Dud and Pete' sketch, which we did in the pilot show, where the two characters discuss the trouble they're having with film stars, 'Bloody Brigitte Bardot and Greta Garbo'.

To create their duologues for the show, Peter and Dudley would work together at home, talking into a tape recorder. When they were satisfied with the piece they'd bring in the recording and it would be transcribed with no changes made. This Peter insisted on, as the speech pattern was most important. He hated 'pay-offs' to sketches where, as he said, 'You expect a musical chord' and he'd fight against any imposed structure. Rehearsals, of course, yielded more jokes which would, or would not, be added. Once the piece had been 'set', Dudley wrote it out in an exercise book in longhand, which helped him commit it to memory. Peter never did. The first 'Dud and Pete' piece in rehearsal ran about three minutes but when it was performed to the audience it more than doubled its length, owing to laughter and ad libs, all Peter's.

Peter was well aware of his appeal to a wide audience. Some years later, we were reunited in *Behind the Fridge*. Having performed this stage revue in Australia, Peter and Dudley asked me to direct the film pieces in the show and restage it for the London production. Peter insisted that

Hemdale, the production company, get a large theatre. 'They'll be coming from north of Watford in coachloads,' he said. 'It's not just the West End we're talking about here.'

He was right. The Cambridge Theatre, one of the largest in London, was procured and was booked out for months before the official opening night. Peter knew this. 'The bookings will be good,' he said, 'Mark my words, the bookings will be good, regardless of what the crickets, the smart West End crickets, say.' Indeed one of the 'crickets', I think it was Darlington, said in his write-up that he didn't see anything particularly amusing in the show but that his eighteen-year-old companion giggled throughout the performance. Peter pounced on this and had the notice put up outside the theatre, signing it, 'W.R. Darlington (aged 93)'.

I'm rambling a bit here, but once you start thinking about Peter this is inclined to happen. The use of the word 'cricket', for example, makes me think of a film piece he did for *Not Only ... But Also*. It was the poem called 'Uncle Arly', by Edward Lear. It was Peter's idea to do it.

> O my aged Uncle Arly !
> Sitting on a heap of Barley
> Thro' the silent hours of night –
> Close beside a leafy thicket:
> On his nose there was a Cricket,
> In his hat a Railway Ticket;
> (But his shoes were far too tight) ...

It's an amazing performance, funny in a surrealistic *Alice in Wonderland* kind of way, very *English*. I can say this, being Scottish. Peter is bearded, wearing a long heavy coat, wide-brimmed hat and long scarf with a large cricket perched on his nose. Throughout the filming, between takes, he was still in character; even the crew treated him as the character, and, while directing him, I forgot completely his real persona and accepted without question what he offered me.

Barry Humphries, who as we know, can also assume character, appears in the film as a gravedigger and he remarked on Peter's 'inner calm' that day. Getting to know

Peter, I realized that crickets, insects and sport were important to Peter. We went to see his team, Tottenham Hotspur, play on many occasions and he never missed a chance to mention them in the show whenever he could, which he does in the 'Art Gallery' sketch. During the 'Leaping Nuns' sketch, he mentions Sister Domination, from Dijon, 'who was transferred from that order to ours . . . at a record fee'. Whilst filming *The Rise and Rise of Michael Rimmer*, Peter asked me to appear in one scene. Harold Pinter also was in the scene and Peter, he and I, spent most of the day, between takes, discussing sporting heroes.

During the run of *Behind the Fridge* Peter got a kick out of the different reactions from the various audiences to which he played. During the previews, when some nights the stalls were full of doctors and nurses, he'd wonder privately how well a certain routine would go, remarking that, 'It went very well last night to that audience of old age pensioners.' But, unlike some of the older comedians of that time, Dudley and he changed nothing radically. They never pandered to the paying public. Peter worked up a very funny piece where he was a comedian of the *Sunday Night at the Palladium* type where the performer, so wanting to be liked, altered his act, line by line, word by word, depending on the reaction of the unseen audience. After each joke he would pause and weigh it up for almost an eternity before going on, suicidally, to a completely different, unconnected subject. He never performed this piece but would do it for me prior to going onstage, adding new lines and bits of 'business' on each occasion.

The years during which *Not Only . . . But Also* was being transmitted are often spoken of as 'The Golden Years of Television'. To me, Peter was at the height of his comedic powers then and is in no small way responsible for the respect that era now commands.

Christopher Hitchens and Dudley Moore

The Other Half of the Sketch

In one of his Bertie and Jeeves stories, P.G. Wodehouse (himself the creator of perhaps the most imperishable double-act and cross-talk in English comic history) speculates on our tendency to think of certain pairs as somehow indissoluble. What – or who? – is Roland without Oliver, Marks without Spencer, Damon without Pythias, David without Jonathan? What was it, muses Wodehouse, that first drew Swan to Edgar?

Well, whether it's Dud and Pete, or Derek and Clive, or Peter Cook and Dudley Moore, there seems in retrospect to have been something as natural in the pairing as Don Quixote and Sancho Panza. Partly it's the incongruity – the tall, thin, spare sardonic one and the short, eager, anxious one. Also there's a subliminal suggestion of the great English class question, the school prefect type and the Bash Street kid in hectic combination. Whether in cap and muffler or in bow-tie and starched shirt, Cook found his ideal foil in Moore, and could make him the object of his drawl (*Bo Duddley*) or of his drone (*The Dagenham Dialogues*). 'The other half of the sketch' was a Wodehouse vernacular for a spouse. How had the Pete and Dud marriage come about, and how had it fared through those long winter evenings?

On a sparkling day in Venice Beach, California, I stepped

off the brilliant sidewalk into a restaurant, named for its address at 72 Market Street, with which Dudley Moore has some kind of *le patron mange ici* relationship. There's a large piano parked in the corner where he sometimes entertains customers without warning but, as he told me when he sat down, he does less and less of this these days. 'I find it harder and harder to play for people who are enjoying themselves. I like people who are listening to be *in pain.*' This makes a promisingly if deceptively bleak beginning, swiftly followed by Dudley's account of a documentary on Auschwitz that he has recently viewed. 'Amazing to think that this was happening while I was alive. Amazing to think' – his voice takes on the appropriate croak – 'that there is anyone who has a worse life than I do.' In my poor understudy of an Alan Bennett nasal whinge, I add that 'There's always someone worse off than yourself.' The correct atmosphere is slowly evolving as the wine is poured.

But in truth I am slightly nervous. Everybody knows that there was a distinct *froideur* between Cook and Moore after they ceased working together, and I don't know quite how we're going to get round it, or even whether we should. Begin, anyway, at the beginning:

'I loved performing with Peter in the latter years of *Beyond the Fringe*, and although I had the least speaking to do in the show I got to perform with him more and more. The dialogue from the floor that we had in *Civil Defence*, where I ask how long it will be before normal service is resumed after nuclear Armageddon, and he says he expects something in the nature of a skeleton service, was the start of it. That and the one-legged Tarzan sketch. Jonathan could play Mr Spiggot, the unidexter artiste, but he never really got his essential optimism. So when, in 1966 or so, I was asked to do a show produced by Joe McGrath, our first director, I asked Peter. But it could have just as well have been Alan. This is what became *Not Only . . . But Also*. It was originally called *Not Only Dudley Moore But Also Peter Cook,* which I later rearranged in alphabetical order to avoid upsetting him.'

Dudley soon realized that he had made the right choice. 'We were improvising in his living-room at 17 Church Row and he started up: "My wife's not a well woman. That's why she doesn't like going to the well ... I met my wife during the war. She blew in through the window on a piece of shrapnel, and became embedded in the sofa, and one thing led to my mother, and we were married within the hour." ' 'The amazing thing,' says Dudley today – having done this from memory just as I have set it down – 'is that it was *just like that*. No warning – he just started coming out with it.' (Later, when I ask him for an encapsulating anecdote about Peter, he returns to this moment as the one that, more than any other, has lodged in his mind.)

'So the show went well. We did a long sketch about a janitor in a West End club where only after a bit do you realize that the club is a public toilet. A khazi. John Lennon (who also brought on some of his poetry from *Lennon In His Own Write*) played the janitor. Peter came up with the line, "This is where the big nobs hang out." I did a parody of the Swingle Singers. Tom Sloan of BBC Comedy called us in and said: "I see a series here." After John died, Yoko Ono wouldn't let us use any of his appearance for *The Best of Not Only ... But Also*, which I wanted to call *The Best of What's Left of Not Only ... But Also*, but the BBC didn't get the point.'

For all this, though, Dudley doesn't talk as if it was fated to happen. 'I don't have any very strong first impression of Peter. All of us thought we were better than the others when the *Fringe* began. I do remember the way he used to come on as a messenger in "So That's The Way You Like It", wearing a crown and carrying a sword and sliding to a kind of halt. And I remember that he never forgot his words. *Ever.* He was more at home with what he wrote than what others wrote, of course, but we tended to keep what he wrote in any case.'

It was when they moved to New York that Dudley began

to take alarm at what he saw as Peter's dependence on the booze. 'It actually affected his performance, though I think I was the only one who noticed.' Moore's memory, which he admits is poor and incomplete, skids between different touring fiascos and nerve-jangling evenings in Australia, New Zealand and Manhattan. 'I remember that once he was plastered on a first night, and I think perhaps that was when he'd just got the divorce papers from his first wife. I remember him taking a pledge to stay off the bottle while we were on the plane to New York, but he didn't keep it. And I remember being on stage by myself for forty-five minutes, doing things at the piano, because he'd passed out on the sofa in his apartment and the door had to be broken down. He appeared in the wings like a ghost and gave me the thumbs-up, and I was so shocked I gave him an off-centre cue but he managed to pull it all off. His lines were coming out a bit slow, but again I think I was the only one who could tell. Jesus he could drink. You'd see the glass go to his mouth and you'd think: "Farking arseholes, that glass'll be lucky if it isn't swallowed." Yet a jazz friend of mine, Francis Megahy, saw the performances in New York and was amazed when I told him Peter had been smashed. He said it didn't show at all. One night, I decided I'd get drunk before the show too, just to see what it was like. It so happens I am a very merry drunk and I came off the stage saying, "That was great wasn't it, just great?" And Peter said, "No, it wasn't. I didn't know what to do. I felt as if my fly was undone." And I turned to him and said, "Well then, now you know what it's like, you cunt."'

What was it like rehearsing and improvising the act, I wanted to know. 'We would get together and improvise into a tape recorder, and then listen. I would do headings of things that we both liked and we would erase the rest and then do it again. We'd do it up to four or five times. A rather higgledy-piggledy approach. Any improvising after that would depend on the response of the audience. But the audience had a tendency to like what we liked, so we didn't alter very much.' Can he remember dropping anything, or lengthening anything, because of the audience response? 'No, I can't. I can remember that a director called Shaun O'Riordan made us do something twice once, because one of his cameras hadn't been working the first time, but of course the second take was no good. The art gallery sketch is still my favourite, because it was so free and easy.' It's no surprise to learn that spontaneity was something that the two of them always agreed upon. 'We were alive to each other's idiosyncrasies and we had a lot of fun. When I think back on it I wince because really it was very risky to rely on that first run-through. There was no safety-net, and no back-up tape.'

Tell me, did you ever get bored with the act, or with each other? 'No. Not once.' But then Dudley qualifies this very slightly. 'We did run out of material for Dud and Pete to discuss. Maybe that's because we always chose odd subjects like Sex and Art and Religion. And we relied a lot on mad reminiscences, like being on the top of a bus while I talk about my experiences at school. Another I remember is of me waking up in a drawer full of socks, and Peter smacking me awake with a cricket bat and saying 'Thank God you're not Jewish.' It slowly emerges that I'm being born again and I'm nine hours late and the doctor is trying to make me cry.' At this point, we sit for a bit over our wine, wondering not for the first time what process of alchemy produced these ideas. 'Oh yeah, and there was one that didn't get shown. It was an Elf and Tinkerbell sketch, quite dirty, with a randy Tinkerbell who has it off with a water-boatman. And another, with a very fat man rolling into a restaurant. It started well but we were never sure how to get on with it.'

What about the *Establishment Club*? What memories of Peter? 'No memories really. I would come in after *Beyond the Fringe* and play until four or five in the morning with my Dudley Moore Trio which was then still in existence. And there were other musicians, like Peter Shade the xylophonist. But I was playing downstairs. So I never saw the upstairs acts. Never saw Lenny Bruce or Frankie Howerd or any of them, including Peter.' There's a very faint squeak of self-pity here, so I say teasingly, 'Don't tell me you were below stairs.' This provokes a digression, not about being below stairs exactly, but about Peter's refusal to 'deal with' Dudley's later success in Hollywood. I had a feeling that this would come up sooner or later. All right, then. Out with it. 'I think he must have been jealous. He never said a word about any of my films; never even said he'd seen them. The only time he even acknowledged one was *Arthur*, and that was only because we were having dinner at Drones one night and the people at the next table spotted me and said, you know, "Oooh there's Arthur. We must buy him a drink." And then questions like, "Where did you get the character of Arthur?" And Peter, before I could say anything, broke in and just pointed to his own chest. And I realized that it was true. Still . . .'

Returning to the *Establishment*: 'Look, it was wonderful downstairs. My bass player Peter McGurk once said that it was just like a faucet being turned on – we got into a groove that was so glorious. But once we tried taping it, and it just didn't work. You couldn't get that *feeling* on tape. It just doesn't keep.' We agree that there is justice in the oft-used American expression 'You had to have been there.'

In a sense, the same applies to Dudley's memories of *Beyond the Fringe*. 'We used to cheer Pete on when he was doing the Judge sketch – we'd settle downstage left and encourage him with gestures. The audience couldn't see us but we were just willing him to take off, and he often did. Mind you, it got longer and longer and sometimes it got very boring. He used to be willing to bore people with endless monologues as long as he could exit on a laugh. I remember once that we did a cabaret for the Young Conservatives, and the reason I remember it is that for once we got no laughs at all. Peter was being unusually lavatorial even for him, talking about some intensive crap he'd been having. The thing ended with an icy silence – the only time it had ever happened to us. Clement Freud came bustling up and said it had been just what the doctor ordered, but we knew different.'

I wanted to know what had happened with the shooting of *Bedazzled*; a memory that seems to put Dudley into a daze of gloom. 'It was rather gawkily written and Peter wanted to have the solo writing credit. I didn't mind that because I was doing the music at the same time for *Thirty is a Dangerous Age – Cynthia*, and I was really overworked. I may have contributed a bit of oil for the machinery, at a few points where it was a little bit stiff. But there was lots in the film that wasn't traditional Dud and Pete or Pete and Dud. There wasn't the same ease as on TV. I think we lost a lot by appearing on film, because there was no improvisation. Just a script and a rehearsal and then we had to stick to it.' Didn't Peter feel this? 'No. He took to filming. Terribly. He was one of the world's worst film actors. He even enjoyed the idea of post-synching because he thought it might improve the performance. But the problem was – he was much too self-aware. And so he was much less good as an *actor*. But he still liked it a lot. He never brooded at all, as far as I know, about the rather iffy reviews and notices that *Bedazzled* got. He just liked the idea of being a movie actor.'

It's not really for me to say what may or may not have conditioned the Cook–Moore relationship. Everybody who has either read or written a biography will know that – with certain epic and heroic exceptions – the number of vivid and active years in any given life are depressingly and remarkably few. But when I asked Dudley to recall anything from the other films in which they both appeared – *The Wrong Box*, *The Hound of the Baskervilles*, *The Bed-Sitting Room*, *Those Daring Young Men in Their Jaunty Jalopies* – he firmly closed the door of memory. A favourite anecdote? No. A particular memory? No. An act of kindness or generosity? No. 'We used to do six months on and six months off on *Not Only . . . But Also*, so I was used to going from a time of seeing him every day to not seeing him at all. Why not? He was a very private person and like all comedians was dedicated to being isolated. I'm as private as he was and I don't like people ferreting about even now. When we did meet and when he was sarcastic to me I would just shrug, and I'd think to myself that he was jealous of me getting on in Hollywood. Or it may have been that he knew I'd told people about his drunkenness.'

As one who has interviewed the odd star in the Santa Monica and Malibu region before now, I can only say that this makes a change – even if not a particularly refreshing one – from the boilerplate stuff about 'how great it was working with Pete' and 'what a wunnerful and professional guy' he was. Perhaps a sense of the ridiculous or the phoney is keeping Dudley from being too fulsome. All the same, his plea of amnesia is sometimes hard to credit. Does he remember the last time they both met, for example? Yes, he thinks it was in the Gay Hussar restaurant in Soho. Does he recall anything about the evening? Not a thing.

A tribute, though, need not depend upon affection. A strong impression will do. And there is no doubt that the impression is strong and deep. Every time that Dudley 'does' a memory of Peter, his voice sinks by an octave or so and assumes an utterly different register of growls and snarls. I venture to ask whether the difference in their 'backgrounds' was a problem, and Moore denies this while incidentally affirming it. 'Peter was always backtracking into the working class. He loved all accents. I always thought he was trying to un-toffee-nose his own voice. Anyway, he had this amazing combination of vowel sounds.' Mimicry, we both agree, is not a paltry achievement. It demonstrates a real interest in the lives of others, perhaps even a carefully guarded sympathy.

'He used to shock the shit out of me,' says Dudley suddenly. 'I used to drop my head in sheer exhaustion at the prospect of what he was about to say. Anything could set him off – it might be this wine-glass – and before you knew it, he could be on a tour of every orifice in the human body. He had a genius for obscenity. I never succeeded in shocking him, though I used to try all right. I could never match him for speed, for one thing. And I usually had to fall back on filthy tales of family life. He was mounting an endless assault on the humour button. He wouldn't stop until he got a laugh. Never mind how much dross there was, he had to come up with a jewel. I can remember him – this was in company, not on stage – going on and on and on and on because he wanted to leave on a laugh line. It was very anxiety-filled for me because I just didn't see how he was going to get out of it. He did of course, but it seemed to take forever.'

Obviously it could be gruelling to be 'the other half of the sketch' in private life. In public, too, for that matter. 'It was at the Bell Sound Studios in New York and we were due to do a Derek and Clive number. With no warning at all, he starts in on "The Worst Job I ever 'ad", and it's all about pulling lobsters out of Jayne Mansfield's bum. I was just stunned – it came out of nowhere. I had to do a very hasty, improvised response – it was all about the worst job I ever had, which was picking up Winston Churchill's bogeys. I don't know where I got it from.'

In a sense, of course, he got it from Peter Cook. Samuel Johnson once remarked that the definition of a wit was someone who was not merely witty himself, but was rather *the cause of wit in others*. (Not Only, But Also, as you might say.) Cook had a quality which Dudley describes as 'insatiable', a determination to work on an audience until he found its funny-bone. But as we know from Joseph Heller (see pages 78–86) he could also provide an audience in himself.

Where did it all *come* from? I remind Dudley of Penelope Gilliatt's *New Yorker* profile of John Cleese, where he recalled overhearing absurd parental conversations about England's spin-bowlers and the muddy wicket, and real-ized that comedy was being spoken all around him. 'Well, he did have these memories of some old retainer at school, and also of some droning old park-keeper who would say things like "Now here's an interesting thing" and then lapse into the most terribly tedious stories. It led to the sketch about "The Most Boring Man in The World".' At this point Dudley's voice drops again and, seemingly without knowing he's doing it, he intones: ' "And here he is – The Most Boring Man in The World." '

The two stopped working as a duo in 1977, but there were a couple more occasions when they did their stuff together. In January 1986, Peter was 'co-host' for the Joan Rivers Show in London and Dudley came over from Los Angeles to be a guest. The next year, Peter was invited to Los Angeles to perform with Dudley in front of a packed house for US Comic Relief. Both of these events provided some ground for reconciliation. Lin, before she became Peter's wife, went to see Dudley at Claridges during his London trip, and told him that Peter minded about the times he'd been in London and failed to call. Moore said that he had got fed up with Peter's sarcasm (he wasn't the only one) but did call. In Los Angeles the two had dinner at Spago with Lin and with Dudley's third wife (or wife-to-be) Brogan Lane. Peter apologized at this dinner for his caustic remarks but reminded Dudley that he had not been blameless in giving press interviews about Peter and the drink. In amicable fashion, the two later did some appearances in London for *The Secret Policeman's Biggest Ball*, a benefit for Amnesty International.

Still, there is an element of melancholy in Moore's memory of their last meetings. 'When he ate or drank he seemed somehow alone. I remember watching him fall on a forkful of food, and slosh the booze about, and thinking that I could see why we were apart. In some way, he was somebody who didn't permit remembrances of himself.'

At this stage, our own meal is drawing to a close and I'm careful not to gulp my wine. Please, I think, let him come out of a reverie with one last good memory. And, without my prompting it, so he does. With a cackle, he recalls how

Peter could 'gum on a moustache and put on a deerstalker and *become* Sir Arthur Streeb-Greebling ... "Good evening ... Good Greebling ... The 'f' is silent, as in fox. Of course, we're training ravens here, training them to fly under water. Knee-deep in feathers." ' The atmosphere lightens, and lunch closes with Dudley 'doing' Peter 'doing' David Frost, as an interviewer of shepherds for the *Bethlehem Star*. 'He had this completely Frost-like way of saying, to someone like Jesus's former landlady, "And you *never* saw him again?" '

Never mind the passage of time or the attritions of friendship, in Dudley's mind he's still around all right.

Shane Maloney

Hanging Out at Hanging Rock

In early 1987 the organizers of the inaugural Melbourne
Comedy Festival invited Peter Cook to officiate at the
festival's formal launch. To their delight and considerable
surprise, he agreed.

For the comediocracy of a city that describes itself as the
humour capital of Australia, this was a *coup* of significant
proportions. So much so that when its Guest of Honour
eventually emerged from his twenty-hour flight from
London, fabulously dishevelled, golf bag slung over his
shoulder, his partner Lin at his side, the welcoming committee could barely refrain from prostrating itself at his feet,
right there at the gate-lounge. 'You come as an emperor,'
local comedy impresario John Pinder told him, 'to accept
the homage of your subjects.'

Pinder is no stranger to hyperbole, but this was not an
entirely excessive description. Although it was some sixteen
years since his last visit, Peter's memory remained fresh in
Australia. To a people who like to flatter ourselves on our
irreverence, he was our kind of Englishman. Pinder's
cabaret, the seed-bed of much new Australian comedy, was
called The Last Laugh, partly in deference to Peter's first
university revue at Cambridge; and tyro Australian comedians were just as keen as their British counterparts to pay
court to the godfather of modern satire.

13. A youthful Peter Cook

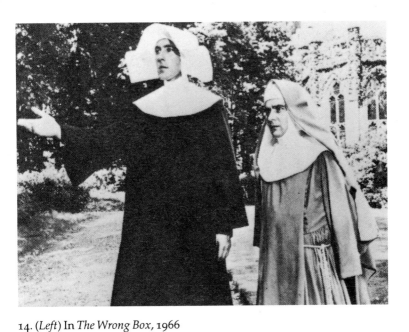

14. (*Left*) In *The Wrong Box*, 1966

15. (*Above*) With Dudley Moore in *Bedazzled*, 1967

16. *Not Only...But Also*, 1970: As 'Emma Bargo', mimicking the closing shot of *Queen Christina*

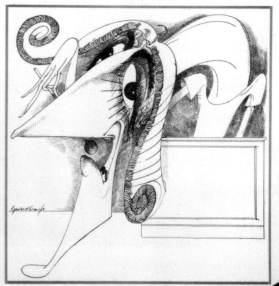

PETER COOK
HERE COMES THE JUDGE
LIVE IN CONCERT

18. Album cover
for *Here Comes
the Judge*, 1979

17. Album cover
for *Good Evening*,
November 1973

"GOOD EVENING"
ORIGINAL BROADWAY CAST

You should not
pay more than
£2.99
for this reco

ALEXANDER H. COHEN and BERNARD DELFONT
present

PETER DUDLEY
COOK MOORE

in

"GOOD EVENING"
COMEDY WITH MUSIC
Directed by
JERRY ADLER

19. With John Cleese as Neville Chamberlain in *Peter Cook and Company*, 1980

20. With John Wells (left) and Willie Rushton on the set of *20 Years On*, 1985

Melbourne Comedy Festival, March 1987

21. With Barry Humphries

23. (*Right*) Press conference with Barry Humphries as Sir Les Patterson

22. With Shane Maloney

24. (*Right*) The stage performer

25. With Lin in Melbourne

26. Flying home: the ubiquitous newspaper

Perhaps what appealed to us most about Peter was his utter indifference to the blandishments of career. In a world where comedy had become an industry, Peter was a reminder of its more anarchic possibilities. He was funny not because that was his job, but because he couldn't help it. The laughter that he provoked was not a commodity to be bartered but an encounter with the absurdities of existence.

I had only seen Peter once before, at a distance and in a manner that seemed appropriately absurd at the time. In 1971, Peter and Dudley toured Australia for nearly five months, premièring *Behind the Fridge* before taking it back to London and on to America. The shows were a sell-out and several weeks into the tour, in an unprecedented and never-repeated move, the Broadcasting Control Board banned Peter and Dudley from live performances on all forty-seven television and 116 radio stations in the country.

Memories differ about the cause of this record achievement. Possibly it was the result of their appearance and something they said on the *Dave Allen Show*. Some hold that it resulted from the broadcast on a Sunday evening of 'The Gospel Truth', a sketch in which Mr Arthur Shepherd (Peter) is interviewed by Matthew (Dudley), a reporter for the *Bethlehem Star*. Although Channel 9 executives had taken the precaution of having a 'panel of expert clergymen' preview the skit and two lines had been excised before it went to air, over three hundred outraged viewers besieged the switchboard with complaints. 'The programme was shown at 8:30, so we were sure that no children were watching,' pleaded station management. To no avail. The Chairman of the Broadcasting Control Board described the sketch as 'the most blatantly offensive reference to homosexuality and masturbation' he'd ever seen.

One particularly obscene word had been used. 'Something a lot of us sit on,' Dudley later explained to the Press Club. 'Not a chair. Short word. Starts with B, ends with M.' The BCB acted firmly and decisively to protect the nation from this filth. For the duration of their visit, no television or radio station in the entire country was permitted to allow Peter or Dudley to go out live and unvetted, under pain of loss of licence.

This did nothing whatsoever to diminish ticket sales to the theatrical shows. And when the Channel 9 network went ahead with a live broadcast of a charity gala for the Freedom from Hunger Campaign at which Pete and Dud were the star turn, the authority of the Broadcasting Control Board suffered a body blow from which it and its descendants have not recovered to this very day.

I was an eighteen-year-old in my first year at university. Student protest was at its height. When the terrible duo appeared on campus in the midst of their battle with the forces of puritanism and cant, they were greeted as heroes. The hall filled to capacity as soon as the doors opened. Speakers were rapidly set up outside to cater to the overflow. When these proved insufficient, the show was piped campus-wide on closed-circuit television. It sure beat the hell out of Hobbes, Locke and the Social Contract.

Many things had changed in Melbourne between 1971 and 1987, but some remained the same. The Chairman of the Broadcasting Control Board had vanished into oblivion, but, yea, Mr Arthur Shepherd's flock were still abiding in the field. And lo, the man was back in town as Guest of Honour of the Comedy Festival.

I had become a bureaucrat and happened to find myself seconded to the Comedy Festival, charged with making sure that the jokes ran on time and the theatrical entrepreneurs involved did not go west with the government grant. Peter, needless to say, more than fulfilled our expectations. Within minutes of his arrival, he'd reduced us to hysterics with a virtuoso display of impromptu invention. When informed that the hotel manager, a Swiss gentleman, had requested an autographed photo for the 'celebrity guest' wall of the hotel bar, Peter immediately launched into a twenty-minute dissertation on the role of the Swiss hotelier in the development of modern comedy. It was, he explained, entirely due to the influence of the Swiss that housemaids announce their arrival with a brisk 'knock, knock'. And it was the hotel management schools of Zurich that first came up with the idea of leaving a small joke on the guest's pillow at night.

Drawn by the sound of laughter, the hotel manager bustled across the lobby and joined us, a look of comprehension settling on his face. This must be his celebrity guest, the famous English clown. And judging by the response of his listeners, a most competent one. Peter, oblivious to the identity of the man in the pin-striped trousers, continued his monologue. Herr Metzger, taking his cue from the rest of us, roared with laughter. While he was in charge nobody could say the Swiss didn't recognize a joke when they heard one.

The Lord Mayor, a fan from the days of *Behind the Fridge*, invited Peter to lunch at the Town Hall. They spent the meal discussing architecture. His Honour, a noted champion of urban conservation, mentioned plans to restore a derelict 1920s picture palace just across the road. It took little encouragement on Peter's part for the keys to be found, and the two of them spent the afternoon wandering through the theatre's cobweb-draped Rococo smoking lounges, Roman Empire Wurlitzer pit and Late Medieval projection box. Just the place, Peter declared, for the world première of his forthcoming feature film based on the secret diaries of Queen Victoria's gynaecologist.

The high point of the official agenda was the press conference to launch the Comedy Festival. Peter was to share the honours with festival patron Barry Humphries, who appeared in the salivating persona of Sir Les Patterson. When he and Peter appeared and the photographers began popping their flashes, the result was like a small thermonuclear explosion. Peter, rendered the colour of Cheddar cheese by the lighting, and beaded with perspiration from the heat of the sun guns, sat in benign bemusement while

Humphries basted him with reminiscences of their early careers.

At the crack of dawn the next day (an event which took place at about 11 a.m. due to the southerliness of the latitude), Peter and satirist John Clarke headed for the nearest golf course. 'My driving hasn't been very good lately,' he warned. 'But my short game is among the shortest on earth.' Positively glowing with ill-health, he wheezed his way through eighteen holes, club in one hand, Superkings in the other.

Although an invitation had been issued by Royal Melbourne, home of the Australian Open, Peter had stated his preference for somewhere a little less formal. Clarke took him to Yarra Bend, a public course favoured by off-duty taxi drivers and shift-working bakers. As they neared the clubhouse, Peter spied a player taking a somewhat relaxed attitude to the posted dress regulations. He demanded to see the pro. If people were allowed to wander about stripped to the waist, he complained, the least the course could do was remove the sign requiring that players wear a shirt. 'I myself would not have bothered', he said, 'had I known.'

One of the main festival attractions was a somewhat anarchic mock trial, conducted in the magistrate's court and involving half the town's legal fraternity. Spirited away by a team of admiring barristers and fed a persuasive lunch, Peter agreed to appear as judge in the case. He did so in full wig and gown with a bottle of gin on the bench in front of him. When he'd finished his summation – half extemporaneous nonsense, half reprise of his famous Jeremy Thorpe monologue – he gave his verdict. 'The sentence I am about to hand down is sponsored by Tanqueray gin,' he began. 'You always get a result with Tanqueray.'

What Peter now needed, it was decided, was a day in the country. Exposure to the therapeutic qualities of the Australian bush would do him a world of good. So first thing the next morning, about noon, we set out for Hanging

Rock. Here, at last, was a chance to escape the demands of the press, the importunings of theatrical producers and the attentions of over-excited fans. The autumn countryside was lush with ripening grain and overburdened grape vines. Lin and Peter could begin to enjoy the free time promised as an inducement for them to make the long journey. A decent lunch was had at Macedon, a town of wooded avenues, the thick deciduous plantings of last century's pioneer aristocracy turning a rich seasonal gold.

We found Hanging Rock deserted, the towering hill of gigantic boulders looking just as eerily compelling as it had in Peter Weir's film. At the start of the trail to the top, a sign advised that this was a nature reserve and that any wildlife encountered should be treated with caution. Peter wondered if perhaps, under the circumstances, we should have brought prophylactics.

His mountain-climbing days well behind him, he ascended the path slowly. 'If we get to the top and there's a camera crew waiting,' he warned at the half-way mark, 'I'll fucking well kill you.' But the only camera was the one Lin had brought. As she snapped the view from the top and Peter lounged like a satyr among the boulders, I did my best to rustle up a koala or two.

I am not, I suppose, the first of my countrymen to have been urinated upon by a marsupial. But I am probably the only one that ever had Peter Cook there to witness the sight. Thirty feet immediately above me, with unerring accuracy, a drowsing furball opened its bladder. Peter, well out of range, found my discomfort highly amusing. And for that, I will remain forever grateful to that bloody koala. It's probably still there to this day, sitting atop Hanging Rock, stoned out of its tiny mind on eucalyptus leaves. No doubt it has long forgotten the sight of that gangly Englishman who could bring laughter even to a remote hilltop at the end of the world. But I never will.

Nor will thousands more. When the Melbourne Comedy

Festival celebrated its tenth anniversary, it marked the occasion by naming its showcase venue for young performers The Peter Cook Room.

Barry Took

The News Quiz

It was always my belief that Peter, who co-wrote the revues *Pieces of Eight* and *One Over the Eight*, which starred Kenneth Williams, saw in Williams an *alter ego* but then realized that while Kenneth could do Peter's material admirably so too could Peter and the partnership ended. They remained friends and in fact worked together in one of the worst films ever made, *The Hound of the Baskervilles* (1977) in which Sherlock Holmes was played by Peter, Dr Watson by Dudley Moore, and Sir Henry Baskerville by Kenneth Williams. (Williams called the script 'a hotch-potch of rubbish' and indeed it was dreadful.) However, in his diary Kenneth wrote of Peter, 'His conversation is infectiously good humoured and enthusiastic. Lovely fellow.'

I only really got to know Peter when he ventured to make occasional appearances on radio. On one occasion we were seated together, although nominally rivals, in the long-running panel game, *Just A Minute*, chaired by Nicholas Parsons. It was a game in which Kenneth Williams, a regular panellist, excelled. His mock indignation when his flow of exotic language was brought to an abrupt halt by other panellists who claimed he had deviated was hilariously offensive. He found his match in Peter, however, as the following extract from the programme shows. The subject was 'My Other Self', and Kenneth got as far as 'My other self ...' when Peter buzzed.

Nicholas Parsons	... and Peter Cook has challenged.
Peter Cook	I thought I'd better get in early, otherwise I might not be noticed; and I have to bring up the possibility of deviation here. The 'other self' which has been talked about ... which self is he talking about? Has he deviated from himself whilst he was talking about himself?
Nicholas Parsons	The only deviation is that the fellow hasn't even started. So, it's a wrong challenge, Peter, but nice to hear from you, and Kenneth still has the subject.
Kenneth Williams	... when we do see something that we didn't notice we ... (*Peter buzzes again.*)
Nicholas Parsons	What is your challenge, Peter?
Peter Cook	We've been subjected to a constant stream of we we's ...

Peter won the point and went on to complete the minute on the subject of 'My Other Self'.

Peter and I had never worked together before our meeting on *Just A Minute* but found an instant rapport. I love mischief, as did Peter, and for a few moments we became a couple of naughty boys, at one point lapsing into a sort of Swedish cross-talk. The Chairman, Nicholas Parsons, commented, 'I think you're playing another game. This is *Just A Minute*.' We were never asked to play together again.

But then came *The News Quiz* with, in its earlier manifestations a *Punch* team, led by the then Editor, Alan Coren, versus *Private Eye*, edited in those days by Richard Ingrams. Richard was usually teamed with John Wells or Ian Hislop, and occasionally with 'hands-off' owner Peter

Cook whose flights of fancy enchanted me. The various producers we had were brave enough to leave much of his ad-libbing in the edited programmes. The following extract is typical. The panellists were Peter, Richard Ingrams, Alan Coren and Nick Clarke. The question related to the Jonathan Dimbleby book on Prince Charles.

Richard Ingrams	It's this week's royal book. There's a new one every week now and the latest one is Charles's apology for himself ...
Peter Cook	I think he's been tremendously brave to reveal that he's met Jonathan Dimbleby – in person, and talked to him for a while.
Alan Coren	I want to read all about these blokes who knocked him about at Gordonstoun and who were all lining up to hang one on him ...
Nick Clarke	They said things like, 'with ears like that you'll never be king'.
Richard Ingrams	We were treated like that but we didn't go whining ...
Peter Cook	I was told I'd never be king very early on. I didn't go whining to the press – no.
Richard Ingrams	You took it like a man.
Peter Cook	I took it like a hermaphrodite, which I was told I was. Whatever it was – I took it.

The delight of *The News Quiz* when it was recorded at The Paris Studio in Lower Regent Street was that there was always a gossipy session in the small back room. There was usually some hot chit-chat about matters of the day winging round the tiny room and Peter would revel in the indiscretions reported by the other panellists, adding a few items of rumour (generally scurrilous) himself. He smoked like a chimney and had no regard for sartorial niceties. He was often sockless, in scruffy tee shirt, slacks and, on one occasion, green shoes. Richard Ingrams and Peter would emerge to be greeted by the audience looking as if they'd drifted into the studio from cardboard city. In my introduction I'd say things like 'Please don't laugh, they've made a special effort' while the audience, who loved them, cheered, applauded, and roared with laughter. As with *Just A Minute* – and I suspect everything else he did – Peter bent *The News Quiz* into a shape that suited him and, once on the trail of a good joke, was unstoppable.

Peter invariably partnered Richard Ingrams who was greatly stimulated and ventured into realms of funny voices, not usually his forte. On one recording there was a question about seaweed, alleged to be radioactive, on the shore near Sellafield. The actual question was 'What doom weed proved to be all washed up?'

Peter Cook	(*In a bogus Scottish accent*) Doomweed? I have no idea but I am willing to spin it out in the hope that my educated friend, Richard Ingrams, will jump in with the answer.
Richard Ingrams	(*Also in an almost impenetrably Scottish accent*) Aye – well, I will. It was in the seaweed on the beaches ... (*In his normal voice*) Hold on, it wasn't in Scotland, was it?
Peter Cook	No. I was doing it in that accent for security reasons. I was asked by Mossad to disguise my voice.

Again from *The News Quiz* a final (mock-autobiographical) memory of that rare bird, Peter Cook:

I remember in the old days, before you were allowed to do satire, you had to do four years of satire in the provinces learning what a joke was. And now these people – these Ben Eltons and all these people – they do satire straight away and it shouldn't be allowed. Four years – you had to be born in Nigeria; you had to go to a prep school and you had to go to college; and then you did your satire. But now anyone can do it. It's a disgrace.

Eric Idle

The Funniest Man in the World

I was talking to Billy Connolly the other day. 'Did you know Peter Cook?' I asked. He turned suddenly serious. 'Oh Peter,' he said. 'Peter was the funniest man in the world. I worked with him on *The Secret Policeman's Ball* and I sat next to him at a Press Conference for an hour and I couldn't open my mouth, he was so funny. I just think he was the best in the world,' said Billy.

Peter *was* the funniest man in the world and all funny people know that. When he died he was universally mourned by all generations of comedians. At the LA tribute to Peter, Richard Benjamin stopped in to say he never knew Peter, he never met Peter and yet he just wanted to come by and stand up and say how great he was. Peter's loss was like that. For months afterwards whenever funny people met, the first subject was Peter. He had friends and admirers all round the globe, all of whom felt his absence, all of whom he had touched. It wasn't just his talent. Lots of people are talented. He somehow seemed to have affected people in a special way. He did for me. He changed my life.

If we can return for a moment to the dark days of 1962, duffel coats, suede shoes, drainpipe trousers, London fogs, Ban the Bomb marches, French cigarettes, John Osborne and jazz. I was coming to the end of a twelve-year sentence in a British boarding school in darkest Wolverhampton. In the holidays I stayed with a friend in Palmers Green, North London. I seem to remember being constantly cold in those days. Our lives were illuminated by visits to the Royal Court Theatre and the West End, where we sat high up in the Gods and hungrily devoured everything that moved. Then one evening we decided to visit the Fortune Theatre to see a new revue. We couldn't get seats, it was long since sold out, but we did manage to get standing tickets at the back of the tiny theatre, which was just as well, because I don't think I could have stayed in a seat. When the curtain went up on *Beyond the Fringe* we laughed until tears ran down our cheeks, we gasped frantically for breath, we thumped each other with great shouts of recognition, we screamed in delight as we rolled and rolled around the back wall. I don't believe I have ever laughed at anything quite so much. It was the shock of it, the freshness, the sheer liberating savagery of its complete dismissal of all things British. Nothing was sacred; not the Queen, not the Army, not the schools, not the Church, not the City, not Advertising, not the Prime Minister, not the late War, not even the impending nuclear holocaust we were all sure was coming. ('Just jump in to your brown paper bags . . .'). It was a complete and total dismissal of everything that had ever oppressed us growing up in post-war Britain, done with the lightest of touches and from a position of complete intellectual superiority. For me nothing would ever be quite the same again. I simply had no idea you were allowed to be that funny. I didn't know you could mock a Prime Minister. (Even more shockingly, mock him to his face, as Macmillan bravely visited the show.) For me it was a total liberation. I instantly learned all the bits off the album and returned to boarding school a different person. It was as if I had suddenly woken up and found that everything that had been oppressing me, restricting me, terrifying me, was now joyously, liberatingly funny.

When I arrived at Cambridge later that year, I had never heard of the Footlights but thanks to *Beyond the Fringe* I knew what was funny. I soon found I had got into Peter Cook's ex-college; Pembroke in those days was *the* comedy College, and his spirit lurked everywhere in the funny voices he had left behind. Everybody's Cambridge is different; mine began as tweed jackets, pipe-smoking, the Jazz Club and sherry and ended up with satire, the Footlights, leather jackets, beer, the Beatles, and, of course, getting laid (which thanks to the Beatles became a little easier). Peter and the great *Fringe* boys had gone off to America leaving a comedy vacuum into which poured the cast of *That Was the Week That Was*. Each week live on our screens the Establishment was pilloried by the TV wits (children of the *Fringe*) until the government put a stop to it by calling an election (which in turn put a stop to them). Frostie became famous, his trademark quiff in every paper, inciting the ire of the great Cook who labelled him The Bubonic Plagiarist, after David's legendary freedom with other peoples' material. (Though to be fair, he always paid. I remember once opening his new book on England and being shocked to read a few of my gags. I had hardly registered my resentment when a case of champagne arrived at the door from David thanking me 'for my indirect help' on his new book!)

The new government wasn't half as funny, though we soon learned that socialist governments can be every bit as repressive and hypocritical. Wilson's government immediately started a war in Nigeria to protect British oil interests, and there seemed to be endless head to head meetings with a man called Smith on a series of boats. Fortunately John Bird came along to remind us that Wilson was just as funny as Macmillan, and a man called Barry Humphries was now holding forth in the Fortune, dressed as an Australian housewife, encouraging staid British audiences to tremble their gladdies.

Then, mercifully, Dud and Pete returned with *Not Only ... But Also* and TV became compulsory viewing again. The

Dagenham Duo mused and amused about everything. Can it really be true that the BBC wiped many of these priceless tapes to save money? Can they really have wiped Spike Milligan's series *Q5*? Did they really erase Alan Bennett's fabulous series *On the Margin* in order to record more episodes of *Horse of the Year Show*? Has there ever been such corporate vandalism from a company claiming to represent the best of British Broadcasting?

Dud and Pete kept us laughing out loud. I will never forget Peter as Greta Garbo nor as a straight-faced Sister in The Leaping Nuns of Norwich sketch, being interviewed as he bounced up and down on a trampoline, a piece which was obviously a favourite as he later recycled it in their movie *Bedazzled*. (Typically, Peter wanted to call this movie *Raquel Welch*, so the billing would read 'Peter Cook and Dudley Moore in *Raquel Welch.*')

I remember soggy days filming *Alice in Wonderland* for Jonathan Miller in 1966, with Peter (appropriately) as the Mad Hatter. On the set at Ealing Studios he would come leaping in with a top hat and that peculiar mad laugh and nasal delivery with which he and Dudley both used to sing–

> Now is the time to say goodbye
> Now is the time to yield a sigh
> (Yield it yield it)
> Now is the time to say Goodbyeee
> Until we meet again, some sun . . . neee day.

Although I went bowling, memorably, with Alan Bennett and Jonathan Miller, I still hadn't met Peter properly at this point, just a polite nod on a movie set. I had watched his every appearance on *The Braden Beat*, where each week, as E.L. Wisty, he would sit on a park bench with his silly hat and moustache and regale us with an inane diatribe about anything that was bothering him. He would also appear frequently on *The Eamonn Andrews Show*, where he would be dangerously, daringly frank, showing neither respect nor mercy to the famous celebrities from Hollywood who sat on the couch beside him.

I think I first really met him with Bill Oddie on the Fulham Road outside the Chelsea Ground after a Tottenham *v.* Chelsea game. Impossibly handsome, but already tipsy from a silver hip flask he sported (there were rumours that he had been beaten up by Manchester United supporters for being funny at their expense). I was far too much in awe of him to say much. Shortly afterwards I remember going to visit John Cleese and seeing him on the set of *The Rise and Rise of Michael Rimmer*, which Kevin Billington was filming in an ex-Masonic Temple in St John's Wood. Who knew that thirty years later we would all be trampling around real ancient temples on a Tour of the Nile?

The seventies were largely Cook-free for me as I laboured alongside that other great giant of Cambridge Comedy, the legendary Cleese. I went to the opening of Peter and Dudley in *Behind the Fridge* in the West End, where the curtain was delayed for twenty minutes while they poured black coffee into Peter to sober him up, and I saw the show again, now called *Good Evening* about a year later in Los Angeles, after their triumphal run on Broadway. In 1982 we finally got to work together on a film that Graham Chapman and Bernard McKenna had written with Peter. *Yellowbeard* was not very successful but it was the most fun I ever had on a movie. We shot the film, a piece of nonsense about pirates, largely on location in Mexico aboard *The Bounty*. It had the funniest group of people in the cast – apart from Peter and Graham, there was John Cleese, Marty Feldman, Spike Milligan, Madeline Kahn, Peter Boyle, a very young Nigel Planer, even David Bowie in a cameo. As with all films, there was acres of time on our hands, which we spent mainly hanging about in a pool at a luxury beach hotel. I remember Peter one day standing waist-deep in the water, bobbing up and down while he philosophized about the Universe in that peculiar nasal E.L. Wisty voice. 'The funny thing about the Universe is, we know where the light comes from but *where* does the darkness come from?' Bob bob bob. 'The speed of light is 300,000 kilometres a second but *what* is the speed of darkness?' That was Peter at his finest, really: the highest intelligence, asking the most serious questions in the silliest possible way. He loved to improvise and was always thrilled if you would play along.

At this point in his life he had given up drinking and one evening he suggested we needed to find some grass. I agreed to accompany him, but where to look? 'No problem,' said Peter, 'we shall find the nearest bordello.' My wife gave me an old-fashioned look, which Peter intercepted, reassuring her with his incredible charm that I should come to no harm. Somewhat sceptically, she agreed to let me go. So off we drove to the local Mexican bordello. Fortunately it wasn't far away. A small door in a white-walled street led into a cantina, a square open to the sky with a band and a bar and lovely girls who were happy just to dance, or there was a low *cabaña* with discreet rooms if you wished to dance horizontally. There were tables for drinking and strings of coloured lights and when we entered it had the air of a private party where the guests had yet to arrive.

Peter was an instant hit. He ran in shouting loudly in cod Spanish, shook the hand of the barman, seized a beautiful tall girl in a shiny red bathing suit and stormed on to the deserted dance-floor where he began the most unimaginable shaking jitterbug boogie. The girls went nuts. They danced around him and he boogied with them all, flinging his arms around, his hair wild, occasionally sinking to his knees or exaggeratedly twisting low. I sat quietly by myself in a corner sipping beer and cursing my inability to cut loose and join him. Everywhere he went he brought joy with him. One minute it was a slow night in a naughty night-club and the next it was a one-man fiesta.

The whole place loved Peter, not just the girls; the band became animated, people flocked in to watch. As he danced away wildly, I envied the freedom of his spirit, the way he could throw himself so wholeheartedly into everything he undertook, whether it was comedy, philosophy or simply dancing in a Mexican whorehouse. And of course every girl in the place was mad to dance with this wild, mad Englishman, who beamed goodwill and, yes dammit, innocence. It went on for hours with the band going nuts and the girls lining up to fandango with this wild spirit. We were filming next day and as midnight approached I made my excuses and slipped shyly away. My beautiful young wife was waiting for me at the hotel; hard enough to persuade her we only went to score some grass without staying all night. My last sight was Peter leading a line of ecstatic ladies in a conga line. He waved cheerily, tapped his nose and yelled, 'No problem, Eric, we're in . . .'

In the morning, we learned what had happened. Peter had taken the tall beautiful girl in the red shiny bathing suit back to her room. She naturally thought he was there for some sex. Once inside, Peter asked casually if she had any grass. 'Of course,' she said, and reached under the bed and brought out a huge load wrapped in newspaper. Peter asked her how much for it. She cited a derisory amount and the deal was made. 'I have to go now,' said Peter. 'What?' She broke into floods of tears. How could he possibly leave? Didn't he think she was beautiful? She was utterly distraught. 'I only wanted some grass,' Peter explained as gently as he could, but she was inconsolable. It wasn't a matter of money. It was honour. It was Mexico. It was her *reputation*. Poor Peter tried hard to convince her that honestly she really *was* beautiful, and *normally* he would have been torn up with desire for her but actually he had only come for some grass.

Dancing on the Nile

Ten years later, we were once again side by side on a dancefloor, this time floating along the Nile. We were on Major Cleese's expedition up the Nile – a legendary attempt to reconcile archaeology, psychotherapy and comedy, and this particular night we achieved it.

The evening had begun amusingly with Peter showing up for dinner and a whole pack of Egyptian waiters picking him up bodily, and running off with him to the back of the boat. People sensed that about Peter; that they could do anything with him and he would go along with it. After dinner, the crew entertained us with some traditional Egyptian songs. 'Right,' said Peter after we finished applauding, 'I think it's our turn.' He rose ominously. 'Come along Eric, time I think for a traditional English dance.' So it was that some of the finest minds of Europe came to perform the hokey cokey for perhaps the very first time on the Nile.

Peter was in great form throughout the three weeks of this unforgettable holiday, John and Alyce-Faye Cleese's magnificent and unbelievable gift to us all, inviting some forty people along to celebrate their 100th birthday. You haven't really visited the Pyramids unless you have visited them with Peter in a pith helmet, taking the pith out of everything.

We had some great evenings too at our house in London with Peter and Lin and great friends at some totally memorable dinners: Peter with Michael Palin, Peter with Stephen Fry, Peter with Robin Williams. The sparks would fly and of course he was drinking too much and smoking too much, but always providing the laughs. And then suddenly, he was gone, and I found myself in Hollywood getting hopelessly drunk, remembering all the good times.

Tania and I were very sorry to miss the May Day tribute Lin organized for him in a church in Hampstead. I got a fax from Michael Palin the next day who told me it was a very touching and funny event, the climax coming with Alan Bennett who said that Peter had only one regret in life and that was saving David Frost from drowning. This brought the church down.

A couple of weeks later I dined with Stephen Fry in Santa

Barbara where he was hiding from the wrath of the British press. He told me a story about Peter which I cherish. David Frost called him up one night and said, 'Prince Andrew is coming to dinner with Fergie, the lovely girl he is going to marry, and they are both tremendous fans. Could you come to dinner? They would really love it because they really want to meet you. Be super if you could make it Wednesday the twelfth.' 'Hang on, I'll just check my diary.' Pause, and rummaging and leafing through diary noises. And then Peter said, 'Oh dear, I find I'm watching television that night.'

Peter was the finest of his age. He wasn't scared of anything. He was not intimidated by power or authority. He was undaunted even by the judiciary and judges. For my generation he constantly did the impossible, he shone light into areas you couldn't believe you could laugh at. He said things which were so fresh you couldn't believe you were hearing them. He changed my life and gave me a whole new way of looking at things. He broadened the mind of the public, increased the range of what could be laughed at and brought comedy kicking and screaming by its heels from the harmless world of Goonery into the harsh new modern world of the Sixties.

The finest company, the nicest man, generous, fair, sensitive and mammothly talented, he made friends effortlessly. He insulted the rich and powerful, perhaps the most important function of comedy, and he brought the gift of laughter wherever he went. He was my hero and I'm proud to say my friend. I miss him dreadfully, but in my head I will always hear his voice. 'Ageing English comic P. Cook died today,' you can hear him say derisively, 'near Neasden. His last request to be buried as far as possible from the Arsenal ground. Bloody typical. Just when Neasden had a chance to be in the quarter-final second leg qualifying round of the Ramsey Cup.'

William Goldman

Peter Cook: For or Against?

So much depends on *when*.

I was talking recently to a writer friend and after our usual moans and whines, he asked what I was up to.

'It's horrible,' I said.

He wondered why tonight was different from any other night.

I explained that someone I cared for had died, and I was trying to put down a memory. As were a number of other people, friends of his. But my problem, doctor, I went on, was that I knew this person the least well of any of the others, and felt something of a charlatan. More than that, I could not shake the feeling that the deceased was perched just above and behind me, disappointedly shaking his head.

He asked who I was writing about.

'Wonderful man, Peter Cook.'

He looked at me a moment. 'The English guy?'

I nodded.

Then he said the most amazing thing: 'God, he was cruel.'

I was simply staggered. 'Peter Cook was as dear a man as I've ever known. And I don't use the word "dear".'

'He was cruel to me. Want to hear?'

I sure did.

'We met and I'd written something and he'd read it and I asked what he thought – big mistake – because he told me.

And he was endlessly rotten, picked at it and went on and on – I'm not saying he was wrong, understand, and God knows he was witty; but he went out of his way to make me feel untalented. And there were other people at the table, listening. It was humiliating. He didn't have to do that.'

My friend doesn't lie, not about pain. But it all rang so strangely. 'When was this?'

He shrugged. '*Fringe* had just opened.'

And suddenly it all made sense. Because *that* Peter Cook knew something the rest of the world didn't: *he was more brilliant than anybody*. And he had to get the news out. Because what if the brilliance didn't last?

That's a terrible burden: to know you're special before the rest of the world has heard. So Peter did was what so many do when they're young – elbow and shove and scratch, making room for themselves at the Inn. (You see, my writer friend was also brilliant, as brilliant as Peter, so of course Peter had to bring him down. When you're young, you don't take prisoners.)

I said this to my friend: 'Peter Cook *was* dear. Maybe he was capable of cruelty then. We all were. But you never knew my guy. You just entered the play too early.'

I got there deep into the last act, when Peter must have known he was going to die.

Oh, he lasted a few years after our initial 'hello', but when the call came that he had gone, no surprise. I remember hoping that his final bottle of wine had been a great vintage, a '45 maybe, even a '61.

We met on the legendary Nile trip – and yes, I was there for the invention of Abu Simbel that Stephen Fry so blessedly relates. And Peter was this genuinely remarkable figure, always hidden by cigarette clouds, who lurched into view, mind on the alert, ready to travel wherever you wanted to go.

The great novelist, Ross MacDonald (try *The Chill*) had an unequalled ability to attack a story where no one else would ever dream. And as he spiralled you along, caught, it made no sense, then less, then suddenly all the sense in the world.

Peter's mind reminded me of that – he was not 'on' in the sense that stand-up comics are on. Because he wasn't a comic. He simply commentated on things and they came out funny, because he attacked the world from a place unique to him.

What was so magical about Peter was this: it was impossible to guess where he was going next.

We were once on a bus in Egypt in the middle of a desert. Noon. Hotter than shit, if you will allow an Americanism. Outside, one of our party, ill, was on her knees in the sand, barfing her guts out.

I was sitting quietly, Cook the row in front, Fry the one behind, both of them smoking madly as we all stared at the poor lady who truly sounded as if she was about to die.

Long silence.

Finally, Peter turned around, looked at Stephen. The trip was coming to an end. Puff, puff. 'What will you be doing back in London, then?'

'Haven't really decided,' from Fry. 'Perhaps some television commercials.'

'Commercials for what?'

'Oh, piles, I expect.'

To which Peter asked the following: 'For or against?'

And for me, sitting there between them, worlds opened. Because I suddenly saw rows of frenzied copywriters, desperately, under deadline pressure, trying to come up with a genuinely catchy slogan for a pro-pile campaign. Or maybe they were against them. Didn't matter. I'd never visited such a place, much less dreamed of its existence.

I remember looking at Peter and I realized he didn't think he'd said anything much. Just getting through a bit of a rough road, watching a travel mate expire.

It was the mind that was the treasure. Effortless, all encompassing. I remember in our later visits, just wanting to be in the presence of that mind, because I knew I'd never

149

been before and wouldn't visit again. You see, Peter was unique as an artist.

Because he was his art ...

John Cleese

Peter Amadeus Cook

It's been difficult coming up with a piece for this Cook book, because I feel I said all I wanted to at Peter's memorial service; his death was the worst loss I've had, so getting up to speak on that occasion was, emotionally speaking, a bit like going over the top at the Somme. And I didn't really want to go through it again, because, after fifteen months, I still get upset.

But then I thought 'I'll have to write something, or people will misunderstand.' So here it is.

The evening before the memorial service I found a paragraph by Elizabeth Kubler-Ross. 'There is no need to be afraid of death. It is not the end of the physical body that should worry us. Rather, our concern must be to live while we're alive – to release our inner selves from the spiritual death that comes with living behind a façade designed to conform to external definitions of who and what we are. Every individual human being born on this earth has the capacity to become a unique and special person, unlike any who has ever existed before or will ever exist again. But to the extent that we become captives of culturally defined role expectations and behaviours – stereotypes, not ourselves – we block our capacity for self actualization.'

Peter was, to a greater extent than anyone else I've ever met, 'a unique and special person, unlike any who has ever existed before or will ever exist again'. I think the reason he affected us so much was that we all recognized his extraordinary freedom of spirit.

Also, he was a genius.

Now as someone who has been called 'a genius' by some journalists, I'd better explain what I'm talking about here. Genius is about being able to do something with preternatural ease. (My big advantage over most of my colleagues is that I think comedy is *harder* than they do, so I spend more time on it.)

But Peter Amadeus Cook found it easy. As Frank Muir once said, 'He could saw it off by the yard.' It just poured out of him, the bastard. Thus, if you wanted a three-minute sketch from Peter, it would take him exactly three minutes to come up with it. Or rather, it would have done if the person with him who was writing it down hadn't interrupted the process by laughing. In the event, it probably took about an hour and a half.

Put him in front of an audience, and something almost paranormal happened. He'd just sit there on his bench and start talking, and after a few seconds perfectly sane, sensible people would start moaning and pawing the air and emitting strange wounded-animal noises. And he would drone on and on, with celestial timing, looking like a huge demented vole, creating physical pain and irrepressible joy.

And Peter did this *effortlessly*, from the early sixties until the late seventies. Then he began to lose it.

This worried some of us. (Maybe we should have been more bothered by the fact we *hadn't* been geniuses for fifteen years, but we didn't think of that at the time.) (We also speculated that because it had always been so easy for him, he wasn't able to sit there and grind it out when it got difficult – that he just couldn't be bothered, as it would have interfered with the rest of his life too much.)

But that was not the only thing that worried us. He was clearly not looking after himself. We didn't *do* much about this, but we did worry, which was extremely good of us.

And then, one wonderful evening in the winter of 1993, he made an appearance on the Clive Anderson show, and to our delight, he was back on his best form. Not just funny, but very sharp, and quick and looking good too. His friends rang each other and celebrated and stopped worrying.

I got tied up with a film, which means that the rest of your life goes in the deep-freeze. So I didn't see him for several months. Then I heard his health was in trouble again. Two events had upset him very deeply, a messy divorce settlement and the death of his mother, and he fell off the wagon.

Just after the New Year, Lin told us his condition was critical; he had been hospitalized. We held our breath. Days later, the news came.

> They told me, dear old Cookie, they told me you
>   were dead.
> They brought me bitter news to hear and bitter tears
>   to shed.
> I wept as I remembered how often you and I
> Had tired the sun with talking and sent him down
>   the sky.
>
> And now that thou art lying, my dear old Nile Cruise
>   guest,
> A handful of grey ashes, long, long ago at rest.
> Still are thy pleasant voices, thy nightingales, awake;
> For Death, he taketh all away, but them he cannot
>   take.

People loved Peter Cook. And I'm not being all touchy-feelie. I do mean 'loved'. He evoked more than affection.

Yet the irony was that he was not a man who thought himself lovable. Except in the last three or four years. At that time, I sensed a real change in him: that he had somehow begun to accept how lovable he was. Some void in him had begun to be filled.

And here's the sad bit: I know that if those two blows had

not hit him, one after the other, Peter was set on a new course onwards and upwards. In other words, if Fate's timing had been as good as Peter's, he would still be with us.

Stephen Fry

Peter Cook

1. A Cook's Tour of Egypt

Picture an oblong swimming-pool, something short of Olympic in length, its perimeter paved. At the top right and bottom left there are steps. You have to imagine now, and this is a sore trial of my powers of description, that the steps are the kind which have hand-holds at either side, tubular hand-holds that are looped back and set into the ground at the outside of the pool, so that they resemble, in profile, the stanchions of a football goal, without the netting.

Hm. If you're like me, then words like 'stanchion' cause you to skip ahead, just as I get lost when thriller-writers start with stuff like 'outcrop' and 'spur' and 'revetment'. So let me put it this way. Imagine that you're standing at the corner of this swimming-pool, on the coping-stones that pave the perimeter. You're at the bottom right, or south-east. As you look straight up, due north, you see the loop of the steps, which resemble an asymmetrical croquet hoop.

It's no good, I shall have to give you a diagram [over]. There, that should be clear now. It is, in fact, a perfectly normal swimming-pool. There should be a diving board top-centre, but frankly that doesn't enter into the equation and I can't be bothered to mess around with the graphics application on my computer a single moment longer.

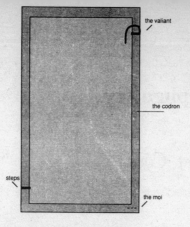

the valiant

the codron

steps

the moi

Fig. 1. The Royal and Not Noticeably Ancient Game of Abu Simbel

So there we have it. A perfectly normal pool. It is set, however, plumb spang in the middle of the Egyptian desert, a mile or so from the colossal monuments of Abu Simbel. Those are the massive, thick-lipped dudes seated majestically, if a touch blandly, next to each other, hands on knees, staring ahead with sightless eyes across the illimitable sands. You must have seen pictures. Actually, I seem to remember that the Egyptian government had the monument moved when the Aswan Dam was built and the original site was to be flooded by the creation of Lake Nasser in fifty-something.

If you're on a Nile Cruise, it is considered more or less obligatory to inspect these gigantic figures at sunrise. Since they stand (or sit) every inch of a hundred miles from the River Nile itself, it is usual to take a three-hour coach trip through the desert to the Royal Simbel Hotel, stay the night, rise an hour before dawn and trot over to watch the first rays of the sun god Ra strike the statuary with his mighty rod of gold before trailing back for coffee and a bun. In that way you can tick off Abu Simbel as one of those sights that you have done.

In April 1992 I am one of a Nile cruise party of forty assembled with sensational generosity by John Cleese and his then fiancée, now wife, Alyce-Faye Eichelberger. Peter and Lin Cook are of our number. It is noon. The coach has drawn up at the Royal Simbel Hotel; we have all inspected our rooms, jumped into swimming cozzies and headed for the pool.

Blisteringly hot, of course. Arabs wear long white flowing things, jellabas and burnooses and yashmaks and heaven knows what else, keeping wisely to their tents, unless disturbed by T.E. Lawrence, Hester Stanhope or Kate Adie. But Englishmen, as Noël Coward put it, detest a siesta.

Not just Englishmen however: some Italians were pool-side too, and a few Americans, adding to the fair number from the United States in our own group. The hotel staff, a mix of Sinhalese, Indians and Egyptians, bustled about with refreshing sherbets and cooling cordials. Well, Heinekens actually.

Most of us tried swimming for a while, fisting a couple of beach-balls back and forth and then climbing out and watching the water instantly evaporate from our skins. Two weeks of slow cruising up the Nile had conditioned us to a strong sun, but even an elephant wouldn't be seen dead in the scorching grill of that desert. Which is to say, an elephant *would* be seen dead in it, which is why they wouldn't be seen dead in it, if you see what I mean.

So, after half an hour of kidding ourselves that we could take it, we gave up the feeble efforts at water-polo, slipped on Ralph Lauren Polo polo-shirts, retired to the shade of the Cinzano umbrellas and started to try and get beyond page ten of our A.S. Byatts and Stephen Hawkingses or raced through our P.D. Jameses and Dick Francises according to taste. Peace reigned for a while.

Had it not been for Peter Cook.

Peter wandered slowly around the pool, a beach-ball in each hand. He noticed that the two beach-balls were each of a size that *jeeyust* allowed them to pass through the hoop of the steps without touching the sides. He wandered down to the south-east corner and bowled a ball up the paving-stones. It passed through the hoop, glancing off the left-hand upright.

'Hm,' he said, to no one in particular, 'a rufford.'

Some of us looked up.

'What was that?'

'If it touches the side before passing through,' said Peter, 'it's a rufford. Two points.'

'Oh.'

He bowled the second ball. It struck the right-hand *and* left-hand uprights, wobbled back and forth and came to rest between them, without passing through to the other side.

'Tsh!' said Peter, walking down to collect the two balls. 'Strottled.'

'Strottled?'

'A strottle between the uprights. One point.'

'So how many if it goes through without touching the sides?'

'A clean Abu Simbel?' He seemed surprised that we had to ask. 'Five for an Abu Simbel. And a trote, of course, is minus two.'

'What's a trote?'

Peter bowled a ball towards the hoop. It veered to the left and, before reaching the target, splashed into the pool.

'A trote,' said Peter. 'Minus two. *And* retrieval duty.'

'So how do you win?'

Peter raised his eyebrows. 'Each team member has two strives per hazard and ...'

'Woah, woah, woah! Two whats per what?'

'Two bowls per go. The first team to reach twenty points wins.'

And those, more or less, were the rules. The hoop, Peter assured us, was called the 'valiant'. A strive consisted of bowling a ball along the 'codron' or paved edge, towards the valiant, hoping for an Abu Simbel, the clean pass through. A natural starting-line or 'moil' was formed at the southern end of the codron by a crack in the paving.

'Moil,' a Jewish member of the party pointed out, 'is the Hebrew word for the circumcision ritual.'

'Exactly!' said Peter, enigmatically.

We quickly divided ourselves into opposing sides for an opening game. Peter was captain of the first 'frett' or team and I was appointed captain of the second. My first strive, I am ashamed to say, was a trote, my second a mere strottle. Minus one, hardly a good opening hazard.

By the time the first game or 'stook' was over, the rest of our party were clamouring to play. We divided ourselves by gender. Carla Powell captaining the Ladies' frett, her husband Sir Charles skippering the Gentlemen. The Ladies won with a thrilling close-out Abu Simbel striven by Tania Idle.

A small crowd from outside our party had gathered to watch and so the first of a series of International Test matches began. The Italians wanted to play the British. Carla Powell forewent her nationality-by-marriage in favour of her native land in order to captain the Italians, and beat us handsomely. There were enough Americans in our party to combine with American guests of the hotel to allow for a Ryder Cup which the British frett clinched with some sensational, though I say so myself as shouldn't, striving from me, as I hit form for the only time that afternoon with three successive Abu Simbels and a rufford, only blotting my copybook with a penalty of minus one for overstepping the moil on the second strive of my third hazard.

By this time the hotel staff had downed trays and were itching to participate, so a full Invitation Tournament comprising the best of three stooks was organized: three national fretts, British, American and Italian versus the Home frett, the Royal Simbel Staff. Peter vanished for a second to reappear with a small vase from his bedroom which was to constitute the Abu Simbel Cup.

It is beyond my powers of description to give you the full details of that historic tourney. Suffice to say that, in a tense

159

strive-off, the Home frett, the beaming staff of the Royal Simbel, finally vanquished Peter's British frett and the Abu Simbel Cup stayed with the hotel.

By now, the sun was dipping with that suddenness common to lands approaching the equator. Eric Idle got out his guitar and, like a Homeric praise-singer choiring the heroes of battle, we treated the exultant and somewhat puzzled victors to a succession of his immortal hits: 'One Foot in the Grave', 'Always Look on the Bright Side of Life', 'Eric the Half A Bee' and 'The Lumberjack Song'.

We left the next morning after paying due court to the great monument: 'Look on my works ye mighty and despair' and all that.

'So we bid farewell to Abu Simbel, land of contrasts,' the guidebook intoned gravely. 'You will stay with us in our hearts for ever.'

A final longing glance at the striving-ground. The codron was coping-stone once more, the valiant a mere hooped stanchion, the moil nothing grander than a crack in the pavement. A light desert wind luffed the Cinzano umbrellas, the staff welcomed a fresh coachload of sightseers. Perhaps they instructed these new guests in what Peter called 'The Royal and Not Noticeably Ancient Game of Abu Simbel'; perhaps they play it there to this very day. I doubt it. You need a Peter Cook for that sort of thing to happen. A Peter Cook? There was, is and ever shall be just the one. His wit, his funniness will be talked about for ever; only those lucky enough to know him can report his alchemic gift for turning a drowsy, overhot day by a pool into an international fiesta that had grown-ups giggling and scampering like children, with the smack of wet feet on stone and the shriek and scream of victory and defeat ringing round the desert. 'Alchemic' is right, for I seem to remember our guide telling us that the ancestor of that word, the old Egyptian 'al hemet', meant 'the magic'.

Arabic gave us 'al kuhl' too, from which we derive 'alcohol' and that's another story ...

2. Al Kuhl

December 1981, London. I'm with friends eating at the La Polla Sorpresa in Hampstead's famous Hampstead. We're brown as diarrhoea, on account of having just flown back from the other side of the world. It's a few months since we left university. Hugh Laurie, Emma Thompson, Robert Bathurst, Martin Bergman and I had been in Australia touring our Footlights show *Botham, The Musical* (a red rag to a bull, this title: earlier that summer Ian Botham had hurled himself at the Australian test side, snatched victory from the jaws of cliché and generally been a bit of a bloody hero) and now we were anti-climactically back in a snowy London. Hugh and I shared a flat in Baker's Passage in Hampstead, together with Katie Kelly, Hugh's girlfriend of the time, Paul Shearer, also from our Footlights year, and other cheerful friends. We were young, fluffy-haired and hopeful. Hugh, Robert and I had spent just about all our cash breaking the journey home in Singapore and treating ourselves to two or three nights at Raffles Hotel. Had it not been for Hugh's impressive ownership of a Barclaycard we would have stayed there much longer, washing dishes and selling our then firm and appetizing young bodies in Bugis Street. Nonetheless, on the strength of a contract with Granada Television and insanely optimistic natures, we decided on that December night that we should treat ourselves to a good Italian.

So there we were, sitting around a large table, enjoying the squirt of garlic butter that jetted from our chicken and sipping large goblets of wine. I should hazard a guess that in those unsophisticated days the wine was Lambrusco, but what the hell. Suddenly, Robert Bathurst leaned forward and, in the charming whisper that has won him friends on all sides, he thundered, 'Don't look now, but isn't that Peter Cook sitting over there?'

We turned in awe. Sure enough, sitting alone, surrounded by dead newspapers, was the Great Man.

I choose my words choosingly. Great Man. The Footlights Club had a room in the basement of the Cambridge Union. This clubroom comprised a miniature bar and a small stage area with a piano and a cute little lighting rig. This was where we rehearsed and, every other Wednesday, held Smokers – small open comedy evenings where people could come along to try out their Punk Noël Coward monologues, their Lawnmower Quickies and their Scorchingly Satirical Songs. All around the room, to depress pretension and remind us just exactly how feeble we were, there hung posters of past Footlights shows: 'Written and Directed by Douglas Adams', 'Starring Griff Rhys-Jones and Clive Anderson', that sort of thing. And then there were the photographs, pictures of Old Footlighters: Graeme Garden, Tim Brooke-Taylor, Bill Oddie, Clive James, Germaine Greer, Jonathan Miller, David Frost, Graham Chapman, Eleanor Bron, Eric Idle, Johns Cleese, Bird and Fortune and, of course, Peter Cook. Most of them, according to the fashions of their time, wore duffel-coats, black polo-necks, college scarves, side-burns and thick-rimmed spectacles. They looked, in short, like Jazz Fans, or, if they were pulling more than usually intellectual faces, like Harold Pinter. Not Peter Cook, though. His photograph showed an impossibly elegant, imponderably handsome young man in a dazzlingly swift suit, a world more sophisticated than anyone else on the walls. I'm sure the Johns, Tims, Bills, Graemes, Eleanors, etc. will forgive me for saying that. After all, it is well known how prodigiously successful the student Cook was, writing Codron revue scripts for Fenella Fielding and Kenneth Williams, hobbing his nob with Soho swingers and generally cutting one hell of a dash.

It's been said so many times you may not want to hear it again, but for us, for our generation, and for generations before us and after us, Peter Cook *was* comedy. He was the *idea* of it. Monty Python was the practice of it, the embodiment of the sketch, of silliness, of verbal and visual brilliance, but Peter Cook was the essence. What am I trying to say? If Python and Vivian Stanshall and *Not the Nine O'Clock News* and so on were the Prime Minister and the Cabinet, then Cook was the Constitutional Monarch. No, that's not quite it.

Let's be frank, Peter Cook was not the greatest comedy actor in the world. He knew this. He knew he was stiff and starey and uncomfortable in fictional performance. He could never have played Basil Fawlty, Norman Stanley Fletcher, Reginald Perrin, Captain Mainwaring or, for that matter, Arthur – in either the film of that name or in *The Holy Grail*. Nor could he have stood in front of a curtain like Tommy Cooper or Eric Morecambe. For all of those who revered the man, this was not a shortcoming in *him*. The shortcoming was that there was never found, on film or television, a format that precisely suited his unparalleled comic gifts. The stories are legion: how people in meetings would ask him to leave because everyone was laughing too much to be able to breathe; how Woody Allen called him Britain's only comic genius; how he wrote the unbelievable Norman Scott/Jeremy Thorpe case judge's summing-up monologue ('he is a piece of slimy refuse, unable to carry out the simplest murder without cocking it up') at the last minute on the back of an old running order in ten minutes flat. He was funny. 'Funny' here is a noun, not an adjective. Whatever 'Funny' is, Peter was it. He *was* Funny.

As a boy listening to the *Not Only ... But Also* records, and then, later, 'Derek and Clive', I, like millions, wriggled and writhed and panted on the floor in the hot breathless ecstasy that only pure comedy can provide. It was sex, drugs, rock and roll, alcohol and adrenalin all in one. Let's not forget the genius of Dudley Moore here, either. When that kind of pleasure has been given you, you don't easily forget. It's the pleasure only great sportsmen and great artists can give. It is the pleasure that gives birth, in your mind, to a Hero.

Peter Cook then, to me and to almost everyone I knew, was a Hero. Of course some friends would, if it came to an absolute choice, pick Bob Dylan, or Eric Clapton, or J. Hunter Thompson or Muddy Waters or George Best or John Lennon or Ian Botham before Peter Cook, but he was up there in the mental pantheon of all of those (the best of us) who are naturally disposed to hero-worship.

It was enough then for us gauche little studes to rehearse our sketches and songs and quickies under his ironic eye in a small clubroom in Cambridge. Just the thought that we were, with however pathetic a baby-step, 'following in his footsteps', was, believe me, enough.

But to have returned from a foreign tour, to be trembling uncertainly on the verge of a 'career' in comedy and then to find one's self in the same room, this was something else entirely.

So there we sat, around the table, stealing covert glances, as excited as a group of schoolgirls who have climbed the stairs to find East 17 in their dorm. The Great Man appeared to be very cheerful, leafing through the papers with the ease and comfort of a member of the Athenaeum reading the *Church Times* in his favourite club armchair. I since discovered that newspapers were one of Peter's favourite occupations. He read *everything*, just as he watched every sport on television. The conversations I had with him subsequently about Indoor Bowls ('seems to me that young Hughie Duff's backhand isn't drawing to the head too well this week'), snooker ('Tony Meo's losing it, I fear') and darts ('hope you caught Keith Deller's nine-dart finish against Jocky at the Lakeside on Saturday') revealed the true connoisseur of minority sports.

It was Bathurst who said the unsayable.

'Shall we ask him to join us?'

What a bleeding *cheek*. We gasped at the impertinent horror of it, yet, somehow, we agreed. Robert was sent over to ask him – 'After all, he can only say no.'

He did not say no. He brought over his vodka and tonic, his pile of newspapers and sat with us as if it were the most natural thing in the world. This was another discovery to be confirmed later. Peter Cook had a gift of affability with strangers that was uncanny. In fact, you might say that to many it was positively off-putting. He got on better with the average passer-by, shop-assistant, waiter, milkman and little old lady than he did with the average producer, comedian, actor, writer or journalist. Actually, come to think of it, that's not uncanny, that's simply good taste.

God knows how sycophantic, drivelling and hysterical we were; yet he didn't show any signs of alarm or irritation. He deconstructed the stories he had come upon in the newspapers with exactly the same brilliance he would have brought to bear had this been a televised interview. Peter Cook never hoarded his wit, never kept it back for a more important occasion. His wit was anyone's; it was like beauty. A beautiful person doesn't look ugly for ten hours in the day and then suddenly explode with pulchritude when it matters, they just *are* beautiful. With Peter there was no technique, no artifice, no contriving, just natural twenty-four-hours-a-day funniness. Some people might call that a fault, describe it as 'being profligate and wasteful of his talent'. Another word, of course, is generous.

As soon as the waiters, who knew and liked him, started to put the chairs up on the tables, we decided it was time to go. Baker's Passage was almost opposite La Polla Sorpresa, so we asked Peter if he wanted to come back for a coffee. A naïve question – how absurdly studenty we still were. Grown-ups in Hampstead, especially if they are Peter Cook, don't come back for coffee, they come back for a drink. And come back for a drink Peter did. I have a dim recollection of having to rush to my bedroom, after the wine and whisky ran out, to open a bottle of Armagnac I had been saving for a family Christmas present. In our innocence, we had probably never seen anyone drink quite so much as Peter did that night. Certainly we had never seen anyone drink so much without appearing to get even slightly drunk. Had I downed as much *milk* as he had alcohol I would have been reeling around hopelessly. But then in this world there are

Good Drunks and Bad Drunks. The quantity they drink is almost irrelevant. I'm sure we all have friends who when drunk are insupportable. They become aggressive, deaf, argumentative and embarrassing. We have all seen how horrific violence on the terraces, in the home or in country market-squares is attributed to alcohol: many have killed their wives, beaten their children or got into knife fights only to blame drink, without having drunk a quarter of a real drinker's average intake. Alcohol isn't a simple chemical, or if a scientist tells you it is, then he would have to confess that its effect on the human brain at least is bewilderingly complex. Peter never yielded to the dark side, never once turned aggressive or rude or loud or bullying or vain. His voice often became slurred, but then it was slurred when he was sober, so that didn't mean much. He sweated a touch and one wouldn't necessarily trust him to remember lines on stage, so there's no avoiding the opinion that it was a *pity* that he used alcohol as much as he did. And, of course, in the end, his liver didn't take kindly to it either. These are all facts that can't be shirked. But, so far as I can judge, alcohol never made him a less pleasant person to be with. Everybody dies, and while it was a terrible thing that Peter Cook left the party early, those of us remaining will all be gone in the twinkling of an eye too, and who is to say that, in the end, it is better to stay long and sober than to leave early and merry? A pity from the point of view of those who enjoyed his company, of course, but from his own point of view?

Well, some say that it was a pity because of the waste. What waste? All right, he never wrote the Great English Novel or became a Film Star or a National Playwright, but then neither did my grandmother. Why is the world so prim, puritanical and judgmental about everyone else's lives? Why this school-report, could-do-better, needs-to-pull-his-finger-out attitude to others? It was as if the world recognized Peter's prodigious talents and decided for him how they should be spent, as if those talents were like

National Lottery money that we absurdly believe we should all have a say in the spending of. Perhaps one can justifiably look at a millionaire, especially one who has inherited his fortune, and condemn him for pissing away his birthright, but when it comes to an inheritance of genius it is an absurdity to claim to know how it should be handled. Peter was not interested in furthering the Art of Comedy, such an idea would have appeared laughably pompous, nor did he believe that comedians are the unacknowledged legislators of the world with a solemn duty to bring down governments and expose hypocrisies. He made just enough money to watch television, play golf, read newspapers, toddle over to Greek Street and help out with jokes at the *Private Eye* offices and live the life he wanted. If he had been left a country house he would have sold it, or turned it into a club; if he been offered a mansion in Beverly Hills with pool, jacuzzi and liveried Mexican gardeners he would have turned it down. He had his daughters, his dear wife Lin and his friends. The only thing to make him uncomfortable was the smell of pity in the air: if anything did make him bitter it was the idea that people thought him bitter. When his friend and partner Dudley Moore became a film star there were many who believed Peter was jealous, and that must have been deeply hurtful, for nothing could have been further from the truth. He was sorry not to have his great collaborator around for more fun, but jealous, never.

That evening in Baker's Passage was the first of many I was to spend with Peter Cook. Over the next fourteen years I was lucky enough to know him better and love him as a friend and companion, while all the time in the back of my mind, whenever I was with him, I could never forget that he was my hero too. He was lucky enough to earn the love of a good, kind woman. He grew closer too to John Cleese, which mattered a great deal to him. While publicly and professionally he rarely regained the comic heights he had scaled in the sixties and seventies, privately he retained every ounce of comic genius.

If I have a regret it is that out of a kind of misplaced guilt I often failed to stay in touch. It's a tricky thing dealing with drinkers: one is very used to their spouses being highly protective and disapproving. Then, one afternoon some time in the late eighties, Lin Cook called me on the phone and put me straight. She would far rather Peter was happy and with friends than sitting alone. Of course she wanted him to stop drinking, because she could see what an effect it was having on his health, but she was too wise to make the mistake of bullying and alienating him. I was not to feel guilty about going out with him. Give him a call. Please.

3. The Voice

I wouldn't want these thoughts on Peter Cook to end with the fumes of alcohol hanging over them. Something I thought about a great deal after he died was the *sound* of Peter Cook. I subsequently discovered that I was not alone in calling up his telephone answering machine in the days following his death, just to be able to hear that miraculous voice once more.

Peter was not a physical clown like Jonathan Miller and other contemporaries. I can't think of many examples of his comedy which don't work as well on audio as on video tape. He had four great voices. E.L. Wisty was perhaps the best known, a nasal, clench-throated delivery that became the archetypal Man In Raincoat sketch voice, and can be heard today in the tones of John Major. I would give anything to be transported back to an early Cambridge revue in which Peter appeared with an usherette's tray filled with gravel and delivered, in Wisty style, the following:

> Grit
> Grit
> I've got lots of it
> Grit
> Grit
> Grit

Then there was Arthur Streeb-Greebling (or Greeb-Streeb-ling, I can never satisfy myself as to which way round it went) the patrician, whisky-soaked Colonel of Old Empire. Peter had this kind of accent perfectly, as you might perhaps expect of a Radleian of his generation. Army officers and empire-builders were voices to which he would have been far more exposed than we are today.

The third and perhaps the greatest voice, however, was that of Pete, as in Pete and Dud. This is the voice of the immortal art gallery sketch and of the Judge and Coalminer monologue. Cuddly Dudley from Dagenham was the real thing, of course, but together, sitting round a sandwich box, corpsing each other outrageously, they contrived, as a couple of Oxbridge graduates, to inhabit these characters without sounding in the least patronizing or snobbish. With all respect to the different geniuses of Jonathan Miller and John Cleese, those two could never have got away with that kind of thing. Pete and Dud developed, with the help of liberal quantities of alcohol and jazz cigarettes, into Derek and Clive, and their influence (I'm sure they won't mind me saying so) can still be heard in the Head to Head duologues of Mel Smith and Griff Rhys-Jones.

Lastly there was the Old Man, which began, I suppose, as a Harold Macmillan impression with the Supermac monologue from *Beyond the Fringe*, and whose variants could be heard in material like that great judge's summing-up from *The Secret Policeman's Ball*.

There's a story about that Supermac monologue which exemplifies Cook's improvisational ability to take things just a little too far. Apparently Macmillan himself came to one performance of *Beyond the Fringe*. Inspired by who knows what devil, Peter added to the main body of the text this extraordinary impromptu flight, in deep, trembling accents:

> And when I've a spare evening, there's nothing I like better than to wander over to a theatre and sit there listening to a group of sappy, urgent, vibrant young

satirists, with a stupid great grin spread all over my silly old face.

The sight of this stupid great grin disappearing from that silly old face and being replaced by a terrible scowl was, I am told, something to see. The audience drew its collective breath in through its teeth and the evening was lost.

Peter's real speaking voice was a curious composite of all of the foregoing. The slight slur I have mentioned, the hint of nasal Wistiness, the suggestion of pukka public-school colonial, the pinch of Dagenham in the vowels and the relaxed open throat of Supermac. It was perhaps the key to what made him funny, as opposed to just witty; while a witty idea was being born the voice could vamp till ready, simply by *repeating*, which was often funnier than any comic idea. Hitler may have said that if you repeat a lie often enough it'll be believed, Peter Cook proved that if you repeated it more than enough it'll be exposed. I'll never forget one of his appearances on Michael Aspel's chat show (Peter Cook that is, not Hitler). The previous guest had been a British actress who had made her name and home in Hollywood. Aspel had asked her if she enjoyed fame in California. She had replied that there was always the problem of charity. As soon as you are well known over there, she said, you are expected to host charity dinners and you get every charity in the US on your back demanding your time and energy. When it was Peter's turn to come on, Aspel asked him how he was.

'Oh, terrible,' said Peter. 'All day long it's been nothing but charity. I charitied my way down from Hampstead in a charity cab, charitying the driver all the while. Then it was charity, charity, charity, all the way through the studio. Charitying in make-up, spot of charity in the dressing-room, loads of charity waiting in the wings. And I fully expect a full night of charity after this.'

Then there was the time when someone remarked to him that it wasn't Elizabeth Taylor's fault that she was putting on weight, it was her glands.

'I know!' said Peter. 'Poor woman. There she is, in her suite in the Dorchester, harmlessly watching television. Suddenly her glands pick up the phone and order two dozen éclairs and a bottle of brandy. "No," she screams, "please, I beg you!" but her glands take no notice. Determined glands they are, her glands. You've never known glands like them. The trolley arrives and Elizabeth Taylor hides in the bathroom, but her glands, her glands take the éclairs, smash down the door and stuff them down her throat. I'm glad I haven't got glands like that. Terrible glands.'

Just the way the words 'charity' and 'glands' were repeated was enough.

Oh hell, I could go on for ever. I've got his voice, as have millions, on cassettes, vinyl and CD so he'll never be far away.

You could write a list of epitaphs which describe a perfect life. They describe Peter's perfectly.

1. He added to the sum of human happiness.
2. He never harmed anyone but himself.
3. He left the world a better place than he found it.
4. He never achieved anything at the expense of anyone else.
5. He made innumerable friends, but not one enemy.
6. He never complained.
7. He was never mean, boastful, envious or vain.
8. He never told anyone else how to behave.
9. He never betrayed a confidence.
10. He made people laugh.

God bless him.

Peter Alliss

A Master Cook at Gleneagles

I knew Peter for more than twenty years and saw him in most of his guises. Indeed you could say anything about him and under the 'right' circumstances nobody could contradict, for he was all things to all people, both good and bad, but through the years I never saw a cruel streak. Through all his ups and downs he kept his undying love of sport and the game of golf was high up on his list of favourite 'things'. He played far more than many people realized and indeed, with a little more effort he could have become a low handicap player. How low? Well certainly six or eight handicap. He had a sound swing, good rhythm and keen eye, but I think it was the game itself that provided him with a fund of ideas. It helped create flights of fancy; the way the rules were constructed, the etiquette, the type of people who made up his own 'fantasy committee'.

Peter started a comedic campaign with an article in *Golf World* to get the whole of Hampstead, both the village and the heath, turned into a golf course for the Ryder Cup. It was a wonderful text, reproduced in the press, which had such a realism about it that I'm sure some who read it really felt that this was a possibility and, even if they disagreed with it, they seemed to think they could read truth between these hilarious lines.

He loved exotic locations, the South of France, Spain, the

172

Caribbean, America, Australia. Wherever he found himself in the line of duty, more often than not he managed to get in a game of golf. He was intrigued by the equipment and the wondrous claims made by the manufacturers, telling one and all in no uncertain terms that if you use their clubs or indeed golf balls it could change your life. He loved the whole scene with an abiding passion.

We first met during the making of the BBC2 series *Pro-Celebrity Golf*. These matches divided their time between the Gleneagles Hotel and the dramatic coastline of Turnberry on the Ayrshire coast. The Pro-Celebrity series were a great delight to me. Ten nine-hole matches played within the space of one week in some of the most wonderful country-side imaginable. The series was supposed to run for two or three years but, as it turned out, it ran for fourteen. A total of 140 programmes were completed. We had so many great stars from the world of sport, business, politics and entertainment.

If memory serves me right, one of the things that stuck in Peter's memory was the sight of the late James Hunt, the World Grand Prix racing champion and his wondrous dog Oscar. Now, Oscar was probably the largest alsatian ever bred in captivity; black and tan in colour, he obeyed his master's commands to the letter. He went everywhere with James and when told to 'sit', whether it be outside the dining-room at Gleneagles, by the car, or alongside the eighteenth green, he would do so, but always alert. But Oscar had one slight failing: when out on the golf course he would insist on crouching down, his nose no more than eighteen inches from the ball about to be driven (which in itself is quite disconcerting), and then, perhaps a split second before the clubhead met the ball, Oscar was up and off down the fairway like a shot from a gun, only to lose sight of it within fifty or sixty yards and come back to the tee and position himself once more for the second drive.

Peter thought this constituted an 'outside agency', indeed this dog that seemed bigger than a timber wolf, was intimidating, so when it came his turn to play, he brought an 'outside agency' along too. This took the shape of a goldfish bowl with one solitary fish going round and round. The fish's name was Abe Ginsberg, his Manager, who in all truth didn't look very Jewish; but Peter assured us he was. When the time came to drive, Peter placed the bowl (with the ever present Ginsberg) some eighteen inches to the side and told Ginsberg to watch for any infringements. Reading this, it may not appear to be funny, but I can assure you it was quite hilarious. The four players drove. 'Ginsberg' was picked up and handed to a long suffering caddy with the instructions not to walk too fast in case he splashed the water out, as Ginberg liked plenty of lubrication! Peter's first tee shot flew straight and true up the middle of the fairway, a well struck medium iron, a five or a six, played as crisply as any professional, right to the heart of the green; but then something strange happened, for he had at least six putts and I'm not sure whether the sixth wasn't hit whilst it was still in motion, thereby incurring penalty shots; but by that time it was too late. This pattern of play continued for the nine holes of the match. Many a good shot was struck but all were dissipated by simply abysmal putting. And again, even Peter's hand-rolled fags couldn't sort out the problems.

Whenever Peter took part in a series he stayed for the whole week, much to the delight of us all. During one we had the elegant E.R. Dexter on board, 'Lord Ted', one of the most beautiful strikers of a ball, whether it be leather or rubber, I've ever seen. Peter informed all and sundry one late-ish night in the sponsor's hospitality room that he had gone to the same public school as Dexter who, with his skill at games and dark brooding good looks, was a monumental figure in the school and not one to be trifled with. According to Peter, he used to dish out punishments for all sorts of sundry misdemeanours.

When it came Dexter's turn to play his match Peter insisted upon refereeing. He turned up on the first tee

27. Newly married: Peter and Lin in Paris, December 1989

John Cleese and Alice-Faye Eichelberger's birthday weekend, October 1989

28. Peter as 'Demis Roussos in Shakespeare's Day', with Sarah Lloyd and Michael Palin

29. With John Lloyd

30. (*Below right*) With John Cleese

31. Guest of Honour at the
Australian Associated Press
Financial Markets charity
golf tournament, Sydney

32. On the beach in Port
Douglas, Queensland

33. Unwittingly attempting to cut a cement cake with Stephen Fry (Sir Charles Powell in background)

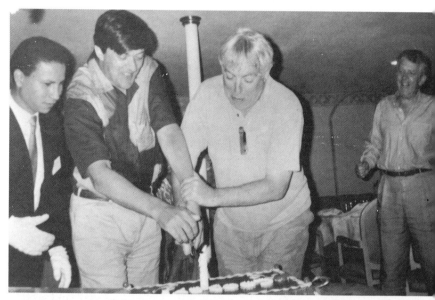

34. Dancing with Tania and Eric Idle

35. (*Right*) Peter demonstrating the game he invented at Abu Simbel

36. The golfer on Hampstead Heath, summer 1993

37. As Eric Daley, ageing rock star, on *Clive Anderson Talks Back*, 1993

38. With Eleanor Bron as Lord and Lady Wrexmire, *Black Beauty*, 1994

39. In the garden with Lin, summer 1994

dressed like Erich von Stroheim, knee-length boots, jodh-purs, leather jacket, scarf, leather flying helmet *circa* 1918, gloves and of course a riding crop. Sitting behind the first tee was a blue-rinsed lady of uncertain years minding her own business. He approached her to ask if she had any make-up in her bag. Although slightly taken aback she said yes. 'May I see?' – 'Certainly.' Peter, with all the aplomb in the world, took some powder and gently rubbed it onto his cheeks, a little lipstick, a bit of eye make-up, a touch of mascara and he announced to one and all that he was ready to take the stage; he had to look his best for the cameras. All this was done in such a way no one took offence, there were smiles, there was happiness. Some of his refereeing deci-sions were bizarre, to say the least, but all in all the match was an absolute delight, although some thought he did go a little bit OTT, but that indeed was Peter Cook.

Geoffrey Strachan

Scripts, Transcripts and Postscripts

I encountered Peter's gracious enthusiasm and gleeful last-minute wit at first hand on three occasions. In the autumn of 1961 I met him at the *Establishment Club* as one of that huge field of ex-university would-be comedy scriptwriters following in his wake (many of whom, unlike me, stayed the marathon course). All of whom had seen and been inspired by *Beyond the Fringe* that summer.

He regaled me with piquant stories from the day's papers. There was a news story from South Africa about the difficulties the South African Government were having deciding whether visiting Japanese businessmen should be allowed to sit on park benches reserved for 'whites' – or whether they should be relegated to the park benches designated for 'coloureds'. (I believe after some cogitation they had decided Japanese counted as 'whites'.)

That evening, I saw him stand up to do his late-night monologue (after his stint in *Beyond the Fringe*) and reduce a packed room to hilarity with a version of that same fluent discourse about the contents of the day's papers. I had never seen a performance like it. No script, no autocue, just unforced, highly articulate conversational wit.

Some ten years later I was an editor at Methuen. I had been struck by the incisive impact made by several of the partly improvised, partly scripted, 'Dud and Pete' dialogues when they were published in *The Listener*. I approached Peter and Dudley to find out whether they would be willing for us to publish a selection of the dialogues in book form. I had a couple of gleeful meetings with Peter in a room bathed in summer sunlight in a house near Highgate Ponds – east of Hampstead Heath – as we sifted through transcripts of the dialogues and made a selection.

These were no ordinary comedy sketches. Peter's and Dudley's performances in them had been achingly funny and the words spoken could only have arisen from their improvisations in character. But what set these texts apart from the scripts of the other sketches in *Not Only . . . But Also* was their verbal richness. The heady mixture of social observation, schoolboy folklore and metaphysical comedy they contain comes vividly off the page at you – like Boswell's conversations with Johnson – whether you have heard Peter and Dudley speaking them or not. (When I first read them, I hadn't.) The gamut of human emotions, fantasies and obsessions they cover – from childish fears of the lavatory flushing to speculation about death and the afterlife – is their glory.

In the autumn of 1971, twelve of the scripts were published in a volume called *Dud and Pete: The Dagenham Dialogues*, with fantastic drawings of slugs, bosoms and other phenomena by Bert Kitchen and photographs of Dud and Pete in raincoats by Lewis Morley and a prologue called 'Caught in the Act' – all done specially for the book.

Dud	Tea's up, Pete.
Pete	Shhh.
Dud	What's up?
Pete	Guard your tongue.
Dud	Pardon?
Pete	Do you not realize we are being bugged?
Dud	Bugged?
Pete	Over the last six years we have been constantly monitored by the KGB.

Dud	Is that the lemon juice people?
Pete	No, it's the secret service of the Russians.
Dud	Who's behind this international conspiracy?
Pete	Yehudi Methuen and Company. Every word we say is taken down and transmitted to Russia ...

Samuel Johnson could hardly have expressed the transcript experience more poignantly.

Twelve years after that I found myself embarking on a correspondence not only with Peter and Dudley, but also with Alan Bennett and Jonathan Miller, about a further book project which eventually led to further genial meetings with Peter. It was autumn now and we met in his cosy upstairs parlour on the west side of Hampstead Heath. His enthusiasm and friendliness were as unforced as they had been in 1961 and his wit was as last-minute and as sharp as ever.

Although the extracts which follow are (of necessity) extremely brief, the whole correspondence was extremely long. I was never quite sure whether Peter was actually reading my letters. He certainly wasn't writing any himself. But he was utterly committed to the project and the outcome was wholly cheerful and triumphant.

12 May 1983

Dear Peter,
I would welcome your comments and help over a plan to reissue a book of which you are a co-author, which goes way back into the past. We have fairly recently started a series called the Methuen Humour Classics. The *Beyond the Fringe* text is a classic of a kind and ought to be made available again. Is this a project of which you would approve in principle? I'd welcome your suggestions. This would not be a book for 1983 but, if we can get everyone's permission, I would like to publish it in the spring of 1984.
  Very best wishes, Yours, Geoffrey

21 September 1985

Dear Geoffrey Strachan,
I'm delighted to hear that you are considering re-publishing the script of *Beyond the Fringe* and I certainly have no misgivings about this, although you may encounter some resistance from Alan, who often has misgivings about work from the distant past. Dudley Moore's address has changed, I think, but you can probably get in touch with him via his agents in the United States . . .

   Yours with best wishes, Jonathan Miller

9 October 1985

Dear Geoffrey Strachan,
. . . I'm sure it would be nice to include some of the additional material which was put in towards the end of the American run after I left it, but you'd have to talk to Peter Cook about that, since most of the extra stuff was his . . .

   Yours sincerely, Jonathan Miller

October 1985

Dear Mr Strachan,
The [original] edition of *Beyond the Fringe* is very corrupt and full of misprints, as it was taken down by the stage manager as he heard it – and very often misheard it – in the Prompt Corner. I'm quite happy to see it reprinted but don't want to feel saddled with the editing. I'm sure the others will feel much the same, though I haven't spoken to them on the subject. Re Dudley, I think 'Dudley Moore, Hollywood' would probably reach him.

   Yours sincerely, Alan Bennett

12 March 1986

Dear Alan,
. . . I would welcome it enormously if you could find time to meet for an hour or two with Peter, Roger Wilmut and myself. Peter suggested that we might meet one day in April . . .

   Yours, Geoffrey

14 April 1986

Dear Geoffrey,
I am certainly very much in favour of the publication of a complete text of the *Beyond the Fringe* scripts. I also think the points raised by Alan and Jonathan are important ... I'm sorry you've had a bit of a problem reaching me ...

Best Wishes, Dudley Moore

13th May 1986

Dear Alan,
We had a good and useful meeting with Peter last week. He is sympathetic to the idea of writing a short postscript to go at the end of the book and I hope each of you may find the time to do this, however briefly.

Very best wishes, Yours, Geoffrey

13th June 1986

Dear Roger,
Until last night I was reading your last batch of stuff from the Cambridge show. There are some good things in this, but also some very slight things. I am quite sure we must be selective about the variorum material. Indeed, Peter Cook rang yesterday and I discussed this point with him and he was in agreement ...

Yours, Geoffrey

August 1986

Dear Geoffrey,
... Reading through the *BTF* stuff is quite painful. So relieved it's all over. I regard the book as a burial more than anything else.

Alan B.

4 September 1986

Dear Geoffrey,
Here – a complete collection of *Beyond TF* music ...
Let me know your thoughts – yea or nay – or may!
'NO SWEAT' as they say here. Nice to have seen you in
London. Keep me posted. Am presently working on
turgid reminiscences.
   Dudley

17 October 1986

Dear Peter,
Many thanks for your hospitality and also for your
help and encouragement yesterday. You said you
would try to write, say, a 500-word postscript to come
at the end of the volume. If you are able to get this in
to me before you go to America that would be
splendid ...
   Yours, Geoffrey

25 November 1986

Dear Peter,
We now have the complete text of *Beyond the Fringe*
from Roger Wilmut ... I am wondering if there is any
chance at all of your getting the text of your own
postscript to me during the next couple of weeks or
so. Otherwise we could probably leave space for it in
the proof, in the hope that you might be able to get
something in to us while we are correcting the galley
proofs.
   Yours, Geoffrey

4 December 1986

Dear Dudley,
... Peter is hoping to write a postscript within the
next couple of weeks. Although we have invited
Jonathan to write a piece he has so far made no
promises on this front ... I think yours and Alan's
work well alongside one another and add quite a lot
to the flavour of the book ...
   Yours, Geoffrey

13 January 1987

Dear Geoffrey,
... I do hope that Jonathan[1] and Peter will be able to contribute something, since I would be fascinated to hear their recollections. Alan's were wonderful to read, although I knew his reaction to writing and doing the show was somewhat tortured at times ...
All the best, as always, Dudley

21 January 1987

Dear Geoffrey,
... I've got the [galley] proofs, having just returned from Egypt (and missed the bad weather).
All regards, Alan

21st January 1987

Dear Peter,
... Ideally, if we are going to include a text from you, we would like to have it by the end of next week ...
Yours, Geoffrey

20 February 1987

Dear Roger,
All the authors have now been sent copies of the page proofs: I have asked them to get corrections to me as soon as possible, so that I can return them, to the printer as scheduled, on Friday 27 February ...
Yours, Geoffrey

3 March 1987

Dear Dudley,
Many thanks for all your help over the book ... I am happy to report the late arrival of a postscript text from Peter. I think our thanks are due to you for a bit of prompting here ...
Yours, Geoffrey

[1] I later met Jonathan at the Tricycle Theatre (we were watching a National Theatre of Brent performance) and he told me he felt he had nothing further he wanted to write about *Beyond the Fringe* at that stage.

Dear Geoffrey,

... I wanted to thank you so much for sending me a copy of the postscript from Peter Cook, which I found delightful and humorous and at the end very moving. Just talked to him on the phone to reiterate my gratitude ...

All the best from, Dudley

Peter's Postscript
Blood from a stone

I never had it so good. As far as I was concerned, the wonderful old showbiz fraud had got it right. I had a flat in Battersea, a Hillman Convertible and the chance to show off every night.

'Don't jeopardize your career by working with these three amateurs' had been the advice of my agent who shall remain nameless (but Donald Langdon is pretty close).

It was a peculiar business assembling the show. Only Dudley and I seemed to want to do it; the other two were perpetually struggling with their consciences. Should Jonathan desert medicine for this frivolous pursuit? Would Alan forsake Oxford and Medieval History for the transient glamour of the Fortune Theatre? Would they ever make up their minds?

In the early days Alan was delightfully shockable. It gave me enormous pleasure to come up with some piece of smut and watch him writhe and moan in agony or amusement, stuffing his handkerchief into his mouth. This handkerchief technique must have had its uses. Sometimes it was employed to stifle his own laughter, at others to conceal his vexation. It was quite hard to tell whether he was having a fit of the giggles or in an almost terminal state of irritation. Happily, he eventually became as filthy-minded as the rest of us.

I look back on the show with nothing but pleasure. I can remember very few rows, though there was one occasion when Jonathan hurled a tea tray across the dressing room in a fit of pique with, I think, Alan. Possibly the latter had been chewing his handkerchief in an insolent manner.

At another time Jonathan became enraged at me. It was often my wont to interrupt the Philosophy sketch by staggering on as an ancient retainer to deliver some incongruous piece of news. One night Rachel Miller was backstage with their newborn son. Grabbing the baby from the willing Mrs Miller, I wandered on saying: 'Excuse me, Sir; your wife's just given birth to this,' to which I think Jonathan replied: 'Go away and put it in the fridge.' I thought this a highly successful piece of improvisation but at the interval Jonathan reprimanded me severely. 'You might have dropped it!' he said. Never having wittingly dropped a baby in my life, I felt a little aggrieved. (He was the one who was clumsy with props.) I seem to remember at a later date carrying Dudley on and saying: 'I've discovered this man in bed with your wife and so I shot him,' to which Jonathan rather cruelly replied: 'Oh well, just drop him anywhere.'

As the show went on, I began to enjoy the 'digressions' more than the written text. I particularly looked forward to Dudley interrupting the Civil Defence Sketch. The barmy ad-libbed questions and answers, usually nothing to do with the subject, were the highlight of the evening for me. I think it was this kind of daft random backchat that led to the two of us working together on television.

There is only one depressing side effect of re-reading the text – I may have done some other things as good but I am sure none better. I haven't matured, progressed, grown, become deeper, wiser, or funnier. But then, I never thought I would.

P.C., 27 February 1987

The book was published in June 1987. Reviewing it in *The Mail on Sunday*, Craig Brown wrote: 'Just as people have been pleasantly surprised at how early Beatles records have stood the test of time, so they will be delighted to find that the recently republished *Beyond the Fringe* scripts are still very funny.'

Five years later, we reprinted *The Complete Beyond the Fringe* and I was able to send copies to Alan, Dudley, Jonathan and Peter. Jonathan had written: 'I'm delighted to hear that you are reprinting *Beyond the Fringe*. I must say I'm somewhat puzzled by the way in which this peculiar old war horse continues to show signs of life after thirty years. It's like reprinting *No, No, Nanette . . .*'

In 1996, after thirty-five years, a further reprint is in preparation.

Lewis Morley

The Wings of Change

If there is any credence to the butterfly wing principle then the slight movement of displaced air resulting from the downward thrust of the wing of an exotic and multi-talented butterfly in the shape of an ex-Cambridge Footlighter, contributed to some changes in the lives of countless people. Many of those involved would not be aware of this, or if they were, would not admit to their status benefiting from this source.

I have no hesitation in admitting that the course of my life was altered by this atmospheric disturbance caused by those two small words housed in one prodigious talent – Peter Cook. My association with him resulted in three important events which were to play an integral part in my life. The *Establishment*, Barry Humphries and Christine Keeler.

I first met Peter when I was commissioned to photograph the front of house pictures for the London production of *Beyond the Fringe*. In this instance it was fortuitous that my partner in a photographic studio was William Donaldson, who also happened to be one of the producers. As the *Fringe* was an iconoclastic theatrical venture, I decided to follow suit by matching the pictures to the production, which also meant breaking theatrical rules – in this instance, photographically. Aside from a few publicity shots taken on stage, the rest of the photocall, which lasted three days, was shot in Brighton, on the beach, under the pier. In London, cavorting in Hyde Park, prowling through the zoo, and attitudinizing against hoardings and other suitable props on the streets around Regent's Park. It was an unforgettable experience directing four highly talented and individual personalities to assume bizarre tableaux which had nothing whatsoever to do with what would be happening in the theatre.

That little puff of wind generated in an earlier clime next found its way into my sails when Peter asked me if I would like to have space for a new studio in the forthcoming venture ... which turned out to be the *Establishment*.

When the club opened, I was firmly ensconced on the first floor above the bar and club premises, happily shooting away. Besides my own clients, I had been appointed by Peter as the *Establishment*'s official photographer, taking pictures for the club's theatre. One of the first artistes photographed was Barry Humphries (another soul that had been gently propelled by that initial zephyr). These winds of chance became winds of change, contributing to a friendship which is still going strong. It was in this same venue that I created a photograph that became an icon of the sixties – Christine Keeler astride that very distinctive chair, publicity shots for a proposed film that was banned ... David Frost later assumed the pose for *That Was The Week That Was*.

The club's membership rapidly expanded, but the club's allotted space on the ground floor could not do likewise. A solution had to be found. The basement was occupied by Dudley Moore and his Trio. Sean Kenny's design studio was immediately above me on the second floor, but there was an empty area at the top of the building and that seemed to be the only solution to the dilemma. Peter approached me and said in his 'Wisty' voice, 'If I offered you a million pounds, would you move to the top floor?' I immediately realized that although the offer was not serious, the request was. Peter had resorted to his 'Wisty' voice to cover his embarrassment. (In spite of his sharp retorts and at times cruel quips, I found him to be a most generous and softhearted person.) He would reimburse me for any out-of-pocket expenses, the cost of building of new darkrooms, etc. I had no hesitation in uprooting and decamping to my new premises. This proved a blessing in disguise, as now I would be insulated by the new club area and Sean's studio from the hordes of members who previously had overflowed and wandered into my studio . . . curiosity leading them up the steps from the club below.

During the *Establishment* years, I saw a lot of Peter, as he was my landlord as well as my client. Besides the theatre photographs for the club, I was photographing for *Private Eye*, in addition to doing personal portraits and other sundry snappings. I saw less of him when the club was sold. I still did work for *Private Eye* and I would see him at the *Eye* offices or he would come to the studio to partake in a photographic session. In 1971, just prior to my departure for Australia, he asked me to take the photographs to illustrate *The Dagenham Dialogues*, a book of Dud and Pete sketches. My last job with Peter was to take photographs for *Behind the Fridge*, a theatrical duet with Dudley Moore. It was during the shoot that Peter learned that I was off to Australia. 'Look,' he said, 'we'll be in Sydney soon after you arrive, so let's get in touch.'

This eventuated and they dined with us. We recalled that it was ten years since the *Fringe*. A lot had happened in that decade. Most of the evening was taken up with nostalgic journeys that always seemed to end up at the *Establishment*. I think we all had a little too much to drink. Peter sat in the garden slapping away at the notorious Hunters Hill (a suburb of Sydney) mossies (mosquitoes), murmuring 'Things have changed – things have changed.' Dudley read a small poem that John Betjeman had written and dedicated to me. It was handwritten on a broadsheet which contained two other printed poems of his, one of which was entitled

'The Crem'. Dudley read this and burst into tears, the other guests at the party were a little confused. They had expected an evening of jollity with a never-ending stream of Pete and Dudisms. It was a very quiet car that drove back to their hotel ... 'At sixty miles an hour all you can hear is the nostalgic sigh.'

It was another two decades before I was to meet up with Peter again. Although during those years I paid London several visits whilst on my European assignments, I never seemed to find time to look up old friends, or even relatives. In 1989, when I was in London to open my one-man show at the National Portrait Gallery, Peter entered my life once more, not in person but in print. There was a great deal of media coverage on the exhibition and one of the less glossy weekend magazines ran an article entitled 'The Photographer the World Forgot'. Various people who knew me or people I had photographed were asked what they remembered of Lewis Morley. I was stunned by Peter's alleged answer: 'Never heard of him.'

In 1993 I was once again in London. This time, I happened to be purchasing some photographic equipment from a camera shop in Hampstead. The proprietor, Keith, whom I had known for several years, informed me that Peter Cook often came into the shop for his requirements. He also told me that Peter only lived across the road and asked if I was going to visit him. I answered 'No,' explaining my reason for not getting in touch, namely the magazine article.

That night I didn't get in until past midnight. My host was waiting up for me ... 'There's a message from Peter Cook to contact him as soon as possible.' It seemed that as soon as I had left the shop, Peter had walked in. Keith told him that he had missed me by seconds; fortunately Keith knew I was staying with another of his customers, a photographer, and so happened to have his number. It was too late to phone back, so I left it until morning. When I tried, I couldn't get through. The phone was constantly engaged. Late in the morning I tried once more; this time the phone rang and after a few rings it was answered by a very harassed voice: 'Yes?'

'Peter?' I ventured. 'It's Lewis, Lewis Morley.'

'Thank goodness you've just caught me. I'm off to Spain . . .' He gave me a date for his return so as we could get together.

On his return, a date was made and on the appointed day I arrived at his house and knocked on the door. I was greeted with literally open arms as Peter embraced me and said, 'Fred – come in.' It was nice to be addressed by the name that he used in the *Establishment* days (my name being Lewis Frederick . . . I was known to friends and family as Fred).

Over cakes and tea we caught up on the lost years. Regarding the magazine article, he assured me that it was not what he had said. I could well believe him, recalling my own misrepresented quotes in the same article. It didn't really matter any more. I had not kept up with Peter's private life. All I knew was that he had not been very well in recent years. As he faced me, I was glad to notice that he appeared very fit. I remarked how well he looked and he told me that he had recently remarried and I should meet his wife.

I was intrigued and tried my best not to conjure up any preconceived ideas. I must admit that when Peter introduced Lin to me I was bowled over; notwithstanding that we could both speak Cantonese, it was the atmosphere she created. I usually find myself a little tense and questioning on first meetings – but Lin had the capacity to relax any tension and soon we were on terms as though we had known each other for much longer than the minute hand on my watch had me believe. Peter himself seemed much more serene in her presence. The sun had lost most of its intensity when I decided to shoot off a few frames of Peter and Lin together. Some of the resulting shots were a little blurred by movement caused by the long exposures due to the failing light.

The next day, Peter and Lin invited me for lunch. It was in a Hampstead restaurant ... a late lunch and the restaurant was virtually empty – just the three of us, eating and conversing on our own little island surrounded by small round tables ... Here we were on the sea of tranquillity. When I left and bade farewell, I didn't know that this occasion would be the last time I would ever see Peter.

During the span of thirty-four years, I have exposed quite a few rolls of film on Peter, and although I do not need those frozen images to remind me of him, I cannot look at those last images taken with Lin without being made aware of the closeness and tenderness that was the sum of them when together. This was the Peter that hid behind Wisty, Pete, Spotty Muldoon and the whole pantheon of other characters he created, characters that have entered the permanent vocabulary of comedy.

Adieu Peter, we miss you.

John Lloyd

The Worst Job I Ever Had

When *Beyond the Fringe* stormed London, I was eight and living in Malta. During the satire boom, I was at West Hill Park Preparatory School, Titchfield, Hants. I gather it was the Swinging Sixties, but they never made it over the wire. While *Not Only . . . But Also* was on air, I was trapped in the precincts of Canterbury Cathedral in a Neville Chamberlain costume. So I never got to go to the *Establishment*, and to this day I still haven't seen *Bedazzled*.

At Cambridge, I learned, embarrassingly late, that Peter Cook was a Legend. I'd heard the name, but that was about it. Naturally, I would no more have admitted this than leafletted the college with the information that I was a virgin and didn't know what claret was. So if the subject came up, I just nodded sagely in a sexually-experienced, claret-man sort of a way.

Many years later, I came to know Peter pretty well as a person, but I never got round to catching up on the fine detail of his career. Most famous people, I think, would have found this either offensive or incompetent. Peter couldn't have cared less. He had the gift of being able to treat everyone absolutely equally, and he made no exception of himself.

In 1979, he appeared in Amnesty International's *The Secret Policeman's Ball*. He had dashed off, especially for the occasion, a staggeringly good pastiche of the Judge's summing-up of the Thorpe Trial. He was astounding, easily the best thing in it, the smash-hit highlight of the evening. In those days I was a BBC radio producer, and I'd been roped in to produce the soundtrack album. The Thorpe Trial piece was so terrific that the Amnesty producer, Martin Lewis, deemed it worth releasing in its own right. To fill out the material, there had to be a 'B' side, and so, as well as producing the record, I briefly became Peter Cook's straight man. It was the worst job I ever had: the straight man who couldn't stop laughing – a sort of dud Dud.

When Peter was the age I was then – twenty-seven – he had done everything, been everywhere, taken the West End and Broadway by storm, won and lost fortunes. He was handsome, talented, rich, famous, adored. He had crammed a lifetime's work (effortlessly, it seemed) into his amazing existence. By the time we coincided, he'd slowed down a good deal, and I got to know him more as a friend than as someone to work with. Because Peter wasn't much inter-ested in working. I think he'd long forgotten what the point of it was. Any 'work' was really an excuse to meet, to have lunch. Well, it was for me, anyway.

All the same, we did quite a few bits and pieces together. He was Richard III in the first episode of *Blackadder*. I produced a series of Duracell radio commercials he was in which won some awards. At the First (and only) Nether Wallop International Arts Festival – the forerunner of *Comic Relief* – I watched agog as Peter and Mel Smith, dressed as synchronized swimmers, got prodigiously drunk for char-ity.

The following year, I was presenting an arts documentary series called *South of Watford*. The producer, John Carlaw, had a very funny idea to do an edition called *Peter Cook's London* which was to have been an exhaustive analysis of the forty yards of Hampstead pavement between Peter's house and his newsagent. I went to see Peter. He was in the throes of a deadline on a script for an American cable channel that he couldn't get down to. So instead of doing *Peter Cook's London* I sat down with him at Lin's computer and did that.

He was a very easy person to work with, I found. He talked and I pressed the buttons on the tape recorder. At the end of the day, I'd take the tape home and type it up, leaving out any waffle engendered while Peter's comic genius accelerated to cruising speed. Not infrequently, he would get stuck. Sometimes he could be prompted into starting again on a different tack, but usually there was really nothing anyone could do to help. When he was on-line, it was like being with someone who was talking in tongues. This brilliant, hilarious, fantastical, credible nonsense poured out. No one else has ever spoken that language.

Peter was, of course, extremely bright. But intelligence, in the conventional sense, isn't much use to a comedian. For a producer or script editor, it's useful in analysing where a thing's gone wrong, why it *isn't* funny. But Peter never bothered to rewrite anything that I noticed, so that was hardly relevant. In any case, intelligence is of no use at all in *creating* comedy. Like scientific discovery, or art, comedy doesn't result from logical processes. Anyone who thinks it does is kidding themselves. Of course, you can start your day by attacking things logically, but that's only the mental equivalent of sharpening your pencil and straightening your gonk. The comedy only comes when it decides that it will. The frustration and misery that results from this inaccessibility is partly what drives so many comedians barking mad. No one knows why they can produce the goods sometimes and not at others.

It's often struck me that the world of original ideas – comic or otherwise – is a kind of parallel Universe where everything already exists; a secret Fingal's Cave; a magical, inexhaustible, underground aquifer. The job of the artist, writer, comedian is somehow to find a way in and get down there with a bucket. There are a number of 'Open Sesames' that may or may not work. Hard graft is one of them. Drink, for some, is another. A third is terror, a fourth, congenital insanity. Most of the time people just hammer away fruitlessly at the exterior and if they ever get in at all, emerge with no more than an egg-cupful of moisture.

But Peter seemed to stroll around in the stuff as if he owned it, soaked to the skin, marinated in it, up to his neck, like a gigantic sea-nymph. He had only to start talking and ideas pumped out of him without stint, as if he were connected to some mighty pipeline. And all Peter's best jokes, like all great ideas – whether $e=mc^2$ or Van Gogh's *Irises* – had a staggering simplicity. How could one possibly not have thought of that before? If he dried up, when the Muse imposed a hosepipe ban, there was nothing to do except pack it in for the day or go for lunch. And on those occasions, we would talk about life.

For someone who made his living as a satirist, Peter was an extraordinarily kind person. I can't ever remember him being nasty about anyone. He managed the neat trick of being both unjudgmental and honest at the same time. He was a good comedian but, rarer than that, he was a good man.

Naturally generous, amongst older comedians he was almost unique in that he was not only interested in what the younger lot were doing, but he *liked* what they were doing. He would say, 'Rory Bremner's brilliant,' or 'Harry Enfield's very funny.' He wasn't at all jealous, and, unlike many comics, he liked to laugh quite as much as he liked to make people laugh. When Peter Fincham and I made *A Life in Pieces* with him for BBC2, we used to meet at eleven in the morning for coffee, and Peter Cook would pull a can of Carlsberg Special out of his briefcase, and the meeting would start and within ten minutes we'd all be weak with laughter till lunch. And that's how I remember him principally: as being very jolly.

So I always wonder why so many people struggled laboriously to go on and on about what his 'problem' might have been. I've never understood this. What problem? I never bought the idea that he must have been miserable because he didn't have a show on BBC1. Why would he want that? Because Gaby Roslin has one? Does that make her a more valuable person than Peter Cook? Or indeed, than anyone? His attitude seemed entirely reasonable to me. It's very hard work turning out a good TV comedy – and who wants to do a lousy one?

He wasn't bored. He had a lot of golf to play. He read every newspaper and magazine. When satellite came in, he had that as well. He was extraordinarily well-informed, fascinated by everything: the *New Scientist*, baseball, a new television series. He had the knack of being able to spot what was interesting about something anyone else would have found mind-numbingly dull.

Of course, Peter's problems are over now. It's a curious thing that everyone's much more frightened of dying than they are of other people dying, yet the deaths of other people cause us far more pain. The deceased suffer no longer but the living have this interminable grief. Peter's death, like his life, took everyone by surprise. He'd always had such amazing powers of recuperation. You'd see him one week and he'd be looking fat and perhaps a bit sweaty and hadn't bothered to comb his hair. The next week he'd be transformed. Fifteen years would have fallen away, he'd be bouncing down the street on his characteristic springy walk – spruce, chipper, bonhomous – and in that big cheerful English face would be these huge, shiny, laughing, Dionysiac eyes. It always took my breath away – how much life there was in him. He had that quality you see in people when they first become famous – sort of lit from within, like some vast cot-lamp. On these occasions, I think anyone who knew Peter felt enormous relief. And probably a dash of foolishness as well, that there might ever have been any cause for concern. Because he gave such a damn good impression of someone who was going to live forever.

Strangely, for someone who, even in his mid-fifties, was

almost ludicrously boyish, he always struck me as one of the few grown-up people I knew. The vanities of fame, and the qualities that it takes to reach the top are such that, inside the bulge of the great celebrity, the baby is usually quite transparent. You can see the inner child and it's not, frankly, one that anyone would wish to get in touch with.

There are two main ways we come to know people. The first is when they offer information about themselves. Peter was never very forthcoming about that kind of thing. What little he did say was always rather innocent and endearing. He was a devoted son. He loved his wife. He was obviously really fond of his daughters. He even liked their boyfriends a lot. He never claimed to have been unhappy at school, or that his life had been a struggle. The other way we get to know people is through their behaviour. They behave badly, or inconsistently, and this makes anyone who is at all curious wonder what it is that makes them tick. In my experience, a disintegrated personality is considerably more common amongst comics than it is amongst, say, bakers or landscape gardeners. But Peter was always wholly and consistently himself. OK, he drank too much. He smoked too much. No one in the world could claim he was tidy. He put off going to the dentist. He never opened his letters. But he was a man without side. Without snobbery, without malice, without greed. And all I can say is: I miss the guy more than I can say.

Quite often at night I think: 'I must ring Pete up . . . damn, I can't .' I miss the midnight chuntering in my study presaging some fatuous missive from his fax machine which, for some reason, he called Betty. I'll always remember him playing cricket in Regent's Park with my then three-year-old son and an entire family of passing Pakistanis. And going to the Limelight Club with him, half-cut, in the middle of the night, where nobody except the doorman recognized him, where he was, nonetheless, instantly surrounded by gorgeous bimbos drawn to his unshielded charm.

I wish I'd done more work with him. Not just because it was always such fun, but to conserve a bit more of that ancient monument for the world: to, as it were, uncover a few more pillars, put a few more stone lions on the record. We always planned to do a movie, a television series, a book; but all that's left are a few scribbled beginnings, raw and untreated, direct from Peter's head:

> There are limitations to the human mind ... as this series will prove.
> Tragically, I was an only twin.
> Pulsars are small and immensely heavy and remind me strangely of my first wife.
> I once spent a weekend in an otter, at the Mark Phillips Otterdrome in Northampton.
> I'm sorry, M'lud, but I'm unable to continue without an injection of nerve gas.
> Nothing pleases Lord Beaufort more than a properly wrapped swarm of bees in velvet.
> Can you remember the 19th? No, but I do remember the awful night I had white sugar on my porridge ...

Sabre-tooth giraffes. The Burberry Apes. The False Passport Office. Cavemen reading by the light of flints. The World's Largest Collection of Porcelain Ants. Secret messages smuggled inside the Olympic Torch. Living in Sherwood Forest with a band of in-laws. Clay Stag-Hunting.

It was the sculptor, Auguste Rodin, who wrote: 'Great works of art, which are the highest proof of human intelligence and sincerity, say all that can be said on man and on the world. An artist worthy of the name should express all the truth of nature, not only the exterior truth, but also, and above all, the inner truth.'

This was what Peter did. The fact that he did it, not through finely crafted busts of Madame Rodin, but via the somewhat lateral method of suggesting that the worst job he ever had was pulling lobsters out of Jayne Mansfield's bottom, is neither here nor there. It's in Geneva.

Clive Anderson

Peter Cook Talks Back

Peter Cook was one of several former members of the Cambridge Footlights who appeared in a BBC radio panto-mime which I had written with Rory McGrath in 1979. In fact, we only just wrote it on time. The programme was produced by Douglas Adams who has since become best known to the reading public as the author of *The Hitch-hiker's Guide to the Galaxy* but is famous in the world of publishing as a persistent late deliverer of manuscripts.

But for a year or so Douglas was a radio producer. Almost as though we sensed how he was going to behave himself in his years as a novelist, Rory and I prevaricated and postponed, excused and absented ourselves as dead-lines came and went and the recording date for the panto came ever closer. At the eleventh hour we resorted to handing our just-about-completed text to a passenger boarding the London train at Cambridge station. We asked her to look out for a very tall, rather cross man called Douglas who would be pacing around at Liverpool Street hoping to receive a very funny package, but not to stay with him while he read it.

On the day of the actual recording (a couple of days later), as no-account young scriptwriters, Rory and I were treated with appropriate disdain by the big name perform-ers who were appearing in the show, and treated with something bordering on tolerance by Douglas, who had been up all night making a few minor changes to render our work something like usable. Peter, though, was spectacularly and unforgettably nice to us. Instead of ruthlessly pouring scorn on our efforts at the read-through as everyone else seemed to be doing, he was unfailingly courteous. Suggesting sparkling improvements to the lines we had written for him, he assumed no airs and graces, but courteously and charmingly he helped things along without condescension or rudeness. What sort of savage satirist was this?

When Peter died, it was this quality of niceness – I still cannot think of a better word for it than that – that I tried to convey in a tribute I was asked to write for the *Independent*. All the comedians and humorists who were asked to contribute appreciations to various papers said the same sort of thing, especially those younger than him. Everyone found him easy to get along with and unpretentious. He did not attempt to lord it over those who approached him in awe. And he totally lacked any resentment towards those, inspired by him, who were succeeding in the world of comedy in which his career was supposed to have peaked years before.

I am happy to put this down to his good nature. He was capable of making scathing remarks and deploying savage wit but without, I think, really wishing to wound. There was no malice in his method. But I think it was also true that he was genuinely comfortable in the company of the overgrown students who make up a prominent strand of the light entertainment industry. He was genuinely entertained by other people's jokes, never fearing that his would ever dry up.

Some people are born middle-aged. Some remain juvenile, however old they get. In this sense Peter was a perpetual undergraduate. The cleverest, possibly; the wittiest, certainly; the hardest working, probably not. But however old in years he might become, he remained the fellow student you meet in a college bar in your first term in whose company you decide you want to spend the rest of your life. The first floor of his house in Hampstead was essentially an elegant college room inhabited by a Bohemian spirit, its walls decorated by mementos of shows and happy events. Newspapers and books and ashtrays were always on hand, the television and video were always there for late night entertainment. When he actually was an undergraduate it sounds as though he had a maturity beyond his years, but in maturity he was a Peter Pan figure who had grown up but had not grown old. And if it sounds like a criticism to suggest that someone in his fifties remained more like someone in his twenties, ask at which age most people are brighter, funnier, wittier and happier.

Years after the radio programme, I found Peter to be a brilliant guest to interview on television, as had many others before me. Not that he chose to reveal much of the inner man. He just made very good jokes about the week's news. About what he had been up to. About anything really. He generally insisted on pursuing unpredictable and original lines of thought. In the wake of some ghastly battle on the continent bringing shame on our country and agony to the face of Jimmy Hill, he would praise British football hooligans for displaying their magnificent fighting spirit. After some scandal or other he did mock the royal family, as every other satirist was doing, but urged them on to greater misbehaviour and even greater expenditure. He would recount some outrageous behaviour of his own involving German tourists, displaying both antediluvian xenophobia and a perfect command of the language. For a talk show he was, in short, the perfect guest. But he cheerily admitted that a chat show he had hosted himself had been dreadful. 'Even worse than this one,' he assured me.

In fact I bumped into Peter quite frequently in broadcasting studios. For some reason I once conducted a discussion on BBC2 between him and the curator of a museum about the relative merits of the art criticism expressed by Rolf

Harris and Sister Wendy Beckett. This was, let me add, a serious programme. And, if you are interested, the consensus was in favour of Rolf Harris. Once we both appeared on Radio 4's *News Quiz*. The four panellists and Barry Took all chipped in with our witty and half-witty remarks about topical events and the programme seemed to be trotting along pretty well until Peter went off on a marvellous piece of whimsy which eclipsed everything and everybody else. Cracking jokes can be a competitive business, but you could not compete with Peter on top form.

About a year before he died we made a special edition of *Clive Anderson Talks Back* in which there were four guests, fictional characters, each played by Peter. It had occurred to me that this sort of thing would suit Peter's talent for improvisation and inspiration and provide a way to exercise and display his extraordinary imagination. But then I suppose all I really wanted to do was to be Dudley Moore for the day. I do not suppose I would ever have got round to suggesting the idea at all but, emboldened by a few drinks at *Private Eye*'s Christmas Party, I raised it with Peter and he cheerily agreed that this would be just the thing to do. But, as I thought he might have had a drink himself, I assumed nothing would come of it.

The very next day he called me to confirm he was genuinely interested in doing the programme in this way and in fact he had already come up with about twenty possible characters he might play. They ranged from the totally bizarre to the completely unbelievable but in any event he was keen.

When we finally made the programme, the interviews were a mixture of improvisation and preplanning. Despite the inventive range of Peter's initial notions, we settled more safely for four fairly straightforward chat-show types, each in their own way representing aspects of Peter himself: a mad judge, the sort of establishment figure Peter's background and education might have turned him into if he had not had had the wit to lampoon them instead – he has always been good at playing judges and patrician politicians; an ageing rock star of the sort Peter was rather like as well; a useless football manager (Peter was a fervent Tottenham Hotspur fan); and a quality controller in a biscuit factory (E.L. Wisty, really) who had been captured by aliens.

We treated the fictional characters as though they were real people. I had a couple of meetings with Peter to sort out which characters he was going to do and to see what sort of conversations we might have. But after that Peter had research meetings with my producer Dan Patterson and his associates Anne Marie Thorogood and Ruth Wallace and they encouraged Peter to flesh out as much as possible about his roles.

So, when we actually did the show I knew about the fictional characters' backgrounds in the same way that I know about the history of a real guest. I was aware of some of the jokes and ideas Peter had come up with in the research meetings. And in the event the interviews on my side were about as sensible as the ones I do with real people. The interview format allowed Peter to go off in any direction he liked, secure in the knowledge that we could always return to the plot with the usual line of talk-show interrogation. And of course Peter was fantastic, even if the Dudley Moore he was working with that day might not have been up to scratch. I wish we had done some more now.

Shortly after the recording, we had a dinner for everyone who had worked on the series. You cannot have a TV series without an end-of-series party. We invited Peter to join us, but when he turned up Dan began to worry that Peter might have been expecting to find the celebrities who had been guests in the series there as well. Film stars, comedians, pop singers, politicians – that sort of thing. But it was not that sort of party. If it worried him to be the only famous person there, he did not show it and settled down to enjoy the company of the production staff, most of whom he had hardly met. Effectively he was at an office party and it was not his office. But as far as I can tell, he had a good time. We certainly did.

I always enjoyed being in his company. More than the further shows we did not make, I regret not having spent more time with him in real life. There was the odd vastly entertaining lunch or dinner, a party here or there, some phone calls which could come at any time. And a picnic in Regent's Park which somehow developed into a cricket match between a team captained by Peter taking on an extended Asian family. I am not sure who won. I am not sure we even had a proper ball. But we did have a ball.

The last time I spent any time with him was watching the World Cup Final: Brazil v. Italy, decided on a missed penalty, after a goal-less match in extra time. Barry Davis did his best to keep us entertained, but I think Peter did better. Some time during the match Peter came up with the idea that instead of pro-celebrity golf, there ought to be pro-celebrity boxing with say, Jimmy Tarbuck taking on Mike Tyson. A typical Cook idea.

If you have to die, you cannot have anything much more poignant at your Memorial Service than Alan Bennett delivering a tragicomic eulogy in his funny clerical voice. Unless it is Dudley Moore singing your jaunty old signature tune, 'Goodbye'.

And not only Dudley Moore, but also a recording of Peter himself in a favourite comedy monologue ready to be played to his grieving family and friends. Indeed, everything was so dreadfully funny, you could have laughed until you cried. But I guess, Peter would have just laughed.

John Bird

3: *The Last Pieces*

There is a character in Conrad's *Nostromo* who makes uncomfortable reading for the satirist, especially one who has been at any time a fashionable satirist. He is Martin Decoud, frequently described by Conrad as 'the brilliant Decoud'. A Spanish-American of good family, we meet him first in Paris, where he keeps himself occupied by circulating in smart journalistic society writing sardonic pieces on the comic-opera politics of his homeland. An example is given of his style:

> Imagine an atmosphere of *opéra bouffe* in which all the comic business of stage statesmen, brigands, etc., etc., all their farcical stealing, intriguing, and stabbing is done in dead earnest. It is screamingly funny, the blood flows all the time, and the actors believe themselves to be influencing the state of the universe.

This doesn't read like Cook, of course, but the attitude to public affairs – possibly excepting the flowing blood – is not a million miles away from *Beyond the Fringe*, the *Establishment*, *Private Eye*, and their successors. Faced with the activities of politicians in particular, all you can do is laugh. The next sentence confirms this view:

> Of course, government in general, any government anywhere, is a thing of exquisite comicality to a discerning mind.

It could be a motto, what now might be called the mission statement, for the 'satire boom' of the sixties and beyond, but Conrad is far from presenting this in a wholly positive light.

Conrad is severe on his own creations, which is what makes the reading uncomfortable, and he doesn't spare Decoud, who, in spite of behaving well – even nobly – at times, is given an unforgiving end, which is held to be the direct result of his satirical cast of mind. 'At the same time he felt no remorse. What should he regret? . . . His sadness was the sadness of a sceptical mind. He beheld the universe as a succession of incomprehensible images.' Of course I am conscious of thinking, or rather worrying, about myself when contemplating these passages: is this the inevitable fate of poking fun at Tory governments on television? Decoud shoots himself, but Conrad is specific about the deeper cause, and this is where the story crosses the legendary destiny of Peter Cook: he is actually 'a victim of the disillusioned weariness meted out to intellectual audacity'.

That Cook had intellectual audacity, and plenty of it, would be contested by few; his mind went to regions the rest of us hardly suspected existed and went there very quickly. As for the disillusioned weariness, we have the picture of Cook's last years supplied by the Press, and by some acquaintances: the inert afternoons in Hampstead with the bottle of vodka, watching daytime television, certainly a recipe for beholding the universe as a succession of incomprehensible images. I was not a companion of his during this period so I am unable to supply anecdotal evidence to confirm or challenge this picture of a sceptical mind dissolving in the fogs of its inevitable destiny.

What does conclusively challenge it, and challenges the idea of a Conradian retribution for a life of misdirected talent, is the quality of the last work that Cook did. I am thinking in particular of the television interviews with Clive Anderson, the improvised tapes for radio with Chris Morris, the Streeb-Greebling conversations on BBC2 with

Ludovic Kennedy; even the late-night phone calls to LBC Radio as Sven, the marooned Norwegian fisherman. It's worth the risk (the risk being that without hearing the performance much of the quality is missed) to quote at length. Sir Arthur Streeb-Greebling recalls his childhood to Ludovic Kennedy:

> **Sir Arthur** My father was a remote, icy man ... almost from the moment I was born he wanted no more to do with me; not very *paternal* as a father. Instead he proposed to have me reared by wolves. Fortunately for me there were very few decent-sized wolves in the Aylesbury area at the time ... so my father decided to have me raised by goats ... My mother by contrast was a saint. Whenever I think of my dear mother I have an abiding image of a small kindly plump grey-haired lady pottering at the sink. 'Get away from the bloody sink!' my mother would yell at her ... we never found out who she was.
>
> **Kennedy** Sir Arthur, your son ... had a somewhat unconventional upbringing.
>
> **Sir Arthur** We had him educated privately, if that's what you mean.
>
> **Kennedy** But not by governesses?
>
> **Sir Arthur** (*furious*) No, by *goats*, not by governesses! Goats! ... It was either that or King's School, Canterbury and I'm not entirely heartless, you know.

Content aside, when you hear the tape, the pacing of this section up to the payoff ('I'm not exactly heartless, you know'), the music of it, is perfect; effortless and surprising in one, a combination not easy to bring off.

I imagine this conversation was scripted, but exactly the same qualities are revealed in the improvised or semi-improvised pieces with Anderson and Morris – who is himself superb, it should be said. This is far from being the dregs of some washed-up has-been scratching around to recreate lost glories, rather it looks like the last work of a considerable creative artist: simple, pared down to essentials.

In 1993 Clive Anderson devoted an entire edition of his celebrity chat show on Channel 4 to a series of interviews with Cook, who improvised in various guises. He produced four characters: a man who claimed to have been abducted by aliens, a judge, a rock star and a football manager – representative figures of his life-long obsessions. These performances are remarkable, not least because there must have been an element of career-importance to the Anderson show for Peter, who apart from the brief Streeb-Greebling dialogues three years earlier hadn't appeared on British television doing his own material since the mid-eighties. The virtuosity and variety of the invention might be taken for granted but compared with the early style which made him famous and which is associated with his name, there is something new here: an insight and even a sympathy in the way in which Cook approaches his characters. The rapt, rather abstract other-worldliness has gone and the comedy has become, not mellower necessarily, but more humane.

Even the character who of the four is closest to an E.L. Wisty figure, the surburban obsessive Norman House – the man who embarked upon the hobby of metal detecting when a borrowed metal-detector unearthed an almost new metal detector – even he is presented as a rounded personality, uncertain in the claims he makes and vulnerable to self-doubt. Mr House had been captured by a process referred to – in a phrase of characteristic Cookian poetry – as 'mental beckoning' by visitors from the planet Ikea. The audience applaud the gag, but the description of the aliens as misshapen because there were

> ... people who arrived millions ago in cardboard
> boxes and were forced to assemble themselves ...
> [but] ... had no instructions

both extends the joke and is a conceit worthy of a sci-fi Beckett.

All four characters are recognizably real people, sharply distinguished not only verbally but physically: House with a wary stillness, the rock star lolling casually, the judge ramrod-straight, the football manager racked by paroxysms of inarticulate energy.

But above all what is impressive is the total absence of charlatanry; there is no striving for effect or outrageousness, nothing of the self-referential tone of a comedian pressing the buttons of a pre-set appeal to his expectant audience. In other words something rare in today's 'entertainment business' climate: no whiff of marketing. Indeed, in the case of the character of the Norwegian Sven, Cook couldn't have assumed the existence of any audience at all. These were simply calls made to Clive Bull's very late-night radio phone-in; no commission, no payment, just Peter Cook creating for creation's sake. And producing a character of great sobriety and great subtlety, funny, poignant and technically extraordinary, the rhythm hesitant, the tone modest and unemphatic, with those slight dislocations of language characteristic of bilingual Scandinavians. Although saddened by the mysterious disappearance of his wife Jutte, Sven makes an honest effort to contribute his experience to a discussion of football hooliganism:

> ... I know it's a very serious subject tonight, but in Norway we have no hooliganism because of our, so many fish programmes on. Every day we have programmes on fish, on TV and on radio, phone-ins, everything, and at the football too, before the match people come on, expert fishermen, showing how to catch chub, and roach and everything like that ... it calms down people, it calms people down.

In contrast to remarks passed – by me among others – about Cook's lack of talent as an actor, there is in the invention and the performance of these late pieces a sense of complete command. He knows these characters from the inside and through experience, yet this supposedly is the work of a disappointed drunk who gave up the promise of a golden talent. On the contrary I'd suggest that not only could no comedian that I know have produced anything like this stuff, it would have been beyond the young Peter Cook too. It is of a different class from those early monologues and duologues, brilliant as they were. The sensationalism of the surface has gone, the sometimes facile surrealism; instead we are given the weight of a persuasively alive, and lived, personality, fully achieved. The word which comes to mind is maturity.

After he died there was some discussion as to whether Cook was or was not a satirist. He himself is on record as denying it, partly because the term is taken nowadays as implying some kind of lofty *purpose*. Perhaps the example of Swift – *Drapier's Letters* being one of the very few instances of a satirical work actually getting a concrete political result, in that case a defeat for the British Government on Irish currency reform – has caused us to expect too much of our satirists. If we forget about purpose and consider satire as an approach or a cast of mind we can be more certain about applying the term to Peter Cook's work, or much of it, whether he would have approved or not. The best definition I know is Northrop Frye's: satire demands 'fantasy, a content recognized as grotesque, moral judgments (at least implicit), and a militant attitude to experience'. Qualities shared by Cook and the fictional character Martin Decoud, and (it should be said) by Conrad himself at times: there is more of him in Decoud than anybody else in the novel.

But unlike Decoud, Peter Cook triumphantly escaped the fate that Conrad says his gifts had marked him out for: these last pieces have no flavour of disillusioned weariness, rather they tell us there was plenty of intellectual audacity to come.

Michael Palin

I Had That Peter Cook in the Back of My Car

I was sitting at my desk trying to write something funny when I heard of Peter's death. Rather than stop when I heard the news, I felt I should slog on. I think I felt that if I didn't some flickering spirit of Peter might find its way to a telephone and leave some abusive observation on my answering machine.

Almost a year earlier a silly story had appeared in one or two of the papers about my cheating at conkers whilst making a documentary on the Isle of Wight. Sure enough, Peter had noticed it and that same evening I came home to hear his voice on tape, sonorously ringing the death knell of the 'nice' Michael Palin. At last, it went on, the truth had been revealed, the thin veil of charm had been sundered and the dark reality laid before the British public. Speaking as a friend, Peter could only express disappointment, confusion and sorrow at my 'suicidal' act. Was winning at conkers worth jeopardizing a career? Why had I done it so publicly? Was it a cry for help? It was the sort of message only someone with time on their hands would have bothered to send. This was how Peter was in the last years of his life, when I began to know him less as a distant bright light, an elder statesman of comedy, and more as a friend.

Some articles appeared after his death bemoaning the 'waste' of his talent, a very Samuel Smiles-ish, 1980s sort of judgement. They seemed to be saying that just because Peter wasn't flaunting it, he hadn't got it. Well, all I can say is their loss was my answering machine's gain. To the end of his life Peter remained the funniest man in the room. But he seemed quite unconcerned with popular acceptance. His was not the gather-round high-octane performance of the joke-teller. He was funny quite softly, often building up a rambling monologue via a series of devastating throw aways. His observations were always acute and he was frighteningly well informed.

Nowadays comedy, like every other tradeable commodity, has to fight for survival. To shout about itself, advertise itself, be accessible and available. Grab the space before someone else does. Peter, I always felt, had seen all that. He had been the new thing. He had been the latest craze. He had been the breakthrough and the Golden Boy and knew well enough that these labels were nothing to do with reality. They were the clichés of the media he mocked and with which he was obsessed. He seemed to take nothing seriously, least of all himself. His preferred title for his autobiography was *Retired and Emotional*.

I first heard of Peter when I was at Shrewsbury School. I must have been sixteen or seventeen and the *Beyond the Fringe* album was all the rage. Much more recherché was *Pieces of Eight*, which impressed me particularly because this was almost entirely written by Peter at some startlingly young age. I was always drawn more to the writers of comedy than the performers.

Beyond the Fringe, like rock and roll, was perceived as something fresh and new and dangerous. To find ourselves laughing at things like the clichés of war heroism was an illicit pleasure to boys for whom the style, and indeed syllabus, of their education was firmly rooted in the past.

It is not easy nowadays to convey the sensational audacity, the explosively liberating effect of hearing the prime minister of the day impersonated, or judges, bishops, police chiefs and army officers mocked. It was shocking and thrilling, but it was done with such skill and intelligence that it could not easily be shot down, dismissed or shrugged off. It was all the more effective for coming from within. Peter's education and background were the very epitome of the Establishment. He knew what he was talking about.

With *Beyond the Fringe*, comedy came in from the end of the pier and out of the chummy comfort of the BBC studios and sank its teeth hard and deep into the fleshy buttocks of the British establishment. The resulting cry of pain and outrage might have deterred lesser men, but not Peter Cook. He was encouraged by it. For that, those who came after, whether on the stage of the *Establishment Club* or in the pages of *Private Eye*, on *That Was The Week That Was* or on *Monty Python*, owe him an enormous debt of thanks. Peter was shrewd enough to know that satire doesn't change a thing. Greed, corruption and deceit will always be with us. But ridicule, well used and well directed, is a potent and much underrated weapon. It can at least stop us taking power and authority for granted. Peter wielded this weapon particularly deftly, and we could ill-afford to lose such a skilled operator.

The first time I met Peter was in 1966, after I had left school and Oxford and taken my first regular job – as the compère of a fast-fading pop show called *Now!*. Peter and Dudley had teamed up to record a sort of Noël-Cowardish cabaret spoof called 'Goodbye', which had stormed the charts, and they were guest stars of the week. Even then, Peter was an exceedingly laid back performer. He wore a three-piece suit and, despite the fact that he couldn't really sing, cut an impressive figure, standing languidly beside the piano, brushing aside a floppy lock of hair whilst Dudley did most of the work. He looked rather like an indulgent parent beside his precocious child. Helen and I had been married three days earlier and had returned from a rain-sodden honeymoon in Ireland in time for me to do the show. So the first photographs ever taken of our married

213

life show Mr and Mrs Palin 'sharing a joke' with Peter Cook and Dudley Moore.

I can remember being bitterly disappointed that they didn't do a Pete and Dud duologue, for I much preferred those to the vague embarrassment of their musical numbers. The Dagenham Duologues from *Not Only But Also* were often sublime. In fact, the more boring the character Peter was playing, the more epic and unforgettable he became.

In some of their best work together, one would watch with almost Attenborough-like fascination as Peter, like some medieval torturer, would slowly and relentlessly pile on the agony, patiently waiting for the moment when Dudley would betray, by the merest movement of the side of his mouth, a hint of a flicker of a smile. That was the opening Peter had been waiting for. Dudley would rarely recover as Peter moved slowly and surely in for the kill. His enormous eyes would widen, the hypnotic monotone would become even more insistent and inescapable. Dudley would pull faces, look away, turn this way and that, munch ever more fiercely on his sandwich, but the trance-like piercing stare would always be waiting for him. And when he was ready Peter would apply the *coup de grâce*. He would ask Dudley a question, thus forcing him to abandon the chewed lip or the bitten cheek-lining or whatever painful method Dudley might have been using to try and survive. Then it was all over bar the shouting. If Dudley survived one question, he would not survive the next. His face would give up the struggle, his eyes would fill with helpless tears, and he would be reduced to communicating only in whimpers.

Peter was tall and slim in those days and yet in all my recent memories he was wider, heavier and jowlier. He never seemed over-concerned about his spectacular change of physique; indeed, he sometimes played up to it. He was one of the very few to wear full fancy dress at John Cleese's fiftieth birthday party. He came dressed as Demis Roussos in a great white swathe of a robe. One night at our house he walked clean through a plate glass door on his way to the lavatory. He was lucky not to have done himself a serious injury, but he was far more concerned about the door. A couple of days later he and Lin sent us a doorstop shaped like a sofa and a small embroidered sign in the style of a sampler reading 'Mind the Door'.

Peter thought order and predictability were serious threats to comedy. He preferred to think on his feet, rather than in a production conference. This made him, among other things, one of the greatest chat-show guests and one of the worst hosts. Much has been talked of his spat with Zsa Zsa Gabor, but this was one small show-stealing moment among many. Whenever Peter ambled his way to the couch he brought with him an air of heightened expectation. Yet when he was given his own chat show, *Where Do I Sit?* it was a dismal failure, taken off the air after only three episodes. The responsibilities of host required different talents – organization rather than improvisation, patience rather than provocation. Peter's wit was neutralized. He cheerfully admitted his failure. 'The trouble was,' he once told me, 'I could have anyone. If I wanted Kirk Douglas, they'd get me Kirk Douglas. But as soon as he sat down I realized there was nothing I wanted to ask him. I'd say, "Hello Kirk" and he'd say "Hello Peter" and then there'd be this awful silence.'

The fact is that Peter was best of all on his own. Long before improvisation became institutionalized as 'Improv' he was the supreme inventor, able to create a world or spin a character out of nothing. No matter how much he'd had to drink, when his eyes grew wide and took on that fixed E.L. Wisty stare you knew that something special was coming. From where no one quite knew, probably Peter least of all. During the four-night run of the 1979 Amnesty Show – one of the Secret Policeman's Balls – a critic took the show to task for lacking a satirical edge. Peter arrived the next night with something he wanted to try out. It turned out to be the hit of the show, a beautifully judged, well-informed, appallingly funny parody of the judge summing-up in the Jeremy Thorpe case. Peter was still honing it in the wings as he waited to go on. I remember him desperately asking around for an original euphemism for a homosexual. Eventually Billy Connolly, with the air of a scholar remembering some medieval Latin, ventured that he'd heard someone in Glasgow use the phrase 'player of the pink oboe'. Two minutes later Peter was on stage as the judge, adding his own twist to Billy's contribution by referring to the witness as a *self-confessed player of the pink oboe*. It was the 'self-confessed' that made me laugh most of all.

His brilliance survived (and anyone who might think it didn't should watch his performance as four different guests on the Clive Anderson show) because his natural and fearsomely quick wit was allied to a superb ear for language. Great comedy comes from getting it absolutely right, not almost right. Peter's talent was to get it absolutely right so often.

But my favourite memories are not great moments at all. They are not even of someone at the centre of things. Peter, as I remember him, played at his own pace. Sometimes, at a party or gathering, when he had had enough of people, and maybe enough of himself, he would be ready to leave, looking for a scarf in the hallway, and sometimes a lift home. If Helen and I had come by car we'd often oblige. Peter would squeeze into the back with Lin and the four of us would head north together. Looking back now, my one regret is that there was never a time when I thanked Peter for all the pleasure he'd given me. It was such an obvious thing to say that I never said it.

Still, at least I got to drive him home.

Eleanor Bron

Peter

I did not particularly want to be in the new film of *Black Beauty*, but Caroline Thompson, the young American director, though slight of form, turned out to have a whim of iron. She was determined that Peter Cook should play Lord Wrexmire and that I should play his wife. I shall always be grateful to her for changing my mind. But for Caroline another ten years or so might have gone by without my seeing Peter except at the occasional charity show; or, as it was to turn out, I should not have seen him again.

It was years since we had worked together. Waiting for the car to pick me up on my first day of filming, I was a little apprehensive. I had had the illusion of being in touch, roughly, simply from hearing news of Peter through mutual friends, acquaintances, the media, but no effort was made on either side and really our paths no longer crossed. Nonetheless I continued to feel the affection for Peter that he always inspired, as well as an absurd and unwarranted mixture of pride and protectiveness towards him. Whenever talk turned to comedy, to the Pythons, and the stream of stand-up comics that has poured steadily for years out of Edinburgh, I always felt bound urgently to point out that there was no one in comedy to touch Peter's genius, his originality or his achievement, either among our contemporaries, or among those who followed on. Once or twice lately, I had heard people speak of him as being in some way 'out of things', a disappointed man who had been overtaken and left behind.

We had first met at Cambridge, introduced by John Bird, who was casting *A Resounding Tinkle*, a play by N.F. Simpson, for one of the university drama societies, a very select one that had no membership but cast, like the professional theatre, from among known Cambridge 'actors'. John had spotted me in a nursery production and came round to Newnham to meet me and to announce that he had just met 'the funniest man in the world'. (So, as Middie Paradock, I got to utter the wonderful first line: 'There's a man at the door wanting you to form a government' to Peter, playing Bro Paradock.) John's next production after this was the Footlights annual revue for which he and Peter and Timothy Birdsall wrote sketches under the name e.e. duncansson, in which I was always cast as a secretary named Miss Rigby ... Peter and Timothy ended the show, which was called *Last Laugh* with a biblical sketch about Moses and miracles and sticks into serpents and general chicanery.

Peter's spirals of fantasy and wit kept us all hilarious most of the time and once we had been to stay with him and his family for a weekend at Lyme Regis they seemed more fantastic still – his background seemed so very stable and rooted in solid tradition. In contrast to this it was an experience to travel on the tube with him, he had merely to lean his head back, half-close his eyes and be seen to be about to make a particular characteristic high growling in the throat that portended the onset of the character of Mr Grole, for the rest of us to be reduced to foolishness and apparently unprovoked hysterics. He had already a range of 'voices' for the persona he adopted. Around that time a lot of us copied the *Goon Show* characters – Bluebottle and

Eccles, etc. – but Peter invented his own. Another early figure was Colonel Rutter (a bit of a voyeur who worked with an accomplice who would keep a pretty girl chatting so that Rutter could lift up her skirt with the crook of his walking stick and view her legs). Peter took great pleasure in the names he made up for his characters. For my Conservative wife in the *Establishment* cabaret, he found the name Lady Pamela Stitty. Everyone assumed that she was intended to be Lady Pamela Berry (a well-known society hostess whom I had never heard of) and nobody ever spotted that the name was Lady Pamela's Titty.

One thing Peter and I had in common was that we were both reading Modern Languages and though I don't remember seeing him at any lectures we did share an examination hall. He always gave me credit for having got him through Tripos by lending him my notes on twentieth-century German Literature – a minor miracle, if true. I had forgotten until recently that he had originally been destined for the Foreign Office, following his father, who had been a diplomat. And this perhaps was where his quite conventional upbringing showed itself because he was the sort of person that parents approved of wholeheartedly – 'that nice Peter Cook' – he was incredibly, effortlessly charming, as well as being extremely dashing and good to look upon. He had the most beautiful blue eyes and enviably long lashes and would look down the side of his cheek at you. When I played Hermione Roddice in *Women in Love*, reading Lawrence's description of her doing this puzzled me at first, until I remembered that it was exactly what Peter did – a sort of haughty, oblique, slightly distancing, testing look. Peter very often was keeping one eye on you to see how you were taking his latest rigmarole. Perhaps this need to know kept him from being the type of actor who entered into his roles in the 'method' style; but it may be that essentially he was always a solo performer, though he could be at his best when bouncing his performance off another person. He improved greatly as an actor. Some of the last characters he created, in *One Foot in the Algarve* and in the Clive Anderson show were rounded and wonderfully observed as well as being as funny as anything he ever did.

The doorbell rang promptly at two o'clock – the car to take me to the location of *Black Beauty*. Instead of an anonymous chauffeur's voice I heard a wild, hyperactive unidentifiable foreigner: Peter, experimenting with a new persona: 'Darling – is a *nightmare*! From Hampstead – the roads – entirely clear – every traffic light is *green*! A nightmare!' Downstairs, Peter bounded along the pavement to greet me. It was wonderful, on our drive to Woodstock, to find him in exuberant form. He was not only very funny but, far from being a sour, wrecked being, he was just as beguiling and far more communicative than he had ever been. He was also wonderfully generous, as we reminisced, towards people whom I had heard he regarded with great bitterness. The notion that he was the man that time forgot was scotched as soon as we arrived at the set. Everyone's face lit up when they saw him. Make-up, wardrobe, the assistants, the sparks, the grips, the entire unit was charmed by him and thrilled to be working with him. When we were in costume and walked into the crowded field where our characters were to preside over a horse race, a tremendous excited whisper could be heard 'There's Pete, it's Pete!' and the extras rushed forward to get his autograph. It was not just that they had spotted a star – this was a man they loved.

We spent a lot of time chatting in his trailer or mine, while waiting to go on the set. Peter loved to gossip. But now he also did something he had never done in the past, which was to talk about himself. He seemed more open than I had ever known him. Some of what he said confirmed thoughts about him that had occurred to me over the years: that because of his upbringing and schooling, women had always been a bit of a mystery to him (and, I suspect, a source of quite a lot of grief). I think his being really rather beautiful and very attractive didn't make that side of his life any easier. No doubt age had helped to mellow him, and from what he told me of Lin, his wife, whom I did not know – describing her with great pride and astonished affection – she had contributed a lot to the change. She provided the kind of support he could thrive on; as, for example, when he was on location making *One Foot in the Algarve*.

Lin, watching the filming, happened to overhear a tourist making a derogatory remark about Peter. At first she was too flabbergasted to react, but a short while afterwards she saw the man again in the village square, went up to him and hit him. It was lovely to see Peter's delight and pride that anyone could leap to his defence in this way.

The voice of Peter's new persona, the extravagant foreigner, would occasionaly infiltrate our conversations. We both began to use it, with mutual delight, until Peter suggested that we ought to do a stage show based around these two people. It was a lovely thought, but I imagined it would remain a thought, until almost exactly a year later he telephoned and reminded me of the idea. I wondered to myself how far we would get. For years now, John Fortune and I have talked about writing together again, and met every so often to discuss it. Peter was far more rigorous than John and I. Once we started we met every week, and quite soon moved into improvising on tape material that we hoped finally to turn into sketches. No doubt what prompted Peter to start working again was the money running out; but what made Peter's death so sad was not that it ended a great long period of tragic waste, as some people implied, but that he was in such a creative period. Though I shall always regret that the show did not happen, I am so grateful to have found Peter again at what was to turn out to be the end of his life, and to find as I did when we walked out onto the set together that, contrary to all rumour, he had not changed, he was just loved by a far huger number of people.

Lin Cook

Paradise in Perrins Walk

Peter's home was his castle. A spacious Grade II listed
house on three-and-a-bit floors with a large beautiful
garden hidden from public view. Looking at it from the
front, the architecture appears Queen Anne. From the rear,
it is undoubtedly Victorian with picturesque, leaded,
inverted strawberry windows. Anyone who saw it from the
garden, would be reminded of fairy tales. It looked that
enchanting.

There are stairs from the second floor with a heavy door
leading directly to the flat roof top, which commands a
panoramic view that only estate agents in Hampstead can
describe. In a rickety wooden shed that housed the water
tank, there were similarly rickety deck-chairs. Peter loved
wandering up there periodically, in the day or in the
nighttime. Sometimes during an evening he would unex-
pectedly say, 'Come up to the roof with me.' This was our
turret in the skies.

In the garden, accessible through french windows in the
dining area on the ground floor, was our paradise, complete
with fig leaves from a mature tree that produced figs in
abundance during the autumn. By this tree, growing at the
farthest corner of the garden, there are hydrangeas, sometimes mauve, sometimes blue. Almost obscured by the
heavy fig branches hanging low, and the hydrangea bushes,

there is a break in the wall dividing our garden from our neighbours; three or four steps connect both gardens. Neither Peter, nor the neighbours who purchased their house a year or two after Peter purchased his, ever felt the necessity to change this unusual feature. In this part of the garden ferns grow tall and wild in the summer months. There are rockery plants and bluebells that seeded themselves wherever they chose. Here too was where Peter repeatedly, but unsuccessfully, tried to create a bog where he hoped newts might live.

In the beds there is an area where the camellia bushes bloom just beneath a majestic magnolia tree. A weedy little eucalyptus that Peter planted one year soon outgrew everything else despite the roots being bumpily visible on the ground because he had not planted it deep enough in the first place. Immediately next to that he had planted a crab apple which has also survived happily enough, and prettily when it is in flower, despite its roots also being obviously visible.

Then there are the assorted shrubs and bushes which he liked to have growing fairly wildly, covering the ground and encroaching on to the lawn. Sometimes if I staked anything up, lifting drooping branches above the ground, I would find the stakes promptly removed by Peter because he preferred branches to be falling about as nature intended rather than 'tidily' straightened up. One of his favourites was a graceful slow-growing acer with brilliant orange and red leaves. This was later complemented with a delicate Japanese acer with green and white leaves although he generally disliked anything with variegated leaves, particularly an ivy plant which we never allowed to grow as freely as it would have wanted to. This was regularly cut back so that part of the garden would not be overwhelmed with its 'awful' variegated leaves.

Bamboo grows in a clump in a large pot. Other enormous tubs have honeysuckle or clematis. One, nearer the house, has a non-flowering climber which we never knew the

223

name of. It is tall, straggly and unhealthy but Peter was no less fond of it. When I asked if we should replace it, he answered 'It has struggled so hard to live, it's a shame to get rid of it; let's leave it be.' It is still there, still struggling, largely because it does not get much sun. That is almost the only plant in the garden that I treat with respect. It is the one plant that has a tough time just to survive, never mind thrive, as everything else in the garden seems to be doing.

An errant gardener, whom we once temporarily employed, removed a holly bush because he did not like the holly. Peter was furious that he hadn't asked us – neither of us would have agreed to that old holly being uprooted – and never wanted to see that gardener around again. Peter wouldn't mention his name, referring to him only as 'that creep, Mr Beard' because he had a beard. It took Peter several weeks, possibly months, before he ceased to mind and complain about that rash act. One day, I came home to find a small holly plant, in much the same place as where the old holly had been. Peter had gone out, bought it, and planted it.

He always asked me to get busy lizzies and tobacco plants in the spring, preferably white ones. Then we would consult about where they should go. Quite often, they would be promptly planted by Peter because he could not be bothered to wait for the weekly visit from our usual young gardener, a quiet hardworking lad we both liked, called Luke. Peter did not potter in the garden much but was always pleased to see me doing so. If he had any 'gardening duties' it would be confined to clearing leaves from the fish ponds, or hosing the garden. This would not be as or when necessary, but at most irregular periods entirely dependent on his mood; when he wanted to, rather than when he 'should', 'ought', or 'must'.

Along the garden walls as well as in several pots, there are climbing roses or rose shrubs. Amongst others we have the cool white Iceberg, Masquerade, Golden Wings, Kiftsgate, Mme Alfred Carrière, Vielchenblau, Blue Moon and

New Dawn. Once, in a garden centre, the name of a climbing rose caught my eye and made me smile. I bought it and took it home, running upstairs to tell Peter as seriously as I could, 'Dearest, there's a Schoolgirl in the garden,' and getting him to go into the garden to see the schoolgirl.

He thought geraniums were vulgar, especially the trailing ones that bloom in profusion. But, precisely because they were 'vulgar', he did not mind them from time to time. On the other hand, he would not put up with chrysanthemums, dahlias, tulips or daffodils. When he did any planting, it never took long because he did not have the patience to dig deep enough. But he would remember to water after planting, firming up the soil with the heel of his shoe.

We shared pride in the garden, and joy at observing life and the goings-on within it, birds splashing in the fountain, or the odd squirrel scampering across the branch of a tree. In one year it might be me, and in another Peter who said, 'I saw the first ladybird today.' We left bread for the robin and cheerily greeted him with 'Hello Robin' whenever he hopped into sight. We looked on fondly if we saw him eating up a worm. I don't recall seeing any spiders in the garden, although over the years Peter had released at least a dozen of them into the garden whenever they were found trespassing in the house. Coming across one in the bathtub would have me in a panic. 'Dar-ling, *please* come *now*.' He soon ceased to be exasperated and became resigned to his role as spider-catcher, doing so expertly with a sheet of paper and a glass, and always taking the prisoner out to the garden, to set it free.

'Let me do it,' he would say if he happened to find me trying to reach an overhead branch, 'I'm taller than you,' and with the greatest of ease he would lower a bough to me.

When I was trailing strands of clematis over a wall or up the branches of a tree, he might again offer his help. 'I can manage,' I usually answered, using two sticks as though they were oversized chopsticks to try and lodge the clematis where I thought it should go.

'Move away, I can reach higher. Is that where you want it?'

'No, the other branch ... please.'

'What's wrong with this one, it looks perfectly fine to me,' and sometimes fine it looked; other times I would insist on having my way. Whenever I needed assistance, he would oblige, effortlessly because he was taller, or stronger. When required, and asked nicely, he might put himself out a bit more, patiently holding a ladder for me whilst I balanced precariously on the very top rung to disentangle overgrowth on top of the garden walls or cut away unwanted creepers.

Visible from the dining room and all the rear room windows in the house, in the front part of the garden, is a fairly shallow ornamental pond with a fountain; a statuette of an angelic looking Cupid holding not a bow and arrow, but a fish that spouts water from its mouth. More pots with assorted plants, and grass that resembles weeds, surround the edge of the pond. Once, when we did a fish count, before the equivalent of a national disaster hit us – when a heron came to visit – there were nearly thirty occupants, including some babies. Each morning, either Peter or I would turn the fountain on and each evening, we would check that one of us had remembered to turn it off.

He loved going out to look at the fishes, recognizing most of them because of their individual colouring or size. Our favourite ones were given pet names. The very first time he spotted a tiny black baby fish, probably an inch long and weighing an ounce, he was thrilled and called me out to have a look. Each year, we looked forward to discovering new babies in the pond and observing their colour change to gold as they grew. In the wintertime, he was concerned that the water should not freeze over and always left the water lamps on; it amused him to see 'the daft fishes' swimming up with their 'noses' close to the lights when he went to look at them. They were supposed to be fed only in the spring and summer, not in the winter months. But in the Cook household, if they were seen swimming about, it was presumed that 'they had come out to play' and might be hungry, therefore they would be fed. It is possible that the fishes in our ponds thought they lived in the tropics because the light and warmth from the lamps that we constantly left on deceived them.

A few years ago, he decided he would like a larger, deeper pond so that he could keep koi carp. This was duly designed and created across the breadth of the garden, in the space between the fig and the magnolia trees. 'We don't need a second pond, it's too much trouble,' I had half-heartedly argued, knowing it to be a waste of breath, as he had already set his heart on his special-deep-pond-with-special-filters-to-keep-water-constantly-fresh-for-koi project.

Whenever Peter made up his mind about anything, whether it was something he would like to own, or to get done, or somewhere he would like to go, he would be impatient to get it organized and would not be deterred by anything, or indeed anyone.

He took boyish delight in netting the larger fishes from the original pond to transfer them to the new pond prior to our getting any koi. I said he might be separating families and we'd be having lovesick goldfishes, which made him call me a 'daft sausage' and smile indulgently at me. He enjoyed having the two ponds, taking pleasure in feeding the fish and watching them swim to the surface for their flakes which he bought from a stall in the local community centre that sold food for pets.

It was at this time that he came to a decision about a grey carp which he tolerated, but had never liked. Originally there were two. I had bought them because I was told that they swim at the bottom of the pond, eating up rubbish, thus helping to keep the pond clean. Not knowing much about outdoor fish at the time when I bought those two carp, I had also purchased a couple of golden orfes. These grew rapidly and darted briskly about, obviously enjoying the good life in our pool, thereby winning Peter over, although initially he did not like them either. The carp, like the orfes, had grown quickly but their movements were slow and there was nothing attractive about them. Then, one of them, for no apparent reason leapt out of the pond one evening. Peter told me it had committed 'hara kiri'; he had found it on the paving stone and buried it so I wouldn't encounter it when I got up. This caused us to be more aware of the lone existence of Ralph, the remaining carp, who continued to swim about morosely, unlike the happy goldfish.

When the carp were small, Peter had already suggested that we get rid of them by taking them in a bucket to one of the ponds on Hampstead Heath. But we had done nothing about it, putting off the deed by saying to each other that it was illegal and we might get caught. Now he was again thinking of moving the carp to a local public pond.

As it happened that weekend, the Sunday morning was glorious and I was able to persuade Peter to take a drive out to the country, and have Sunday lunch at a pub on the way. We talked about where we might drive to and I suggested I could take him to Enfield where there are several Waterworld centres dealing with ponds and equipment, selling all varieties of goldfish and aquatic creatures. It might be interesting for him to have a look.

'Let's take Ralph with us,' he said.

'Why?' I asked, thinking that he might be contemplating using the unwanted Ralph to swap for a goldfish or two at the shop. However, that was not what Peter had in mind.

'There's bound to be a stream that we will pass on the way. We can release him there,' he explained as a matter of fact. The idea seemed sound enough.

'Pull up on the side, darling,' Peter said.

'Here?'

'Yes,' he answered. 'We have just gone over that hump, it's a bridge. There will be a stream below.'

I looked back and indeed what he said was true. I waited in the car with the engine running, ready for our getaway after the deed. Peter went to the middle of the bridge which was not at all high and, leaning over as far as he could, discharged Ralph, last seen swimming away to a new adventure.

Back in the early days, the first time we noticed that a small goldfish was swimming lopsidedly, obviously unwell, Peter had tenderly scooped it out to put it in a bowl, bringing it into the house so that we could keep an eye on it. We hoped it would recover but when it died days later, that was our first experience of a death in the pond. Neither of us could help feeling sad although it was just a goldfish. It was our goldfish and its little life mattered to us.

One major drama we experienced was the time when the pond was visited by a heron. We were concerned and agitated when we could not see any fish swimming about in the pond. Then we caught sight of one, two ... five! We were relieved and slightly comforted. Peter decided to rescue the remaining fishes in case the dreaded predator returned. We drained the pond and were pleasurably surprised to find nearly ten survivors, the sighting of each one greeted with an excited exclamation from me, 'Here's one,' or 'There's another one by the lily!' whilst Peter stayed cool, calmly saying, 'I've got it,' or 'I've got another one,' until they were all caught. The spare bathtub in the house was half-filled with pond water and half with water from the tap; that was how Peter said it was to be. Green bits from the pond were added and the fish were moved there for close to a week before they were returned to the pond.

One summer when he thought our koi were taking too long to grow, he decided to buy half a dozen large ones. Much as I liked pleasing him, I wasn't keen to drive out to Enfield on that particular day but he found someone else, a minicab driver, who not only did so willingly but also enjoyed the experience as well as the generous fare earned for the trip. Arriving at the Enfield aquatic centre, the driver had been disconcerted to find out how much the koi cost and rang Peter who still told him to go ahead with the purchase, paying for it with his credit card details.

Peter would generally be drawn into the garden at least a couple of times a day. Often, he would also have the impulse to wander out at more unusual times. We constantly had variations on a conversation along these lines:

'I'm just going to give the fish their midnight snack.'

'Please don't go out in your dressing gown, darling. The mosquitoes will get you. Please don't go out barefoot!'

'No, they won't,' he would retort as he padded out. 'I won't be long.'

And, when he got back into bed, invariably he would risk an 'I told you so,' or sometimes he might receive a more sympathetic 'Oh dear,' as he said, 'I've been bitten,' showing me where he had been attacked, as well as boldly displaying a not-too-clean pair of soles.

Several years ago, during a particularly hot summer, there seemed to be a virus infecting ponds and fishlife. Bits of their scales dropped off, revealing white patches, and they looked rather pitiful. Worse, the affected ones seemed to be being picked on by the healthy ones, who went straight for the open wounds of the poorly fish. A pet shop recommended drops which would help clean the water and clear the infection. We were pleasantly surprised that this worked and life in the pond went back to normal for a longish while.

Then, months later, we noticed that certain fishes were again being chased about, taking refuge when they could amongst some of the pond plants. Not wanting them to be hurt, we caught those that risked being harmed, and put them in a bucket for a couple of days, before deciding it was safe to return them to the pond. This happened every now and then, although we did not always separate the fishes. Sometimes we would do no more than shoo the bullies away, hoping those few fishes that we were feeling sorry for would somehow be all right and manage to fend for themselves.

Just by chance, I happened to be reading about goldfish one evening whilst Peter was watching television. 'What's so funny?' he wanted to know when I started giggling. Unable to tell him, I pointed to a paragraph in the magazine and he too joined me in laughter – because when goldfish mate, they chase one another around in the pond. Our concern had been thoroughly misplaced.

When I was in the garden, usually for hours on end and mostly during weekends, Peter would regularly open a window to watch or to make conversation, wanting to know what I was up to. On occasions when he had come out to join me, I had never failed to react with a startled shriek before saying to him, 'Don't frighten me like that!' because I wasn't expecting to find him suddenly standing next to me, smiling, cigarette in hand. He would usually be there to tell me, 'I am just popping out for a minute,' to get cigarettes, considerately asking at the same time if I'd like anything from the shops, or to see if I'd like to go out with him for a quick lunch.

'Let's have a barbecue,' he once suggested.

'We don't have a barbecue unit,' I answered.

'We can make one up can't we? There's plenty of bricks in the garden. Food cooked over a fire tastes so much better.'

'Well, they have disposable barbecue sets now, shall I get one from Andrews [the local hardware store]?'

'Yes. Can you please get me some cigarettes too.'

'Who do you want to invite?' ·

'No one. We don't have to invite anybody.' And he was right. Often, nothing pleased him more than an impromptu barbecue. With a DIY kit from the garden centre and the bricks we had, we did build a small barbecue unit in the patio area, sometimes cooking elaborately with fish wrapped in foil, steaks, skewered vegetables, and as much as we chose to eat, other times nothing more than hamburgers and sausages. Our outdoor table was a rectangular slab of marble permanently fixed to the base of an old-fashioned sewing machine. We had no shortage of fuel as there are two large aluminium storage bins filled with pieces of coal for the fireplace.

For major races, like the Grand National or the Derby, Peter would always place a bet. Then, instead of watching the race with me, he would say he could not bear to do so and disappear into the garden, asking me to call him in when it was over and he would watch the re-run. If I was already in the garden, I would be sent indoors with instructions to give him a shout when the race was over. At other times, when he made bets on a football or boxing match, or golf, he would be glued to the television screen, commenting or heckling throughout, regardless of whether there was company or not. He might be on his own in the living room on the first floor, with me downstairs and it would not be unusual for me to hear him swearing out loud or calling out triumphantly, his voice hoarse from the excessive yelling, encouraging whoever it was that he wanted to win.

Peter is the only person I have ever met who always bet on a football team or a boxer or a golfer that he did not support. The first time I noticed this was when we were watching the finals of a golf tournament together. He told me he had placed a bet on a golfer who was playing against Greg Norman. I had turned on him in disbelief and said, 'I thought you wanted Greg Norman to win!' 'I do,' he said. 'This way, if Greg loses, I won't be quite so upset, because I'll win a lot on the bet. Whereas, if he wins, that will make me happy and the money won't matter.' Where golf was concerned, he consistently rooted for Greg, although he had other favourites too. And, if the local betting shop ever wondered why Peter always backed an opposing team and never Tottenham Hotspurs – a team he was reputed to support – when major matches were being played, now they have the answer.

By the original pond near the house, there is a vast vase-shaped container made of stone; it is filled with lavender. In the raised garden beds by Peter's pond, there are more climbing roses, honeysuckle, poppies, rain daisies and a young weeping cherry. A buddleia that seeded itself was left to grow but often pruned. Just here, there is a battered garden bench nearly falling apart, where the summer before Peter died, we had sat and laughed whilst an old friend of his, Lewis, took pictures of us.

I had protested, 'I don't want my photograph taken. My hair is a mess.'

'Stop it! Just relax,' Peter said, encircling me in his arm. I was happy then and Lewis had a fleeting glimpse of our life together.

This was just one aspect of a private Peter Cook, my husband, calm, contented and happy in his home and especially his garden, whom no one, no journalist, no friend, no family member really knew. Only me, because I was his wife, loving him and having the privilege of sharing his life fully for twelve of the twenty-four years that he lived in his beloved home ... his castle with the enchanted garden.

Epilogue

The Man Who Invented the Wheel

*During the last few weeks I've been trying to think of something
absolutely original and devastating. I've been trying to lay my
hands on some idea that'll revolutionize the world in some way.
Something like fire, or the wheel. 'Course, it's no good thinking of
those two because they've already been invented, but something
along those lines. It's a very good thing to do, you know. I mean,
look at the man who thought of fire. He could have made an
absolute fortune. As soon as he thought of it he should have
patented it, and every time anybody lit a fire they'd have had to
pay him a royalty. But being a rather primitive person he didn't
think of that.*

*The same thing happened to the bloke who thought of the wheel.
Actually nobody really knows who was the first person to invent
the wheel. It's all shrouded in mystery. Apparently, in primeval
times, there were these two primitive people, who were both
working on inventions in their caves. They were called Drodbar
and Gorbly. Two extremely primitive people. Then one day
Drodbar came out with a great smile all over his hairy face, and
he said, 'Guess what – I've just invented the ban-dan-bladder-
stiddle. It's absolutely brilliant. Brilliant!'*

*And so Gorbly came out, and said, 'Hello, Drodbar – I hear
you've invented the ban-dan-bladder-stiddle – congratulations.
Er – what exactly is it?' And Drodbar said, 'It's a wonderful*

device, that will revolutionize the world. It's very simple. It's just a round thing that's easy to push along, that's all.'

And then Gorbly went white, and said in a strangled voice, 'It hasn't by any chance got spokes in it, has it?' 'Yes, it has as a matter of fact,' said Drodbar. 'How the devil did you know?' And Gorbly said, 'That's not a ban-dan-bladder-stiddle, you stupid idiot, that's a wheel, and I invented it first – how dare you steal my idea?' And a great fight broke out between them, and if the man who invented fire hadn't come along and threatened to set light to them both they might have killed each other.

Anyway, there was a great dispute, and all the hairy old Neanderthals met together at Stonehenge – a lovely place – to decide who really thought of it first. And eventually, after days and days of argument, they come to the conclusion that although it seemed likely that Drodbar thought of his ban-dan-bladder-stiddle before Gorbly thought of his wheel, nevertheless they were going to give the credit to Gorbly because he thought of a much better name for it.

I think they were right, actually, I mean think of going into a garage and asking them to put a bit more air into your ban-dan-bladder-stiddle. Still, you can't help feeling sorry for poor old Drodbar, you know. He went into a great depression and went round mumbling and moaning about his wretched old ban-dan-bladder-stiddle – eventually he was run down by the world's first pterodactyl-drawn chariot. A terrible end.

I know lots of people who've thought of things just a little bit too late. Poor old Spotty Muldoon – he thought of splitting the atom the other day. If only he could have had the idea about thirty years ago. He'd have made a bloody fortune.

Appendix

compiled by Roger Wilmut

Chronology of Peter Cook's work
Books
Videos
Records, Tapes & Compact Discs

Chronology

This Chronology of Peter Cook's work includes most of his performance appearances on stage, broadcasting or film. Interviews and appearances as a chat show guest are not included (although many of his interviews were as entertaining as a performance); these included Parkinson *(five times),* Clive Anderson, Jonathan Ross, Russell Harty *and* Fantasy Football League. *Appearances on panel shows are not listed; these included* Just A Minute *on Radio 4,* Have I Got News For You *on BBC2,* Tell the Truth *on ITV, and* Whose Line Is It Anyway? *on Channel 4.*

Abbreviation used throughout, PC = Peter Cook.

Dates given for radio and television are transmission dates (programmes were usually pre-recorded); some detailed date information is no longer available. Dates given for films are year of first release.

1937
Born 17.11.37, Torquay.

1954
At Radley College school, appeared in his House play as the Wicked Fairy (the part originally taken by the author) in *The Love of Four Colonels* (Ustinov); and in the Dramatic Society play as Dol Common in *The Alchemist* (Jonson).

1956
Still at school, appeared as Don Adriano in the Dramatic
Society production of *Love's Labour's Lost* (Shakespeare); his
school magazine said he was 'the very recipe of fantastic; a
measure of Malvolio, an atom of Aguecheek, and a pinch of
Polonius, the whole garnished with sprigs of Shallow, Jacques
and Quince. Here was a wonderful display of virtuosity' – an
assessment which was prescient given particularly his 1993
triumph in *Clive Anderson Talks Back*.

Also wrote a verse play for marionettes, *The Black and White
Blues*, and a one-act farce *He Who Laughs*.

1957
Entered Pembroke College, Cambridge University, reading
French and German.

1958
Cambridge Amateur Dramatic Society production of the
complete version of *A Resounding Tinkle* by N.F. Simpson.
Directed by John Bird. PC appeared as Bro Paradock.

1959
June: Cambridge Footlights revue *Last Laugh*, directed by
John Bird. Cast included PC, Timothy Birdsall, Adrian Slade,
John Bird, Eleanor Bron and Geoff Pattie. PC's sketches
included 'Guilty Party', 'Entitytainment', 'Friends and
Neighbours', and 'Mr Grole' (the duologue on a park bench
which later became known as 'Not an Asp'; his straight man
was Timothy Birdsall). Alistair Cooke wrote an enthusiastic
review in the *Manchester Guardian*, commenting 'If the West
End does not soon hear of John Bird, Patrick Gowers, Geoff
Pattie and Peter Cook, the West End is an ass.' The show
was subsequently produced in Oxford with a professional
cast by William Donaldson under the title *Here is the News*.

Wrote thirteen out of a total of thirty-two sketches for the
West End revue *Pieces of Eight*, at the Apollo Theatre from
23.9.59. Other sketches written by Harold Pinter, Sandy
Wilson, John Law and Lance Mulcahy. Directed by Paddy
Stone. PC sketches included 'Not an Asp' (performed by

Kenneth Williams and Peter Brett) and 'If Only' (performed by Kenneth Williams and Fenella Fielding).

1960
President of Cambridge University Footlights Club.

June: Cambridge Footlights revue *Pop Goes Mrs Jessup*. Directed by John Wood (John Fortune). Cast included PC, David Frost, Mike Burrell, Hugh Walters and Peter Bellwood. PC's sketches included 'Ducks' and 'Interesting Facts' (another sketch with PC as a park bench bore).

Beyond the Fringe opened at the Edinburgh Festival 22.8.60, written and performed by PC, Dudley Moore, Alan Bennett and Jonathan Miller; this version, which ran for over an hour, included many of the most famous sketches, but a number of items were subsequently cut. It made an immediate impression, sufficient for it to transfer to London the following year (see below). Sketches included 'Royal Box', 'So That's The Way You Like It' and 'The End of the World'.

1961
Wrote ten out of a total of thirty-one sketches for the West End revue *One Over the Eight*, at the Duke of York's Theatre from 5.4.61. Other contributors included John Mortimer, Lionel Bart, N.F. Simpson and John Bird. Directed by Paddy Stone. PC sketches included 'Interesting Facts' (performed by Kenneth Williams and John Howard) and 'Critic's Choice' (performed by Kenneth Williams and Lance Percival).

Beyond the Fringe ran for one week at Cambridge from 21.4.61 and a (badly received) week at Brighton from 1.5.61; then opened at the Fortune Theatre London on 10.5.61. Ran for over a year and then continued with a substitute cast until 24 September 1966 (transferring to the Mayfair Theatre in 1964). It was PC's barbed and pointed impersonation of the Prime Minister, Harold Macmillan, which more than anything else branded the show as 'satirical' (to the irritation of the cast). Other sketches included 'Sitting on the Bench' (the monologue about the miner who wanted to be a judge – there were many later versions of this, sometimes called 'Judge', 'Miner' or 'Down the Mine'), and 'Civil War'. It was an immediate smash hit, attracting rave reviews(particularly from Bernard Levin, who described the cast as 'great, good men') and became widely popular beyond the theatre audiences from the continuing availability of the record (see below in the records listing). Almost overnight it killed off 'old-fashioned revue' and opened the way for the explosion of satirical comedy throughout the 1960s.

October: opened the *Establishment Club* in Soho. Writer/ performers included John Bird, Eleanor Bron, John Fortune and Jeremy Geidt. Guest artists included Lenny Bruce and Frankie Howerd. Produced by PC and Nick Luard.

1962
Bought controlling interest in the satirical magazine *Private Eye*.

Beyond the Fringe opened at the John Golden Theatre, New York, on 27.10.62, running for about a year.

The show from the *Establishment Club* performed in Chicago in October, then in Washington in December and from 23.1.63 at the Stroller's Theatre Club in New York, also playing Toronto, Ottawa and San Francisco. PC contributed material and acted as producer (with John Krimsky) but did not appear.

PC and John Krimsky produced *The Muffled Report* at the Stroller's Theatre Club, New York.

1963
PC and John Bird appeared in and wrote for the would-be satirical show *What's Going On Here?* for NBC in New York, 10.5.63; directed by Jonathan Miller, producer Ed Sullivan. Cancelled after two editions because of incompatibilities.

1964
Beyond the Fringe returned to New York in a revised version, with Paxton Whitehead replacing Jonathan Miller. New sketches included 'The Great Train Robbery', 'One Leg Too Few' and Dudley Moore's 'The Weill Song' for which PC wrote the words.

Set up the Establishment Theatre Company in New York with Ivor David Balding and Joseph E. Levine to present plays off-Broadway; plays included *The Knack* (Ann Jellicoe) and *The Ginger Man* (J.P. Donleavy). Produced *Square in the Eye* (Jack Gelber) at the Theatre de Lys, New York.

Television version of *Beyond the Fringe* broadcast on BBC2 on 12.12.64 (66 minutes).

Appeared performing E.L. Wisty monologues in the autumn season of Bernard Braden's comedy/consumer series for ITV, *On The Braden Beat* – his first appearance to a mass audience. Monologues included 'World Domination League', 'Royalty', 'The Tadpole Expert', 'Are You Spotty', 'C.P. Snow', 'Peace Through Nudism', 'O'er Hill and Dale', 'A Bee Life', 'The Man who Invented the Wheel', 'The Plib', 'Food for Thought', 'Spindly Legs', 'Man's Best Friend' and 'The E.L. Wisty Festival of the Arts'. (All these were issued on a record and more recently a cassette, see listing below.)

1965
First TV series of *Not Only ... But Also*, seven 45-minute programmes fortnightly from 9.1.65 on BBC2. Produced by Joe McGrath, written and performed by PC and Dudley Moore – their first real pairing and the first appearance of the Pete and Dud characters. (Additional writing by Joe McGrath, Robert Fuest and Jonathan Abbott.) The shows also included performance items by various guests, musical guests and the Dudley Moore Trio. Sketches included 'The Ravens' (which introduced another regular PC character, Sir Arthur Streeb-Greebling), 'Painting on Television', 'The Guide to the North Circular Road', the leaping nuns, and the Pete and Dud sketches 'Sex Fantasies', 'Art Gallery', and 'The Worst Thing in the World', plus a filmed interpretation of the Edward Lear poem 'Incidents in the Life of my Uncle Arly'. Moore wrote an opening theme tune, and their closing theme song 'Goodbye' (aka 'Goodbye-ee'), used throughout, rapidly became popular and remained their signature tune in later years. Guests included John Lennon (in a film illustration to one of his poems), Barry Humphries, Peter Sellers, Anna Quayle and Eric Sykes. Various sketches from this and the two subsequent series made their way onto records, cassettes, and a video (see below).

Appeared in gala show *Artists Against Apartheid* at the Prince of Wales Theatre, London 22.3.65.

PC and Dudley Moore's single 'Goodbye-ee' entered the top 50 in July, staying there for 10 weeks and reaching no.18; PC's single 'The Ballad of Spotty Muldoon' also entered the top 50 in July, staying for five weeks and reaching No.34.

Appeared with Dudley Moore in the teenage pop programme *Ready Steady Go*, performing 'Goodbye-ee', broadcast in July on ITV.

Appeared with Dudley Moore in TV variety show *The New London Palladium Show*, broadcast live on ITV 26.9.65.

Appeared with Dudley Moore at the Royal Variety Performance at the London Palladium, 8.11.65 (broadcast on ITV 14.11.65).

Produced *The Mad Show* at the New Theatre, New York.

1966
Not Only . . . But Also – second series, seven half-hour programmes weekly from 15.1.66 on BBC2 plus a 52-minute special 26.12.66. Produced by Dick Clement. Written by and starring PC and Dudley Moore. Sketches included 'Frog and Peach' (with PC as Sir Arthur Streeb-Greebling), 'Bo Duddley', the *Thunderbirds* spoof, the blue movie ('and your bra and panties'); and Pete and Dud discussing music, sex and sickness, and visiting heaven and the zoo. Guests included Cilla Black, Dionne Warwick, Dusty Springfield and Marian Montgomery; John Lennon appeared in the Christmas Special.

PC and Dudley Moore performed 'Goodbye-ee' in the pop magazine programme *Now!* compered by Michael Palin, ITV South Wales and West Country only, 20.4.66.

Appeared in Jonathan Miller's de-Tennielised production of *Alice in Wonderland*, broadcast on 28.12.66 on BBC2. Cast included PC as the Mad Hatter, Alan Bennett as the Mouse, John Bird as the Frog Footman, Peter Sellers as the King of Hearts, and Anne-Marie Mallik as Alice. Music by Ravi Shankar.

Film: *The Wrong Box*, directed by Bryan Forbes, screenplay by

Larry Gelbart and Burt Shevelove based on the novel by
Robert Louis Stevenson and Lloyd Osborne. Cast included
Ralph Richardson, John Mills, Michael Caine, PC (as Morris),
Dudley Moore (as John), Nanette Newman, Peter Sellers,
Tony Hancock and Wilfrid Lawson. Complicated farce
involving conflicts over the proceeds of a lottery; PC and
Dudley Moore survived the tricksy production well enough
for their performances to impress Stanley Donen and lead to
him directing *Bedazzled*.

Produced *Monopoly* at Stage 73, New York; *Serjeant
Musgrave's Dance* (John Arden) at the Theatre de Lys, New
York; produced, with Rita Fredericks and Paul Stoudt, *The
Kitchen* (Arnold Wesker) at the 81st Street Theatre, New York;
and, with Fredericks, *A Hand is on the Gate* at the Longacre
Theatre, New York.

1967
Film: *Bedazzled*. Directed by Stanley Donen. Script by PC,
based on an idea by PC and Dudley Moore. Starring PC,
Dudley Moore, Eleanor Bron, Michael Bates, Raquel Welch
and Barry Humphries. 1960s reworking of the Faust Legend
with PC as the Devil (aka George Spiggott) and Dudley
Moore as Stanley Moon. Spiggott offers Stanley seven wishes
in exchange for his soul – these include Stanley being a
tycoon, a pop star and an intellectual, all in the hope of
attaining the love of his life (Bron); however Spiggott
manages to spoil every wish. Included a re-working of the
leaping nuns from *Not Only . . . But Also*.

1968
Series for ITV, *Goodbye Again* written by and starring PC and
Dudley Moore. Produced by Shaun O'Riordan: 18.8.68,
24.8.68, 14.9.68. Sketches included Dud and Pete in a doctor's
waiting room and in jail, and 'Sherlock Holmes – the Case of
the One-Legged Dog'. Guests included Warren Mitchell and
Donovan.

Film: *A Dandy in Aspic*. Directed by Anthony Mann (who
died during filming) and Laurence Harvey. Screenplay by
Derek Marlowe, based on his own novel. Starring Laurence
Harvey, Tom Courtenay, Per Oscarsson, Mia Farrow, Harry

Andrews and Lionel Stander. Cast also included PC (as Prentiss) and John Bird. Convoluted spy thriller; PC and Bird appear in straight roles.

1969

Film: *Monte Carlo or Bust* (aka *Those Daring Young Men in their Jaunty Jalopies*, aka *Que Temerari sulle loro Pazze, Scatenate, Scalcinate Carriole*); Italian–French co-production directed by Ken Annakin. Screenplay by Jack Davies and Ken Annakin. Starring Bourvil, Lando Buzzancana, Walter Chiari, Tony Curtis, Gert Fröbe, PC (as Major Dawlish), Dudley Moore (as Lt. Barrington), Jack Hawkins. Noisy and spectacular comedy about vintage motor-rallying: a follow-up to *Those Magnificent Men in their Flying Machines*.

Film: *The Bed-Sitting Room*. Directed by Richard Lester. Screenplay by John Antrobus, based on the play by himself and Spike Milligan. Starring Ralph Richardson, Rita Tushingham, Michael Hordern, Arthur Lowe and Mona Washbourne. PC and Dudley Moore appear as Police Inspector and Sergeant. Imaginative but uneasy version of the surreal stage play depicting post-nuclear-holocaust Britain. PC spends most of his role precariously suspended from a balloon instructing everyone to 'Keep moving'.

1970

Not Only . . . But Also – third series, seven 45-minute shows fortnightly from 18.2.70 on BBC2 (in colour). Produced by James Gilbert, written by and starring PC and Dudley Moore. Sketches included 'Emma Bargo' (the Greta Garbo spoof), 'The Ludwig Van Beethoven Show', 'The Making of a Movie', and 'The Glidd of Glood'; while Pete and Dud discussed racial prejudice, the futility of life and writing, and re-enacted Dud's birth with a wardrobe replacing his mother. There was also an improvised 'Poets Cornered' series with guests, who included Spike Milligan, Barry Humphries, Frank Muir and Ronnie Barker.

Film: *The Rise and Rise of Michael Rimmer*. Directed by Kevin Billington. Screenplay by PC, John Cleese, Graham Chapman, Kevin Billington. Starring PC as Michael Rimmer, Denholm Elliott, Ronald Fraser, and including John Cleese, Graham

Chapman and Dennis Price. Satirical story of a business efficiency expert (PC) who uses opinion polls to rise into the British Government and eventually, after submitting every question to a referendum, becomes President. PC appeared somewhat detached from the proceedings.

1971
Where Do I Sit? – disastrous chat show with PC as host, started 19.2.71 on BBC2 (thirty minutes) and cancelled after three editions.

Not Only ... But Also – two half-hour special editions for the Australian Broadcasting Commission, subsequently broadcast in Britain on BBC1 under the title *Pete and Dud Down Under*, 18 and 25 June 1971. Sketches included Pete and Dud meeting Australian cricketers, 'The Funnel-Web Spider' (Streeb-Greebling), 'Shirts', plus 'Bollards; and 'One Leg Too Few' from *Beyond the Fringe*. With Barry Humphries.

Appeared (as Elmwood) with Dudley Moore and Spike Milligan in *An Apple A Day*, a surreal comedy by John Antrobus, broadcast 9.7.71 on BBC1.

1972
Stage show in Australia, *Behind the Fridge* with PC and Dudley Moore. Then ran to packed houses in London from 21.11.72 to 25.8.73 at the Cambridge Theatre. London version and a couple of film inserts directed by Joe McGrath. Sketches included 'Hello', 'Come in', 'So Much Tolouse', 'Gospel Truth', 'On Location', 'Mini Drama' (these last two in a rather blacker tone than PC's previous work), and 'Tea for Two' in which Pete and Dud discussed women's rights.

Film: *The Adventures of Barry Mackenzie* (Australia), directed by Bruce Beresford. Screenplay by Barry Humphries and Bruce Beresford based on the comic strip by Humphries and Nicholas Garland. Starring Barry Crocker and Barry Humphries, with PC (as Dominic), Spike Milligan and Dennis Price. Raucous adventures of an Australian innocent in pommie-land. PC appears as a BBC producer whose invitation to Barry to appear on television leads to a remarkable on-air exposure and the burning down of Television Centre.

1973

Behind the Fridge ran in America under the title *Good Evening*, in Boston from 12.10.73, in New York at the Plymouth Theatre from 29.10.73 to 30.11.74, then on tour from February to August 1975. New material included 'Soap Opera' and revivals of 'Frog and Peach', 'One Leg Too Few' and 'Sitting on the Bench' (under the title 'Down the Mine') in an expanded version detailing the adventures of some nude ladies.

1974

Television version of *Behind the Fridge* transmitted on BBC2 7.3.74 (forty-five minutes).

1976

Appeared in the Amnesty gala show *A Poke in the Eye With a Sharp Stick* at Her Majesty's Theatre, London, 1, 2 and 3 April. PC appeared in the Monty Python trial scene, performed 'Not an Asp' with John Fortune, and did his 'Sitting on the Bench' monologue in the expanded version from *Good Evening* ... Film record of the show and the backstage events released as *Pleasure at Her Majesty's* the following year, directed by Roger Graef.

Appeared with Dudley Moore on the American TV variety show *Saturday Night Live*, 24.1.76.

Film: *Find the Lady*. Canadian-English co-production (video only in UK) (aka *Call the Cops!*, and *Kopek and Broom*, on American video). Directed by John Trent, screenplay by David Main and John Trent. Starring Lawrence Dane and John Candy, with Mickey Rooney, PC (as J.C. Lewenhak) and Dick Emery. Knockabout comedy with Dane and Candy as two inept cops trying to trace PC's kidnapped socialite niece; PC is wasted in a straight role.

1977

Wrote a weekly column in the *Daily Mail* newspaper, 'Peter Cook's Monday Morning Feeling', from 31.1.77 to 14.11.77.

Appeared in the Amnesty Gala *The Mermaid Frolics* at the Mermaid Theatre, London, 8.5.77, performing 'E.L. Wisty from Beyond the Veil' and 'Sitting on the Bench'.

In June, appeared in a sketch with Dudley Moore on US television in ABC News Report special on the Queen's Jubilee.

Film: *The Hound of the Baskervilles*, directed by Paul Morrissey. Screenplay by PC, Dudley Moore and Paul Morrissey, loosely based on the novel by Conan Doyle. Starring PC (as Sherlock Holmes), Dudley Moore (as Dr Watson, Ada Holmes, and Mr Spiggott), with Denholm Elliott, Joan Greenwood, Terry-Thomas, Max Wall, Kenneth Williams, Hugh Griffith, Irene Handl, Roy Kinnear, Penelope Keith, Spike Milligan and Jessie Matthews. Described by PC as 'a mess', largely due to Morrissey's incompatibility with what was more or less the *Carry On* style. Includes yet another re-working of the 'One Leg Too Few' sketch.

1978
Presented ITV pop series *Revolver*, 22.7.78 for 7 weeks. PC appeared as the manager of a dance hall who hated the music and the audience. With Chris Hill, Les Ross and a wide variety of bands. Directed by Chris Tookey, produced by Mickie Most.

Appeared in BBC Radio 2's pantomime *Black Cinderella Two Goes East*, with Richard Baker, Tim Brooke-Taylor, Rob Buckman, John Cleese, Graeme Garden, David Hatch, Jo Kendall, Bill Oddie and Richard Murdoch; script by Rory McGrath and Clive Anderson. Produced by Douglas Adams. One hour; 25.12.78.

1979
From about now until 1992 PC made various guest appearances in Radio 4's *The News Quiz*.

Appeared in the election day comedy show *Why Vote? It Only Encourages Them* on BBC Radio 4, 3.5.79, with Roy Hudd, David Jason, Alan Coren and Richard Ingrams. Broadcast in two parts, the second after the polls had closed (thus permitting political comment).

Appeared in the Amnesty Gala *The Secret Policeman's Ball* June 27–30th, doing his sketch 'Interesting Facts' with John

Cleese, in a sketch 'Balloon' with Eleanor Bron, with the entire cast of the gala in 'The End of the World', and in a new monologue 'Entirely a Matter for You' (on the Jeremy Thorpe Trial). Film record of the show released under the same title.

Appeared in two episodes of Granada's after-dinner-speeches series *M'Lords, Ladies and Gentlemen*, ITV 21.7.79 and one other date.

Appeared in *Friday Night ... Saturday Morning* – 'A Way of Ending the Week with the Cambridge Footlights'. Produced by Iain Johnstone. Cast included Martin Berman, Emma Thompson, Hugh Laurie, with PC as guest. 16.11.79 BBC2.

1980
Appeared in an edition of Spike Milligan's series *Q9*, BBC2 8.7.80. Written by Milligan and Neil Shand, also appearing: John Bluthal, Bob Todd and David Lodge.

Appeared in *Peter Cook and Co.* with Rowan Atkinson, John Cleese, Terry Jones, Beryl Reid. Written by PC. Directed and produced by Paul Smith, executive producer Humphrey Barclay. Broadcast ITV 14.9.80 (sixty minutes).

1981
Appeared in US TV situation comedy series *The Two of Us*. Produced by Charlie Hauk, who co-wrote with Arthur Julian; starring PC (as Robert Brentwood) and Mimi Kennedy. Based on LWT's 1976 series *Two's Company*, with PC as a very English butler to a very American lady. Twenty-five-minute shows, 6.4.81 for four weeks and 14.9.81 for twenty-four weeks. Ran (erratically) from 16.10.83 on ITV. (No connection with a later ITV series of the same title, starring Nicholas Lyndhurst.)

Appeared as one of *An Audience with Dudley Moore*, a show in the occasional series in which famous people entertain other famous people. Directed by Ken O'Neill. ITV 26.12.81.

1983
Appeared in the fund-raising one-night show mounted by Adrian Slade, *An Evening at Court* at the Theatre Royal

Drury Lane, 23.1.83; with John Cleese, Tim Brooke-Taylor, Graham Garden, Bill Oddie, Rowan Atkinson, David Frost, Eleanor Bron, Julian Slade, and French and Saunders. Directed by Humphrey Barclay. PC performed his sketch 'Inalienable Rights' with Cleese.

Film: *Yellowbeard* (USA), directed by Max Damski. Screenplay by Graham Chapman, PC, Bernard McKenna. Starring Graham Chapman, Peter Boyle, Richard 'Cheech' Martin, Tommy Chong, PC (as Lord Lambourn), Marty Feldman, Martin Hewitt, Michael Hordern, Eric Idle, Madeline Kahn, James Mason, Susannah York, John Cleese, Stacey Nelkin, Nigel Planer and Beryl Reid. Spoof swashbuckler, a sort of Monty-Python-meets-Mel-Brooks-on-the-high-seas.

Appeared in first episode of Rowan Atkinson's TV series *Blackadder* (15.6.83 BBC1) as Richard III. Written by Rowan Atkinson and Richard Curtis.

1984
Film: *Supergirl*, directed by Jeannot Szwarc. Screenplay by David Odell. Starring Faye Dunaway, Helen Slater, Peter O'Toole. PC appears in the unlikely guise of Supergirl's maths teacher in a twee DC Comics spin-off.

1985
Appeared as E.L. Wisty in *Twenty Years On* with David Frost, a reworking of *The Frost Report* format; five weekly shows on ITV from 27.7.85.

Appeared in an episode of the comedy series *Who Dares Wins*, starring Julia Hills, Rory McGrath, Jimmy Mulville, Phil Pope and Tony Robinson. Script by Colin Bostock-Smith, Andy Hamilton, Guy Jenkin, Rory McGrath, Jimmy Mulville and Tony Sarchet. Directed by John Stroud. PC appeared in a book-plugging 'interview' with Rory McGrath. November/December 1985 on Channel 4.

Appeared in *Kenny Everett's Christmas Carol*, with Kenny Everett, Michael Barrymore, PC, Spike Milligan, Willie Rushton and John Wells. Written by Barry Cryer and Neil Shand, produced and directed by John Bishop. BBC1 24.12.85 (thirty minutes).

1986

Assisted Joan Rivers as chat show co-host in *Joan Rivers – Can We Talk?* on BBC1, 10.3.86 for six weeks. In the event PC contributed very little to the proceedings.

Appeared as E.L. Wisty in a second series of *Twenty Years On*, ITV 19.7.86 for four weeks.

Film: *Whoops Apocalypse!*, directed by Tom Bussmann. Screenplay by Andrew Marshall and David Renwick based on their TV series. Starring Loretta Swit, PC (as Sir Mortimer Chris), Michael Richards, Rik Mayall, Ian Richardson, Alexei Sayle and Herbert Lom. Satirical nuclear holocaust with PC as the British Prime Minister involved in escalating international tension where everyone involved is incompetent or venal.

Hosted and performed in one episode of Channel 4 variety show *Saturday Live*, 22.3.86; also appearing: John Fortune, John Wells, John Bird. PC impersonated President Marcos and Lord Stockton (Harold Macmillan), appeared with John Fortune in a new park bench sketch, and, in a sketch with John Bird, as Kubla Khan's jobbing builder on the stately pleasure dome.

1987

PC was guest of honour at the first Melbourne Festival of Comedy, which ran for three weeks from April 1st.

PC and Dudley Moore performed 'One Leg Too Few' in the live TV special *Comic Relief '87* on the American 'Home Box Office' channel.

Film: *Mr Jolly Lives Next Door* – a 'Comic Strip' film given a limited cinema release before transmission on Channel 4 on 5.3.88. Directed by Stephen Frears, screenplay by Adrian Edmondson, Rik Mayall and Roland Rivron. Starring Mayall, Edmondson, PC (as Mr Jolly) and Peter Richardson, with Nicholas Parsons, Dawn French and Jennifer Saunders. PC appears as a mad axe-murderer who seems almost gentle by comparison with the manic performances of the Comic Strip regulars.

249

Film: *The Princess Bride* (USA), directed by Rob Reiner. Screenplay by William Goldman, based on his novel. Starring Cary Elwes, Mandy Patinkin, Chris Sarandon and Robin Wright, with PC, Billy Crystal, Wallace Shawm and Andre the Giant. Witty, charming and affectionate sword-and-sorcery spoof with the hero overcoming all odds including death itself to rescue his princess. PC appears as a more-than-usually eccentric bishop.

1988

Film: *Without a Clue* (USA), directed by Thom Eberhardt. Screenplay by Gary Murphy and Lawrence Strawther. Starring Michael Caine, Ben Kingsley, Jeffrey Jones, Lysette Anthony, Paul Freeman & PC (as Greenhough). Kingsley is Dr Watson, a brilliant detective who hides behind the fake Sherlock Holmes character he manipulates (Caine). PC appears as the editor of the *Strand* magazine.

About this time PC made periodic anonymous appearances as 'Sven' on the phone-in show *The Clive Bull Through the Night Show* on LBC Radio (initially unknown to the show's presenter or producer).

1989

Film: *Getting It Right* (USA) directed by Randal Kleiser. Screenplay by Elizabeth Jane Howard, based on her own novel. Starring Jesse Birdsall, Helena Bonham Carter, PC (as Mr Adrian), John Gielgud, Jane Horrocks, Shirley Anne Field and Lynn Redgrave. Uneven but entertaining romance about a thirty-one-year-old virgin and his difficulties with women. PC appears as a villainous salon owner.

Film: *Great Balls of Fire!* (USA), directed by Jim McBride. Screenplay by Jack Baran and Jim McBride. Starring Dennis Quaid, Winona Ryder, Alec Baldwin & Steve Allen, with PC as an English reporter. Stylized biography of Jerry Lee Lewis.

Appeared in the Amnesty gala show *The Secret Policeman's Biggest Ball* August 30–Sept 2 (subsequently shown on ITV on 28.10.89). Performed 'One Leg Too Few' and 'Frog and Peach' with Dudley Moore.

1990

Appeared as Sir Arthur Streeb-Greebling in *A Life in Pieces*, a series of twelve five-minute interviews with Ludovic Kennedy based on the gifts listed in the song 'The Twelve Days of Christmas'. Daily from 26.12.90 on BBC2.

1991

Appeared in *The Craig Ferguson Story*; Scottish stand-up comic Craig Ferguson being given advice on his act during a tour of Scotland. With PC (as Ferguson's father), Gerald Harper, Frankie Howerd and June Whitfield; producer Charles Brand. Channel 4 12.9.91.

Provided the voice for the cartoon hero of *It's Roger Mellie – The Man on the Telly*, based on the character from *Viz* comic. Other voices by Harry Enfield; directed and produced by Tony Barnes. Five short cartoons daily on Channel 4 from 30.12.91. (Also issued as a video.)

1992

Appeared in the ITV series *Gone to Seed*, a comedy drama about a family-run garden centre in London's Docklands written by Tony Grounds. Directed by Sandy Johnson and Nick Laughland, produced by Tim Whitby. Starring Alison Steadman, Jim Broadbent, Sheila Hancock and Warren Clarke, with PC as con-man Wesley Willis. 13.11.92 for six weeks.

1993

Appeared as compère and as 'Robert Maxwell' in *Bore of the Year Awards* with Angus Deayton, Ian Hislop, Michael Palin, Harry Enfield and Richard Ingrams. Directed by Janet Fraser Cook, produced by Ian Hislop and Harry Thompson. BBC2 20.3.93, 1 hour.

Appeared in *Arena* – 'Radio Night' with David Attenborough, Professor Asa Briggs, Alistair Cooke and Spike Milligan, broadcast 18.12.93 on BBC2 and Radio 4 simultaneously. PC impersonated 'Radio'.

Appeared in *One Foot in the Algarve*, a ninety-five-minute Christmas special featuring the characters from *One Foot in the Grave*. Starring Richard Wilson and Annette Crosby; written by David Renwick, produced and directed by Susan Belbin. PC appears as accident-prone freelance photographer Martin Trout, who trails Victor Meldrew during a disastrous Portuguese holiday thinking he has a valuable roll of film. Broadcast 26.12.93 on BBC1.

Appeared being interviewed as four different characters in *Clive Anderson Talks Back*, 17.12.93 on Channel 4: as Norman House (a biscuit quality controller who has been abducted by aliens), Alan Latchley (a football manager), Eric Daley (a rock megastar), and Sir James Beecham (a judge who has shot a defendant). This turned out to be PC's last major performance – an improvised comic tour de force.

1994
Film: *Black Beauty* (USA/UK) directed by Caroline Thompson. Screenplay by Caroline Thompson, based on the novel by Anna Sewell. Starring Sean Bean, David Thewlis, Jim Carter, Peter Davison, Eleanor Bron, PC (as Lord Wexmire), the voice of Alan Cumming and several horses. Faithful and effective version of the Anna Sewell classic about the life of a horse; PC plays a haughty aristocrat.

1995
Died 9.1.95

A memorial service was held on 1.5.95 at the Parish Church of St. John-at-Hampstead, conducted by the Reverend Philip Buckler, The Vicar of Hampstead. Readings and tributes by Auberon Waugh, Alan Bennett, John Cleese and Eleanor Bron, with an address by Dr Sidney Gottlieb; music: 'Love Me Tender' sung by the Radley Clerkes, a piano solo by Dudley Moore, 'Fear No More the Heat o' the Sun' (Finzi, Shakespeare) and hymns 'To Be A Pilgrim' and 'The Lord of the Dance'. Finally a recording of PC as E.L. Wisty performing 'O'er Hill and Dale' was played, and Dudley Moore and the Radley Clerkes sang 'Goodbye'.

Books

Beyond the Fringe
Script published 1963 by Souvenir Press and subsequently by Samuel French Inc. in USA (including items from *Beyond the Fringe '64*); and in 1987 under the title *The Complete Beyond the Fringe* by Methuen London Ltd (reissued in 1993 by Mandarin Paperbacks); this included a revised and corrected text of the London production plus items from the earlier and American versions, and postscripts by Bennett, Moore and PC.

Bedazzled
Novelization by Michael J. Bird of the film script by PC and Dudley Moore. Published 1968 by Sphere Books.

Dud and Pete – The Dagenham Dialogues
Twelve Dud and Pete sketches published 1971 by Methuen, reissued by Methuen in paperback 1988 and by Mandarin Paperbacks in 1991 and 1995.

Good Evening
Script (of the American version of *Behind the Fridge*) published 1977 by Samuel French, New York.

Videos

The Best of What's Left of Not Only ... But Also
Sketches from the three BBC Television series, including some colour items. p. 1990

Derek and Clive Get the Horn
Derek and Clive material filmed in 1978. p. 1993.

Peter Cook Talks Golf Balls
PC, in four characterizations, talks about golf and other things. p. 1994.

Roger Mellie – The Man on the Telly
The five cartoons broadcast on Channel 4 in December 1991 for which PC provided the hero's voice.

Many of the films mentioned in the Chronology have been released on video.

Records, Tapes and Compact Discs

(Note that all the LPs, EPs and singles and some of the tapes are long since deleted.)

Pieces of Eight (stage show)
LP Decca LK 4337 (mono) SKL 4084 (stereo) p. 1959
Includes 5 sketches written by PC (who does not appear).

One Over the Eight (stage show)
LP Decca LK 4393 (mono) SKL 4133 (stereo) p. 1961
Includes 6 sketches written by PC (who does not appear).

Two extracts from *One Over the Eight* issued on single Decca 45F 11342 (mono).

Four extracts from both above shows issued on EP Decca DFE 8548 (mono).

Beyond the Fringe – extracts, recorded at the Fortune Theatre, London, July 1961; with PC, Bennett, Miller, Moore.
Mono LP Parlophone PMC 1145; reissued 1976 on EMI One-Up OUM 2151. (see also end of this section).

Beyond the Fringe – original Broadway cast (cast as above) – extracts.
USA & UK mono LP Capitol W1792 p. 1963; USA stereo LP Capitol SW 1792; UK stereo LP Capitol ST 11654. Reissued on USA compact disc Capitol C21Y-92055 p. 1989, cassette Capitol C41E-92055. Some items on EMI CD set 7243 8 540452

Two excerpts from above on single Parlophone 45-R 4969 p. 1963.

Two excerpts plus two Dudley Moore Trio items on EP Parlophone GEP 8940 p. 1965.

Beyond the Fringe '64 – original Broadway cast (Miller replaced by Paxton Whitehead). Excerpts.
USA LP Capitol W 2072 (mono) SW 2072 (stereo) p. 1964. Reissued 1996 on EMI CD set 7243 8 540452

Original *Beyond the Fringe* LP and excerpts from the two American LPs reissued 1990 on cassette EMI ECC1 and 1992 on compact disc EMI CDECC1.

Bridge on the River Wye (original record)
Spike Milligan, Peter Sellers, Jonathan Miller, PC. Script by
Milligan.
LP Parlophone PMC 1190 (mono) PCS 3036 (stereo) p. 1962.
Reissued 1992 on cassette EMI ECC 25.

The Establishment (theatre club show)
Items recorded live; PC does not contribute.
Mono LP Parlophone PMC 1198 p. 1963.

Peter Cook Presents the Establishment
Items recorded live in U.S.A.; PC wrote some items but is
not present.
USA mono LP Riverside RM 850 p. 1963.

Both Establishment LPs reissued on cassette EMI ECC 26 p.
1992.

The Misty Mr Wisty – monologues from the soundtracks of
on the Braden Beat.
Mono LP Decca LK 4722 p. 1965. Reissued as part of double
cassette Speaking Volumes 522 101 4 p. 1994.

Not Only Peter Cook ... But Also Dudley Moore
Six sketches from the soundtracks of *Not Only ... But Also*
Mono LP Decca LK 4703 p. 1965.

'Religions' from above LP included on LP *40 Years of
Television Comedy Spectacular*, BBC REB 249, cassette RMC
4048.

'By Appointment' recorded at the Royal Variety Performance
14.11.65, with Dudley Moore.
Mono E.P. Decca DFE 8644.

Goodbye-ee/Not Only ... But Also (with Dudley Moore)
Single Decca F 12158 p. 1965.

'Goodbye-ee' also included in LP *40 Years of Television – The
Comedians Sing*
BBC REB 251, cassette RMC 4050.

The Ballad of Spotty Muldoon/Lovely Lady of the Roses
Single Decca F 12182 p. 1965.

Isn't She A Sweetie/Bo Duddley (with Moore)
Single Decca F 12380 p. 1966.

Once Moore with Cook
Eight sketches from the soundtracks of *Not Only ... But Also*
(with Moore)
Mono LP Decca LK 4785 p. 1966.

'Father and Son' from above LP included in *The World of
British Comedy*
Mono LP Decca PA 39 p. 1969, cassette Decca KCPA 39; and
on *Fun at One*, stereo LP BBC REB 371, cassette ZCF 371.

'The Music Teacher' from above LP included in *More Fun at
One*, stereo LP BBC REB 399, cassette ZCF 399.

The L.S. Bumble Bee/The Bee Side
Single Decca F 12551 p. 1967.

Bedazzled – film soundtrack music by Dudley Moore (with
vocals by PC and Moore)
Mono LP Decca LK 4923, stereo LP Decca SKL 4923 p. 1967.

Bedazzled/Love Me (from above LP)
Single Decca F 12710.

Goodbye Again
Sketches from the 1968 ITV series (with Moore)
Mono LP Decca LK 4981 p. 1969.

Not Only ... But Also
Six sketches from the soundtracks of the TV series (with
Moore)
Mono LP Decca LK 5080 p. 1971.

The World of Pete and Dud
Compilation from LK 4703, 4785, and 5080 (with Moore)
Mono LP Decca PA 311 p. 1974; reissued cassette Laughing
Stock LAFFC 32 p. 1991.

Behind the Fridge – excerpts from the stage show (with
Moore)
LP Atlantic K40503 p. 1973.

Good Evening
Sketches from the American stage version of *Behind the
Fridge* (with Moore)

USA stereo LP Island 9298 p. 1974; reissued on USA LP Antilles AN 7047; reissued in 1994 as part of double cassette on Speaking Volumes 522 101 4.

The Clean Tapes – The Very Best of Peter Cook and Dudley Moore
Sketches from *Not Only . . . But Also* plus studio item.
Stereo LP Pye Cube HIFLY 26 p. 1978; reissued on cassette Castle Classics CLAMC 295 p. 1992.

Derek and Clive – Live
Thirteen duologues (with Moore)
Mono LP Island ILPS 9434 p. 1976; cassette Island ZCI 9434; 8-track cartridge Island Y81 9434; cassette Island KM 202.

Derek and Clive Come Again
Seventeen duologues (with Moore); stereo LP Virgin V2094 p. 1977; cassette Virgin TCV 2094; stereo LP Virgin OVED 110; cassette Virgin OVEDC 110; cassette Virgin VCCMC005 p. 1994; compact disc Virgin VCCCD 005 p. 1994 (containing four extra tracks).

Derek and Clive Ad Nauseam
Fifteen duologues (with Moore); stereo LP Virgin V 2112 p. 1979; cassette Virgin TCV 2112; stereo LP Virgin OVED 162; cassette OVEDC 162; cassette Virgin VCCMC 011 p. 1994; compact disc Virgin VCCCD 011 p. 1994 (containing six extra tracks).

Amnesty 1976 show *A Poke in the Eye with a Sharp Stick*
Includes PC performing 'Asp' and 'So That's The Way You Like It'
Stereo LP Transatlantic TRA 331.

Amnesty 1977 show *The Mermaid Frolics*
Includes PC performing 'E.L. Wisty Beyond the Veil' and 'Miner'.
Stereo LP Polydor 2384.101, cassette 3192.450

Amnesty 1979 show *The Secret Policeman's Ball*
Includes PC performing 'Entirely a Matter for You', 'Balloon' and 'The End of the World'
Stereo LP Island ILPS 9601; cassette Island ZC 19601; cassette Laughing Stock LAFFC 9 p. 1992.

Here Comes the Judge – Peter Cook in Concert
Includes 'Entirely a Matter for You' from the above LP plus
two studio items.
Stereo LP Virgin VR4 p. 1979

Amnesty 1989 show *The Secret Policeman's Biggest Ball*
Includes PC and Dudley Moore sketches.
Stereo LP Springtime HAHA 6003.

Private Eye records:
Including, variously, PC, Dudley Moore, William Rushton,
Barry Humphries, Richard Ingrams, Christopher Booker, John
Wells

7" mono 'flexi-disc' single-sided singles issued with *Private
Eye* on dates given:
His Master's Vass p. 2.10.64
I Saw Daddy Kissing Santa Claus p. 18.12.64
Lord Gnome Presents Private Eye's Rites of Spring p. 1.4.65
The BBC Gnome Service p. 23.12.66
The Abominable Radio Gnome p. 8.12.67
The Loneliness of the Long-Playing Record p. 14.2.69
Dear Sir, Is This a Record? p. 5.12.69
Hullo Sailor p. 14.12.69
Just for the Record p. 14.12.70
Farginson p. 21.3.75
The Sound of Talbot p. 5.12.80
Record Damages p. 11.12.87

Private Eye commercially issued records:

Private Eye Sings Private Eye
Single Artists and Repertoire ARP 1212 p. 1962/3

The Neasden Single/The Trouts
Single Spark Records SRL 1059

Private Eye's Blue Record
LP Transatlantic TRA 131 p. 1964.

All but last four flexi-discs included on LP *Private Eye's
Golden Years of Sound* LYN2745/6 p. 1973.

All but the last two flexi-discs included on *Private Eye's
Golden Satiricals* LP Springtime HAHA 6002 p. 1981.

In 1994, a double cassette titled *An Evening with Peter Cook and Dudley Moore and E.L. Wisty* (taken from *The Misty Mr Wisty* and *Good Evening*) was issued on Funny Business/ Speaking Volumes 522 101 4.

After his death, Laughing Stock issued *The Peter Cook Anthology*, LAFFC 39 p. 1995, including items from *Beyond the Fringe* and *Beyond the Fringe '64*, from *Not Only ... But Also* and the Amnesty shows.

In Autumn 1996 EMI issued a 3-CD set comprising the complete London version of *Beyond The Fringe*, using the tapes from two complete performances from which the original LP had been drawn (now in stereo); plus extracts from the LP of the original Broadway version and the complete LP of the 1964 Broadway version. EMI CD set 7243 8 54045 2.

Notes on the Contributors

Peter Alliss: professional golfer/sports commentator. Born 28.2.31. Turned professional 1946; 8 Ryder Cup caps; 10 World Cup caps (England); winner of 20 European Tour events; writer of 22 books on golf. Presents golf for ABC TV in the USA; presents golf for BBC; also worked on TV golf in Canada and Australia. Twice Captain of the Professional Golfers Association. First President of the Ladies PGA European Tour. All round good egg, etc!!

Clive Anderson: for many years Clive Anderson was a barrister. He is currently a chat-show host. He hopes to have an even less popular occupation some time in the future. He has written comedy scripts for television and radio programmes and one and a half books. In his private life he lives in London with about seven million other people.

Michael Bawtree, Australian-born and educated at Radley and Oxford, has lived in Canada since 1962. He has worked variously as an actor, book critic, TV host, dramaturge, playwright, director and educator. He was Associate Director of the Stratford Festival (Ontario) in the early seventies, founded COMUS Music Theatre of Canada, was Arts Planner at the Banff Centre – and then founder and director of Banff's Music Theatre Studio Ensemble. Since 1990 he has been professor and director of drama at Acadia University, Wolfville, Nova Scotia, where in 1995 he spearheaded the founding of the Atlantic Theatre Festival. He is currently the Festival's Artistic Director.

Peter Bellwood: screenwriter Peter Bellwood went up to Cambridge in 1958. He appeared in three Footlights revues, becoming President in his final year. He then endured a spell in advertising before being lured to America by Peter Cook to appear in *The Establishment*, an off-Broadway success which was followed by two national tours. Later, he turned to writing, creating the libretto for the 1970 Broadway musical, *Elmer Gantry*, starring Robert Shaw. A film assignment took him to California in 1971, where he has remained ever since, trapped like a fly in Hollywood's sticky web. His screenwriting credits include *Highlander*. He lives in the country with his wife, daughter and assorted furry animals.

Alan Bennett first appeared on the stage in the revue *Beyond the Fringe*. His stage plays include *Forty Years On*, *Habeas Corpus*, *The Old Country*, *Enjoy*, *Kafka's Dick*, *The Madness of George III*, and an adaptation of Kenneth Grahame's *The Wind in the Willows* for the National Theatre. He has written many television plays, including *An Englishman Abroad*, the series of monologues, *Talking Heads*, and *A Question of Attribution*. His collection of autobiographical writings, *Writing Home*, was published in 1994.

John Bird was educated at a Nottingham grammar school and Cambridge University, where he was a contemporary of Peter Cook. He began his professional career as a theatre director but joined Peter Cook in the founding of the *Establishment Club* in London and New York. Since then he has confined himself mostly to television, both as a straight actor and in comedy, often in collaboration with John Fortune and with Rory Bremner. He lives in Surrey with his partner Libby Crandon, a pianist, and numerous animals.

Eleanor Bron, actress and writer, graduated in Modern Languages from Cambridge University. She first became known in satirical cabaret, with John Bird, Peter Cook and John Fortune, at the *Establishment* night-club in Soho, London and later at The Strollers in New York. She went on to become equally admired as a dramatic actress in films, television and on the stage. As well as writing for television, she has written two autobiographical books, *Life and Other*

Punctures and *The Pillow Book of Eleanor Bron*, and translated *Desdemona – If You Had Only Spoken* by the German author Christine Brückner. Her first novel, *Double Take*, was published this summer. She appeared with Peter Cook in two films, *Bedazzled* and, more recently, *Black Beauty*.

John Cleese was born in 1939 in Weston-Super-Mare. He took science 'A' level at The Clifton College Sports Academy, taught for two years and then studied Law at Cambridge. He then became a comic and married many times.

Lin Cook: spring 1982 to January 1995, Peter's acquaintance, platonic friend, dearest friend, girlfriend (one of), 'constant companion', 'live-in' permanent relationship, wife, widow.

Stephen Fry was born the year Cosy Socks won the Victoria Cup at White City[1] and educated at Sunnyvale Kindergarten, Chesham Preparatory School, Cawston Primary School, Stout's Hill Preparatory School, Uppingham School, the Paston School, the Norfolk College of Arts and Technology, Norwich City College and Queens' College, Cambridge, some of which establishments did not throw him out. As well as popping up from time to time on stage and screen, Stephen Fry has written *The Liar*, a novel; *Paperweight*, a collection of articles, stories and essays; and, with his best friend Hugh, who is very nice, three collections of sketches culled (out of season) from BBC TV's *A Bit of Fry and Laurie*. Stephen Fry, who is Rector of Dundee University, lives in Norfolk and London. After writing *The Liar* he maintained that he would not write a second or a third novel, but perhaps a fourth. *The Hippopotamus* was it. His hobbies include cooking his godchildren and leaving out commas.

William Goldman is an American novelist and screenwriter. He has also written non-fiction books about Broadway, about Hollywood, and about what it was like to be a judge at both the Cannes Film Festival and the Miss America Contest (in the same year) and live to tell about it. He has won two American Academy Awards, one British Academy Award, and three lifetime achievement awards from various writers' groups. As he enters his fifth decade learning his craft, he is,

[1] 1957

from all verifiable reports, as immature as ever. He plans to continue writing until he gets it right.

Jonathan Harlow, contemporary of Peter Cook at Radley. After National Service and History at Cambridge, civil servant in Botswana. Then Masters degree at London Business School and work for businesses in Zambia and Guyana. Since 1978, teacher of Economics and History at Backwell School (N. Somerset). Now 58, living with doctor-wife and two of their three children in Winterbourne, South Gloucestershire.

Joseph Heller, the novelist (*Catch*-22, etc), lives in New York and is an honorary visiting fellow of St Catherine's College, Oxford, which he attended in 1949 as a Fulbright Scholar. He was acquainted with Peter Cook for more than thirty years and now very deeply regrets that the friendship wasn't closer and could not continue longer.

Christopher Hitchens writes the *Fin de Siècle* column for *Vanity Fair*.

Barry Humphries was born and educated in Melbourne. Since the late fifties he has divided his time between England and his homeland, performing in a series of one-man theatrical events, and, more recently, television appearances which have won him the Golden Rose at Montreux. He is the subject of two individual biographical studies and the author of several books, including his autobiography, *More Please* (winner of the J.R. Ackerley Prize for Autobiography), which Auberon Waugh described as 'An extraordinary cocktail of a book . . . a literary masterpiece.'

Eric Idle brackets born '43 close brackets stop. Educ. Pem. Coll. Cantab. Footlights Frost TV sixties kids show *Do Not Adjust* led Monty Python etc. etc. etc. to movies *The Grail*, *Holy Brian* and so on. *Rutland Weekend TV* yawn yawn *Rutles* parody for NBCTV Jonathan Miller ENO *Mikado* tra la, Gilliam *Munchausen* shaved head and a hangover, 'Always the Bright Side' hit single, *Pass Butler* play, *Hello Sailor* novel. Yank wife. Two kids, one boy one not. *Casper*, as Ratty *Toad in the Willows* etc. *Owl and Pussycat* book of. Living abroad. Provence sick to death of. California happy with koi, kids, puppy, and wife etc. etc.

John Lloyd: a radio and television producer by trade, John Lloyd originated *Quote Unquote* (1976), *The News Huddlines* (1976), *The News Quiz* (1977), *To The Manor Born* (1978), *Not The Nine O'Clock News* (1979), *Blackadder* (1983) and *Spitting Image* (1984). These days he is married, directs commercials, and concentrates on his three-part series *Harry* (1990), *Claudia* (1992) and *Caitlin* (1995).

Victor Lownes joined Hugh Hefner in 1954 as Playboy's Advertising and Circulation Promotion Director. When Playboy launched their famed Playboy Clubs Lownes was both Hefner's partner and a key management figure. When the Clubs expanded to Europe, Lownes moved to London. Fired by Hefner in 1981, Lownes watched in horror as all that he'd built up came crashing down. Lownes enjoyed a close friendship with Peter whom he met in Chicago in 1960, a friendship which never prevented Cook's *Private Eye* from libelling Lownes (or, come to think of it, Cook). Lownes wrote his autobiography, published as *Playboy Extraordinary* in England and as *The Day the Bunny Died* in the US.

Elisabeth Luard, married to Nicholas Luard for over thirty years, is an award-winning food writer and natural history painter whose smallest claim to fame is a spell of stamp-licking at *Private Eye circa* 1960. She spent her early adult life bringing up four children in southern Spain and France. In 1978 she had her first West End exhibition and provided the illustrations for Miriam Rothschild's *The Butterfly Gardener*. In 1986 she published the highly-acclaimed *European Peasant Cookery* on which was based her TV series *The Rich Tradition* (BBC 1994). Her first novel, chosen for the W.H. Smith Thumping Good Read award, appeared in 1994, and her autobiographical *Family Life* was published in May 1996.

Nicholas Luard: author and conservationist. Founded the *Establishment Club* in partnership with Peter Cook and was proprietor of *Private Eye* in the early sixties. He is the author of eighteen books, including the international bestselling novel *Gondar*. His latest, *Silverback*, was published in May 1996. Among his non-fiction works are *Andalucia – A portrait of southern Spain*, and *The Last Wilderness*, an account of his expeditions across the Kalahari desert. As Chairman of the John Muir Trust, the third largest conservation landowner in

Scotland, he divides his time between Scotland, his hill farm in Wales, and London, and continues to travel widely.

Shane Maloney is a novelist and columnist, the author of crime thrillers *Stiff* and *The Brush-Off*. He has been at various times the Director of the Melbourne Comedy Festival (retired), the Public Relations Officer of the Australian Boy Scouts' Association (escaped), a contestant on *Sale of the Century* and *Jeopardy* (stumped) and a swimming pool lifeguard (sacked). He is currently the Deputy Director of the Brunswick Institute, a weather-board think tank financed by his wife (much obliged).

Joe McGrath: writer/director. Has worked extensively in film, stage and television. Recipient of BAFTA Award on three occasions (one for his directorial work on *Not Only . . . But Also—*). Received the Standard Award for best film, and co-authored Oscar-winning short film *Great!* Besides writing screenplays and sitcoms, has concentrated mainly in comedy direction. Apart from Peter and Dudley, has worked with Peter Sellers, Orson Welles, Shirley MacLaine, Leonard Rossiter, Spike Milligan, Michael Bentine, Frances De La Tour, John Cleese and most leading comedy figures, both in the United States of America and in Britain.

Dudley Moore was born and brought up in Dagenham and won a music scholarship to Oxford. He made his professional stage debut in *Beyond the Fringe*, later reuniting with Peter Cook to create the television series *Not Only But Also* which featured the comic duo of Dud and Pete, and the stage revue *Behind the Fridge*. He has starred in numerous films including *Bedazzled*, *10*, *Arthur* and *Unfaithfully Yours*, and composed the music for many others. He has co-presented the television series *Orchestra!* with Sir George Solti, released several albums, the latest of which is *Songs Without Words*, and starred in his own American television show *Dudley*. He lives in Los Angeles.

Lewis Morley: born Hong Kong 1925. Returns to UK 1945, with family after four years internment in Hong Kong. Two years National Service, followed by three years Art school. Works as commercial artist in London. Escapes to Paris to paint and study art. Returns to marry illustrator Patricia

Clifford. Forsakes brushes for camera after success as photographer. Freelances for *Tatler* as photojournalist. Theatre front of house photography, including *Beyond the Fringe*, results in friendship with Peter Cook and studio in the *Establishment*, where that infamous chair-straddling photograph was taken. Migrates to Australia 1971. Given One Man Show, National Portrait Gallery, London 1989. Large retrospective 1993 in Sydney, where he still resides with wife, son and father-in-law.

Michael Palin was born in Sheffield in 1943. A founder member of the *Monty Python* team, he has written and performed in numerous successful films and television series, including *The Missionary, Time Bandits, A Private Function, A Fish Called Wanda, East of Ipswich, American Friends* and *GBH*. His many published books, apart from the *Monty Python* titles, include *Ripping Yarns, More Ripping Yarns* and *Dr Fegg's Encyclopeadia* (with Terry Jones); several children's books including *The Mirrorstone, Small Harry and the Toothache Pills, Limericks* and the *Cyril* stories; the bestselling *Around the World in 80 Days* and *Pole to Pole*; a play, *The Weekend*, first performed in London's West End in spring 1994; and, most recently, a novel, *Hemingway's Chair*. He is married with three children and lives in North London.

Adrian Slade: three years reading law at Cambridge convinced Adrian Slade he did not wish to be a lawyer. He drifted into advertising in which he remained for the next thirty-two years, the last twenty with an agency he co-founded. In parallel, abandoning cabaret performing, he became a Jo Grimond Liberal. Having failed to become an MP he was elected to the GLC in 1981 and led the GLC Alliance group until abolished by Mrs Thatcher. He became the last ever Liberal Party President (1987) and first Joint President (with Shirley Williams) of the merged Liberal Democrats (1988). Current occupations: media training, company publicity and chairmanship of the Orange Tree Theatre and charity ONE plus ONE.

Geoffrey Strachan read Modern Languages at Cambridge, President of St Catharine's College Midnight Howlers 1957–58; contributed scripts to Footlights revues 1956, 1958. As editor, later Publisher, at Methuen, 1961 to 1995, published *Dud and Pete: The Dagenham Dialogues* and *The Complete Beyond the Fringe*; also books by Patrick Barlow, Beachcomber, Steve Bell, Arnold Brown, Graham Chapman, John Cleese, Jilly Cooper, Ivor Cutler, Terry Gilliam, Jeremy Hardy, John Hegley, Eric Idle, Terry Jones, Dillie Keane, B. Kliban, Tom Lehrer, Frank Muir and Denis Norden, Michael Palin, Monty Python, Alexei Sayle, The Comic Strip, Sue Townsend, Katharine Whitehorn, Roger Woddis, Victoria Wood.

Barry Took (aged 68) was involved in both the old worlds of Music Hall and Camp West End Revue, and the satire boom of the 60s, when he wrote regularly for *Not So Much A Programme*, and *BBC3*. His major writing achievements include the radio classic *Round the Horne* (co-written with Marty Feldman) and *On the Move* which starred Bob Hoskins. Other work includes writing for and with Marty Feldman the award winning TV series *Marty*. His recent work has included writing and presenting the BBC TV letters programme *Points of View* and chairing BBC Radio 4's *The News Quiz*.

Auberon Waugh has published five novels and eleven other books, including an autobiography *Will This Do?*, an account of the Nigerian Civil War, *Biafra Britain's Shame* and an account of the trial of Jeremy Thorpe, *The Last Word*. He joined the *Daily Telegraph* in 1960 and *Daily Mirror* in 1965, and has written regular columns in the *Catholic Herald*, the *Sun*, the *News of the World*, *The Times*, the *New Statesman*, and *Private Eye* (for sixteen years). He was political correspondent of the *Spectator*, and returned in 1976 to write *Another Voice*, for the next twenty years. He has reviewed books regularly for *Books and Bookmen*, the *Standard*, the *Daily Mail* and the *Independent*. He currently writes a thrice-weekly column, *Way of the World*, in the *Daily Telegraph*, a weekly one in the *Sunday Telegraph*, edits the *Literary Review* and runs the Spectator Wine Club.

John Wells taught at Eton before joining the editorial board of *Private Eye* in 1963. He has acted in the West End and at the National Theatre, in films and on television, written a novel, *A Melon for Ecstasy*, with John Fortune, a television series, *Return to Leeds*, with John Bird, in which they between them played all the characters, and two serials – *Mrs Wilson's Diary* and *The Dear Bill Letters*, with Richard Ingrams. Both ran in the West End as shows, one directed by Joan Littlewood, the other by Dick Clement. He has translated and directed operettas, including *Candide* with Jonathan Miller, written a history of the London Library, *Rude Words*, biographical plays about Swift, Wesley and Benjamin Robert Haydon and a book, *Princess Caraboo*, co-scripting the film about her.

Roger Wilmut: born 1942, Stratford-on-Avon. Books: *The Goon Show Companion* (1976), *Tony Hancock 'Artiste'* (1978), *From Fringe to Flying Circus* (on the Monty Python generation) (1980), *Kindly Leave the Stage* (on theatrical Variety 1919–1960) (1985), *The Illustrated Hancock* (1986), *Didn't You Kill My Mother-in-Law?* (on 'alternative comedy') (1989). Compiled two books of comedy sketches: *No More Curried Eggs for Me* (1982) and *Son of 'Curried Eggs'* (1984). Text-edited *The Complete Beyond The Fringe* (1987) and *Monty Python's Flying Circus – Just the Words* (the complete Python scripts) (1989).